INNOVATION IN LOCAL ECONOMIES

Innovation in Local Economies

Germany in Comparative Context

COLIN CROUCH AND HELMUT VOELZKOW

OXFORD
UNIVERSITY PRESS

OXFORD
UNIVERSITY PRESS

Great Clarendon Street, Oxford OX2 6DP

Oxford University Press is a department of the University of Oxford.
It furthers the University's objective of excellence in research, scholarship,
and education by publishing worldwide in

Oxford New York

Auckland Cape Town Dar es Salaam Hong Kong Karachi
Kuala Lumpur Madrid Melbourne Mexico City Nairobi
New Delhi Shanghai Taipei Toronto

With offices in

Argentina Austria Brazil Chile Czech Republic France Greece
Guatemala Hungary Italy Japan Poland Portugal Singapore
South Korea Switzerland Thailand Turkey Ukraine Vietnam

Oxford is a registered trade mark of Oxford University Press
in the UK and in certain other countries

Published in the United States
by Oxford University Press Inc., New York

© Oxford University Press 2009

The moral rights of the authors have been asserted
Database right Oxford University Press (maker)

First published 2009

British Library Cataloguing in Publication Data
Data available

Library of Congress Cataloging in Publication Data
Data available

Typeset by SPI Publisher Services, Pondicherry, India
Printed in Great Britain
on acid-free paper by
the MPG Books Group

ISBN 978–0–19–955117–0

1 3 5 7 9 10 8 6 4 2

ACKNOWLEDGEMENTS

The research project on which this book is based, *Local Production Systems in Europe*, was funded by the Volkswagen Stiftung and supervised by Helmut Voelzkow with the assistance of Colin Crouch and Theo Leuenberger. The authors are grateful to the generous assistance of the Stiftung, which made possible direct, case research in the various sites reported in the studies. The full report, which also includes work on the biopharmaceutical cluster, BioValley, in Switzerland, was presented to the Stiftung in 2006 as *Local Production Systems in Europe*, and subsequently published in German as *Jenseits nationaler Produktionsmodelle? Die Governance regionaler Wirtschaftscluster. Eine international vergleichende Analyse* (Voelzkow (with Elbing and Schröder) 2007).

CONTENTS

LIST OF FIGURES

LIST OF TABLES

NOTES ON CONTRIBUTORS

Colin Crouch is Professor of Governance and Public Management at the Business School of the University of Warwick. He is also an External Scientific Member of the Max Planck Institute for the Study of Societies at Cologne, and a Fellow of the British Academy. His most recent books include *Social Change in Western Europe* (1999); (with others) *Local Production Systems in Europe: Rise or Demise?* (2001); *Postdemocrazia* (2003) (in English as *Post-Democracy* [2004]); (with others) *Changing Governance of Local Economies: Response of European Local Production Systems* (2004); and *Capitalist Diversity and Change: Recombinant Governance and Institutional Entrepreneurs* (2005).

Ulrich Glassmann is an Assistant Professor in Comparative Politics at the University of Cologne. He is the author of *Staatliche Ordnung und räumliche Wirtschaftspolitik* (VS-Verlag, 2007). He is currently working on his *Habilitation*, which deals with social norms and welfare regimes.

Simcha Jong is a Lecturer in the Department of Management Science and Innovation, University College, London. His research and teaching concern strategic management, innovation, and entrepreneurship, with an emphasis on the life sciences sector. He was awarded first prize in the 2006 PRIME Early Career Competition and a DIME WP European Framework Grant for qualitative research on university entrepreneurship.

Maarten Keune is Senior Researcher at the European Trade Union Institute, Brussels. His research interests include economic sociology and neo-institutionalist analysis; European integration and enlargement, employment policy and welfare states; and industrial relations. His recent publications include articles on flexicurity, work relocation, and the impacts of globalization and privatization on collective bargaining and labour markets.

Geny Piotti is a Researcher at the Max Planck Institute for the Study of Societies, Cologne, and Lecturer at the University of Osnabrück. Her PhD on local development in Eastern Germany and Southern Italy was awarded the Saraceno Prize by the Association for Industrial Development in the Mezzogiorno (SVIMEZ). She was editor of the special issue *'La Cooperazione Locale nella Germania Est'* in *Sviluppo Locale* (2005).

Pernilla S. Rafiqui is a Doctoral Student at Stockholm School of Economics, where she is working on the use of institutional theory in economic geography and the evolution of the furniture industry in Småland. Her research also includes economic development and urban growth in Southeast Asia. Among her recent works is *Institutional perspectives on the road and forestry sectors in Laos* (Swedish International Development Cooperation Authority, 2003).

Martin Schröder is a Researcher at the Max Planck Institute for the Study of Societies, Cologne. His interests include political economy and economic sociology, welfare states, varieties of capitalism, and research on firms.

Sabine Elbing is a Doctoral Student in social sciences at the University of Osnabrück. She earlier trained and worked as a ship broker. Her research interests concern governance structures in film and TV production.

Örjan Sjöberg is Professor of Economic Geography at the Stockholm School of Economics. Focusing on the geography of economic change, his research interests also include urban, population, and development geography. In addition to conducting work on Sweden, he takes an interest in socialist and post-socialist societies and in the developing world, with a focus on issues such as rural development, migration, and urban change.

András Tóth is Senior Research Fellow at the Institute for Political Science of the Hungarian Academy of Sciences, Budapest. He has carried out several studies of economic change and adjustment in Hungary.

Helmut Voelzkow is Professor of Comparative Social Sciences at the University of Osnabrück. He has published within the fields of economic sociology and comparative European sociology. His recent works include *Jenseits nationaler Produktionsmodelle? Die Governance regionaler Wirtschaftscluster. Eine international vergleichende Analyse* (with Sabine Elbing and Martin Schröder, 2007); *Die Europäische Union—Marionnette oder Regisseur?* (edited, with Patricia Bauer, 2004).

1

Introduction: Local and Sectoral Diversity Within National Economic Systems

COLIN CROUCH AND HELMUT VOELZKOW

The now extensive literature (cf. Deeg and Jackson 2007;Hall and Soskice 2001*b*; Hancké, Rhodes, and Thatcher 2007) on the diversity of capitalism has been mainly concerned to demonstrate the importance of different national forms. Given the importance of legal and political institutions in shaping differences, and given the concentration of these at the level of the nation state, this has been a reasonable preoccupation. However, it must not blind us to either the emergence of global, European, and other supranational economic governance or diversity within countries caused by distinctive regional or sectoral attributes. In this book we concentrate on the latter, and particularly on where they come together in geographical concentrations of certain economic activities. We seek neither to discredit the idea of national varieties of capitalism nor to treat the local sectors we identify as eccentric deviations from otherwise dominant national forms: diversity of the kind we identify may well be present in a very large number of localities and sectors, as it tends to accompany the production of certain goods. We present the local and the sectoral playing out their specificities against the background of the national, and in some cases making use of a capacity to reach beyond the national to access institutions available at European or even global level. We are particularly concerned to seek out cases where local divergence from an ostensible national model might produce contrasts and tensions that are actually useful for firms making adjustments and changes, making use of a variety of institutional possibilities—some local, some national, others even international. This enables us to avoid the slide into a claustrophobic determinism, excluding scope for actor-centred institutional innovation, to which neo-institutional analysis is sometimes prone. This is also one of the core conclusions of Douglas North (2005). He underlines that too much conformity has not proved beneficial to economic performance in history, as it leads to inflexibility which hinders processes of change. Systems that allow for greater variation and experimentation have in general been better at adjusting to changing circumstances, and at adopting innovations.

The method logically suggested by this kind of research, and used in this project, is the case study: only through the detailed investigation of specific examples can one learn the details of particular institutional arrangements. But it is a method with weaknesses. First, case studies cannot be used to demonstrate what is typical or even likely; only what is possible. This suits our task here, which is to demonstrate how, in certain circumstances, economic activities might be organized in ways that are not fully consistent with what is often depicted to be a particular national model. If we are able to do this, we are able to demonstrate that there are alternative *possibilities* to what seem to be the main institutional forms. We here follow in the footsteps of Charles Sabel and Jonathan Zeitlin (1997) in their study of alternative paths of industrial development, *A World of Possibilities*. It is an exercise well worth undertaking, as the search for what is statistically typical—or, less methodologically respectable, the positing of 'stylized facts'—does not exhaust all knowledge. For example, if we learn that 85 per cent of firms in a particular sector in a particular country have failed to find sources of finance other than those typical of the national system, we have certainly confirmed that typicality. However, we have not eliminated the reality of the remaining 15 per cent, and it remains an interesting and legitimate research task to discover through case studies what they have been doing, and how. At the same time, we must never lose sight of the fact that our case studies themselves will never enable us to make statements about typicality at all.

Our starting assumption is therefore that, even though certain national institutions may dominate a particular national economy, there are likely to be regions or smaller localities where different institutional patterns survive and possibly thrive. A number of studies have explored this dimension (Crouch et al. 2001, 2004; Storper 1997). Similarly, different industries or economic branches within a national economy may have access to different institutional arrangements than those given by the national model (Herrmann 2006). Institutional specificities are particularly likely to concentrate where locality and economic branch come together in geographical concentrations of particular activities, or clusters. For reasons that will be explained below, we selected the following sectors: furniture-making, motor-vehicle manufacture, biopharmaceuticals, and television film-making. At the centre of the work was the German economy, as this is frequently depicted in the literature as one with particularly rigid, interconnected institutions and offering little scope for local variation. For each of the selected branches we selected a local cluster in Germany and one in a comparator country. Selection of the comparators is also discussed below. Before we come to this and introduce our case studies, it is necessary to develop further the theoretical basis on which the research rests.

Studying Capitalist Diversity

Dominant within contemporary institutional analysis of national economies is the 'Varieties of Capitalism' school. This is a general term for a number of comparatively designed international studies, which analyse institutional differences in capitalist countries and the socio-economic consequences following from each national institutional order. This school cannot easily be subsumed under conventional scientific disciplines. Political scientists, researchers in the field of public administration, sociologists, as well as economists are attempting to overcome conventional borders of their disciplines, in order to generate a holistic image, containing various national or regional forms of capitalist production systems. The discussion has been shaped by a growing number of contributions. An early protagonist was Michel Albert (1991), who invented the differentiation between Rhenisch and Atlantic capitalism. His analysis is mainly noted today for its differentiation between shareholder and stakeholder capitalism. Other contributions have been the edited collections of Berger and Dore (1996), Crouch and Streeck (1997),Hollingsworth, Schmitter, and Streeck (1994), Hollingsworth and Boyer (1997), Kitschelt et al. (1999), and Whitley (1992, 1999). But the most systematic has been that edited by Hall and Soskice (2001b).

Stressing institutional differences between capitalist countries does not imply ignoring the basic common features applying to all of them. Private ownership of the means of production, more or less complex enterprises, competitively organized markets, etc. exist in all capitalist countries. However, and this is the main thesis of the school, important differences exist in the national institutional environment between countries and 'country families', which justify the term 'varieties of capitalism'. And these institutional peculiarities, argues a subsequent thesis, build decisive explanatory variables, illuminating such complex issues in international comparison as the diverging importance of economic sectors, diverging growth dynamics, the varying distribution of income, or—in more general terms—the variance of social structures in different countries.

Central to the approach is tracing the connection between the independent variable (differences in national institutional arrangements) and the dependent variable (differences in performance). According to Hall and Soskice (2001a) there exist different patterns of innovation. These are caused by national institutional arrangements, the latter again explaining national trajectories of economic performance. In some countries like Germany incremental innovation dominates as the general pattern; while in other countries like the USA or (within Europe) the United Kingdom, radical innovation appears to dominate, finally also creating differences in the sectoral composition and growth dynamic of the respective national economy (Porter 1990; Soskice 1997). By analysing empirically the differences in institutional arrangements for national economies, the discourse on the varieties of capitalism generated a few 'national models'. National cases are classified according to their institutional qualities and as such they are viewed as being part of 'country families' with a specific innovation and production regime. These innovation and production regimes are then pointed to as carrying specific strengths and weaknesses within an increasingly global competitive environment.

A common starting point for these analyses has been the study of certain institutional spheres. Economic actors in these, it is assumed, behave according to the rules provided for them by the specific institutional arrangements, which thus coordinate and 'govern' them. Because of this, institutional sectors are analysed with respect to their dominant modes of coordination. Particular attention is paid to certain of these spheres:

- As shown by various studies, national capitalisms diverge in *corporate finance*. Two major variants are usually distinguished: in some countries, for example, Germany, credits are offered to firms by so-called *Hausbanken*, which are very often under public control. In other countries, like the UK, firms rather appear to seek for investment capital in the private capital market (Vitols 1995; Zysman 1983).
- Important differences also exist in the field of *corporate governance* and structure. While in some countries the policy of firms is more oriented towards the short-term interests of shareholders, in others the corporate board also considers the interests of other stakeholders (especially employees). Research on corporate governance deals with the question of which interests influence the action of enterprise management. This does not only affect the cleavage line between capital and labour but also that between capital and enterprise management. Thus, in some countries *Hausbanken* directly influence the policy of firms, while in others corporate policy may depend much more on the development of the private capital market (Fligstein 2001). Such differences in the inner structure of firms have specific consequences. Short-term-oriented action dominates enterprises, which have to respond to the pressure of capital markets; while long-term-oriented action can be found among firms operating on the basis of stakeholder models and where credits are given by 'patient' actors rather than by 'impatient' investors at the stock market.
- A further sphere concerns *industrial relations systems*. There are countries dominated by ideologically fragmented and conflictual industrial relations systems (France, Italy), as well as those dominated by pluralist bargaining systems (UK) or countries which have constructed corporatist arrangements (Sweden, Germany). The state is somehow concerned in all industrial relations systems, either through industrial and welfare law or through the law providing general acceptance of collective wage agreements (Crouch 1993).

- *Vocational training* is also offered within different institutional frameworks: in some countries training is dominantly offered by state agencies, in others it is rather offered on a free market for vocational and further training. In further different countries skills are diffused in-house or through enterprise networks (Crouch, Finegold, and Sako 1999; Soskice and Finegold 1988). The 'dual system' of vocational training in Germany demonstrates how even hybrid mixes of state infrastructure and corporatist arrangements may provide the demanded skills.
- *Relations between firms* in market economies are of a competitive nature, but differences in the form and the intensity of these relations lead neo-institutionalists to the hypothesis that they also will be shaped by national peculiarities. In liberal market economies market relationships seem to dominate, while in some forms of coordinated market economies there will also be cooperation between firms, often mediated by strong associations.
- *Innovation systems* are an increasingly important aspect of the ways in which at least some sectors in advanced economies operate (Lundvall 1992). They concern relations among firms, and between firms and universities, other research centres, and various public institutions. The structure of these can have important implications for the extent to which innovation taking place within an economy is radical or incremental.

Complementarity and (In)coherence

There is a tendency in much research in this field to seek underlying similarities among the institutions of these different spheres that appear within an individual country. Often there is then a further reduction, as differences among countries are pressed into a small number of 'models' or 'country families', which all host a comparative institutional infrastructure (Rhodes and van Apeldoorn 1997; V. Schmidt 2002). In order to achieve this, the single results of the research undertaken are put together into a holistic image, which gives the impression of strong coherence. The basic element that allows fusing the individual results of national particularities into a small number of models lies in the concept of a *complementary order*, implying in turn assumptions of the mutual *coherence* of the institutions in such an order.

Theoretically speaking, the variety of combined institutional particularities of sectors—this follows from the complementary order assumption—must be very limited, because institutional particularities mutually have to fit together. Certain combinations reinforce each other; others exclude each other due to their mutual disfunctionality. For example, a system of corporate finance that rests on incremental innovation of existing and successful products, thus oriented towards long-term projects, 'fits' into a system of vocational and further training, which invests with large efforts into the qualification of employees. Vice versa, a system of corporate financing that is oriented towards the maximizing of short-term profits, 'fits' better into a system of vocational and further training that directs investments into the qualification of employees accordingly. However, if these employees have only been qualified very poorly by the firm, due to the low investments that are generally activated for human resources, then it does not make any sense to keep these exchangeable employees in the firm when crisis is ahead. 'Hire and fire policies' on the level of the firm 'fit' a system of short-term entrepreneurial strategies as much as the relatively high stability of employment 'fits' production systems with long-term orientations.

This approach to discussing economic institutions has had an influence far beyond the academic literature. For example, everyday political debate in Germany often posits a 'German model' that does not only comprise a number of characterizing institutional particularities (like the distinctive banking system, the 'dual' training system, employee participation in firm-level decision-making, collective wage bargaining) but also constitutes a linked, coherent structure through the complementary order of these characteristic institutional particularities. They are seen as fitting together in their functional logic and because of this, mutually reinforce each other. Thus, from this complementary order evolves the specific 'performance' of the German model, which on the one hand shows a relatively high level of income combined with a relatively low wage differential, but on the other hand a relatively high rate of unemployment under current economic circumstances. The model also guarantees a comparative advantage in 'diversified quality production' (DQP), but suffers from weaknesses in the branches of the 'new economy'.

The complementary order thesis serves well for depicting the path-dependences, 'lock-ins', and institutional stability with which national economic arrangements certainly abound, but it serves less well for advancing our understanding of institutional change. In this perspective, change is rather unlikely to happen or can only be thought of as a symmetrical movement of a whole 'national model', including all institutional sectors. Research methods that concentrate on identifying the typical and on generating stylized facts are fully consistent with this determinist kind of functionalism. In contrast, an approach that looks for diversity behind the typicality, and for the untidiness and lack of fit and complementarity likely to result from such diversity, will be more likely to find situations in which entrepreneurial actors in both the economy and public policy may find scope for innovation that escapes the determinism. There may even be *creative incoherences* within national innovation and production systems, when internal diversity produces a loose coupling of different institutional spheres, leading to the creation of autonomous subsystems and governance structures on the sectoral and/or local level. Actors may establish their own governance structures, diverging from the national model. For example, Höpner (2001) has shown that while several large German firms have switched to the shareholder value model of corporate financing, other institutional arrangements (including the system of labour participation, the cooperation between labour and capital, the dual system of industrial relations) have largely been unaffected (see also Deeg 2001).

This leads us to consider more carefully the use made of the idea of complementarity. We have above referred to it in the meaning that is increasingly being given to it in neo-institutionalist literature, that is more or less 'functional fit'. But this is problematic. Not only is functional fit notoriously difficult to determine in social institutions except in rather pointless *post facto* analysis, but also this meaning clashes with the other major usages of the term that readers may expect to have in mind (for more extended discussions see Crouch 2005: ch 2, 2009). These are the following:

1. *Complementarity meaning where components of a whole mutually compensate for each other's deficiencies in constituting a whole.* This is the strictest but, curiously, also the everyday sense. It defines two phenomena (in our case institutions) as complementary when each can be defined in terms of what is lacked by the other in order to produce a defined whole. While such cases are encountered in institutional analysis, they are rare, as they depend on the identification of perfect matchings of a kind that can usually only be found in mathematics and physics. However, we can occasionally find such instances, and there are some in the subsequent chapters of this book. They provide particularly interesting examples of empirical institutional configurations, embodying important cases of local and sectoral 'deviations' from national models.

2. *Complementarity in the economist's sense.* More common are examples of the economists' concept of complementarity as part of the production function. This is defined clearly in terms of two goods, a fall in the price of one of which will lead to a rise in the demand for the other. Aoki (1994) has extended this concept to institutions, defining institutions as complementary when the enhancement of one will assist provision of the other. Hall and Soskice (2001a), Deeg (2005) (but using the concept of 'coherence'), and Amable (2003) have followed this approach. While this works well as a *post hoc* discovery by research, the ensembles thereby discovered might not be the only viable ones, as Amable (ibid.) himself points out. They might also be changed by innovative action by social actors. They do not imply necessities. Further, unlike the previous definition, they do not imply that the two items identified are necessarily enough to produce some kind of whole when combined.

3. *Complementarity as mutual effects.* Pierson (2000a: 78) refers to configurations of complementary institutions as being those 'in which the performance of each is affected by the existence of others'. While this is similar to 1 (reciprocal reinforcement), it is much weaker, as it specifies

only 'affected by'. It also loses the tension that was present in the idea of goods that required ingredients making different contributions to the whole. But many authors use complementarity in this weak sense. There is some notion that institutions go together, but how is not specified; it could mean similarity or elective affinity, leading us to the very opposite of complementarity in its strongest sense.

Successful institutions are likely to contain complex combinations of similarities (we operate more easily in contexts where everything is familiar to us, even if there is no objective advantage to such similarity in itself) and differences that enable us to take advantage of the compensation and balance offered by complementarity in its first, strongest, sense. The logic of similarity argues that institutions with similar properties will be found together; that of complementarity that those with balancing, even sometimes opposed properties will do so. Theories of similarity are likely to reflect a model of societies as having been shaped by more or less conscious design, at least of the fictional social contract kind, as one might expect powerful shaping forces to seek some degree of homogeneity in the structures they produce. Theories of complementarity, however, reflect an evolutionary functionalist logic, as they assume that evolutionary survival has privileged those social forms in which different institutions operate together in a way that balances the whole.

If similarity dominates among institutions, there is likely to be very limited scope for innovation and institutional entrepreneurship. Schumpeter (1993 [1912]) described entrepreneurship in terms of making 'new combinations', and subsequent students of entrepreneurial creation have continued to find this useful (Garud and Karnøe 2001). It should be noted that this formulation explicitly does not see enterprise as creation *de novo*. It is assumed that some components already exist; what the entrepreneur does is to put them together in new and creative ways—and if this is true of economic entrepreneurs, it will also be the case for institutional ones, institutions being more difficult to create than products. The important point to note is that new combinations can be made only if the environment provides a diversity of such components: if everything is more or less the same, nothing exceptional can be expected from new combinations within the uniformity. This is why we aim to understand here whether and how institutional diversity is accommodated in national economies.

Schumpeter's concept also includes something of the disruption of entrepreneurship: it is certainly not a functionalist approach. This leads us to look out for 'productive incoherences' as particularly interesting cases of where local, sectoral, or other departures from national systems present complementarities in the strictest sense of the term: institutions that do not appear to 'fit' together at all in a logico-functionalist sense of complementarity seem, in practice, to create an institutional ensemble that is distinctive and 'successful'.

Levels of Analysis

As noted, some contributions to the study of capitalist diversity reduce the range of this diversity to just two types. For these authors, therefore, it is not only the German economy but also all those that they call 'coordinated' that will be highly unlikely to engage in radical innovation technologies; these latter occurring only in 'liberal market economies', which turn out to be equivalent to the Anglophone nations. This approach, by insisting on a rather strict form of functionalist complementarity, invites us to seek out a number of potential productive incoherences. For example, how else could one account for the Finnish and Swedish presence in radical innovation in advanced telecommunications (Berggren and Laestadius 2000)?

More flexible than the Varieties of Capitalism school in its capacity to see important diversity within the institutional forms of non-Anglophone countries are the national innovation school (Lundvall 1992; Nelson 1993; Nelson and Winter 1982), and the approach to national competitive advantage adopted by Michael Porter (1990). The former authors maintain that clusters of institutions at the *national* level will determine the application of science and technology within an economy. They examine government policy, the structure of universities and other advanced research institutions, and their relationship to firms. They develop theory about why particular ensembles of national institutions favour the production of particular kinds of science-based goods and services, but they do not reduce these national ensembles to just two types. Porter, looking more broadly at diversity of economic activities, and not just those that are science-based, reaches similar conclusions. As a result, writers in these schools have no difficulty in differentiating the Nordic countries from Germany, or indeed from each other.

However, the national innovation school authors, as their name implies, insist on the nation state as the crucial level, and in fact are more bound to the nation state than the varieties of capitalism school, as they do not align national forms to wider 'families'. In doing this, they can point to strong arguments. As part of modern state-building, governments have either directly constructed higher education and advanced research systems, or produced fiscal and other regimes that have facilitated particular kinds of institution (Jong 2007). They have not necessarily consciously willed the particular outcome, but they have been key shaping actors: systems of higher education and research change at national borders. Similarly, corporate law, patent law, and law governing the forms of trade associations have all been produced at the level of nation states. Within the European Union some, though by no means all, of these legal structures are gradually passing to the European level, but this process is very recent. For most of the nineteenth and twentieth centuries nation states founded and guarded these structures. Further, because nation states have been such significant actors in shaping economic and legal frameworks, business associations and trade unions have tended to concentrate their own structures at the same level, even if they also have local and regional branches and various international activities.

Much of the existing critical literature on capitalist diversity (Bertoldi 2003; Crouch 2005; Goodin 2003; Regini 2003) also concentrates on the national and other macro-levels. However, as Trigilia (2004) asks: if the national level is the main determinant of economic diversity, why are not the industries seen as nationally 'typical' distributed evenly across the national territory? In other words, why do clusters exist? That they do exist, and that they cannot all be explained in terms of physical geography, is well established; and not only for traditional sectors (Crouch et al. 2001) but also in the so-called high-tech ones (Crouch et al. 2004: Part III; Kenney 2000; Saxenian 1999; Swann, Prevezer, and Stout 1998). This diversity does not necessarily contradict national innovation system or national competitive advantage theories, which can easily accommodate the idea of further sub-national concentrations of governance, provided the local specialisms are consistent with the national framework, which has to be regarded as dominant. Therefore, to anticipate the cases at the heart of our own research, neither these theories nor that of the varieties of capitalism should have any difficulty with the fact that some areas of Germany specialize in high-quality motor vehicles, others in machine tools, and others again in chemicals. But they may have more difficulty with the biotechnology specialism of the Munich region, as this appears to require a different structure of innovation institutions from the presumed national one. Similarly, while these theories (unlike varieties of capitalism) have no difficulty explaining how Swedish institutions can support advanced biotechnology and telecommunications, they would have more difficulty with the small firms and consumer orientation of the southern Swedish furniture industry (Kjær 1996). Indeed, the fact that this sector is partly characterized by small- and medium-sized enterprises (SMEs) provides problems for nearly all accounts of the Swedish economy, which stress its domination by large enterprises.

Local specialisms that seem to 'defy' the logic of a national system in this way suggest that the nation state is not necessarily always the most important level for determining the institutional environment of business. In some cases the 'defiance' may be real. For example, according to Aniello and Le Galès (2001), French specialized local economies based on small firms are often located in areas where late nineteenth century Catholic communities deliberately set out to resist the French republic and its centralizing tendencies. Similarly, Bagnasco (1977) and others have related the industrial districts of central Italy to the previous dominance there of a 'red' political culture resisting both the dominant, state-dependent large corporations of the north-west, associated with post-war Christian Democratic industrial policy, and the equally Christian Democratic but economically backward south. (The Italian case disturbs a further frequent generalization: an association of the political left with state-dependent large firms and of the right with entrepreneurial SMEs.)

Other cases of divergence from national models are far less dramatic, and simply constitute part of an overall variety that lives alongside and possibly in a symbiotic relationship with any national system. Two institutional components may be different, but that difference only becomes a deviance when it can be demonstrated that they somehow contradict each other. For knowledge of that we depend on the strength of institutional theory, which claims to be able to demonstrate what kinds of institution fit together well, and which impede each other. However, this knowledge is in its infancy. Not enough research evidence yet exists to enable us, for example, to delimit the boundaries of functional equivalence, or to determine precisely where a usefully balancing complementarity becomes a plain lack of fit.

We have above criticized the fashion for dealing in 'stylized facts'—encouraged by many economists in the name of 'parsimony and elegance'—which can easily become an invitation to deal in stereotypes and over-generalizations. Accounts that remain at the level of stylized facts can be likened to artistic guides designed for the day-tripper: if you go to Paris, make sure that you go to the Louvre, the Quay d'Orsay, the Musée des Arts Modernes .... That will not do for an academic study of art collections in Paris, and it is remarkable that social-scientific accounts of national economies often fail to go far beyond the tourist guide level. But, to take the analogy further, it is unlikely that we shall learn anything about what is today inspiring young Parisian artists by looking round the great museums. We are more likely to find clues if we look at small galleries and exhibitions of art from remote parts of the world; or, more likely still, to discover the destinations of their travels around the world. (One recalls the dramatic impact on an earlier generation of Parisian artists of Gauguin's travels to the South Pacific.)

This very last point reminds us of a further problem with the concept of national systems. It assumes that units within a country are fully dependent on institutions made available within it. In some respects this is true. If a firm is located, or has some of its activities located, within a particular national jurisdiction, it will be subject to the laws of that jurisdiction (cf. Boyer 1996). To the extent that a firm needs frequent inter-personal contacts for its activities—which is strongly the case in knowledge-sensitive sectors (Trigilia 2004)—it is partly dependent on its locality. However, many other resources are internationally mobile. The southern Californian high-tech economy is not dependent on the products of the Californian or even the US education system, as the region's universities and firms recruit doctoral students and research staff globally. German high-tech firms are not dependent on the German corporate finance system, as they can attract venture capital from the UK or the USA. There is today in general a growing range of internationally available institutions, particularly for large enterprises; this is a fundamental part of globalization. Capital, standards, trading rules, product markets, even some forms of labour, are available on a global basis, at certain points without reference to nation-state jurisdictions. As an economic entity the contemporary nation state has to be strongly relativized in institutional theory.

On closer inspection, therefore, the idea of a national system starts to seem less solid. It can be at least variegated and at most directly challenged by local institutions; and it may be in competition with both supranational regulatory regimes and internationally available institutions, services, and persons (Brose and Voelzkow 1999). These questions become even more acute when we consider parts of the world where national systems are weak. This is for example the case with the countries of Central and Eastern Europe. Most of the institutions of the state socialist period seem to have been swept away very rapidly during the early 1990s; that regime had in its time swept away most pre-existing institutions; and even before that, in much of Central Europe the 'national' level had in any case had a short-lived period following centuries of foreign domination. Further, during two decades of post-communist reconstruction, governments and other institutional actors in this part of the world have been presented with various powerful exogenous models; the idea of national systems remains elusive. For those countries that have entered or that are working towards entering the EU, there is the *acquis communautaire*; for all there is the World Bank, the International Monetary Fund and the OECD, and individual multinational firms considering major investments in production. These exogenous forces do not simply offer ideas for consideration; they offer important inducements for compliance. How then are these national systems to be described?

Towards a Non-Functionalist Approach

We have now challenged many of the rather functionalist dominant assumptions of neo-institutional analysis. First, in common with the national innovation system school, we have cast doubt on the adequacy of theories that posit very small numbers of system types. Second, we have challenged the assumption that the nation state is the sole appropriate unit of analysis, though we have not sought to deny its major importance. We have encouraged examination of lower as well as higher levels of jurisdiction, as well as lateral influences brought about by actors within a system reaching out to exogenous influence. Third, we find the claim that national cases can be allocated unambiguously to one or other of a small group of identified types problematic, because it prevents us from seeing the diversity, tension, even contradictions, that may be vital to the innovative capacity of actors within a particular nation state. Finally, by seeing how changing combinations of components, even within a hypothetically sealed system, can produce change, we have cast doubt on the neo-institutionalist assumption that a country's standing within a typology of institutions will not change.

This discussion seems to lead to the conclusion that mixed institutions are always likely to be more useful for change and innovation, and more resilient, than those that reproduce similar characteristics over a wide institutional range. However, some empirical studies seem to demonstrate exactly the opposite: that 'pure' cases perform more highly than mixed ones. A reasonable conclusion must be that, while some ostensibly incoherent patterns will provide useless sets of capacities, others will not do so. Microanalysis is essential if we are to discover where which logic applies.

Our alternative approach here uses such microanalysis. It depends also on seeing institutions as both constraining and capable of being changed and manipulated. This closely resembles the concept of the random walk. The previous trajectory of such a walk determines the starting point of the next step, but that step is left free to move in a variety of directions. If, as is often the case with institutional development, it is possible to identify mechanisms of path dependence (Crouch and Farrell 2004; Mahoney 2000; Pierson 2000*a*, *b*; Thelen 2004), the trajectory may be predicted more closely (technically, a random walk on a complex plane (Arthur 1994)). A number of authors have recently begun to explore these more flexible possibilities of neo-institutionalism. Crouch (2005) and Ebbinghaus and Manow (2001) have explored how empirical examples of an institution are likely to be complex hybrids of pure forms, different ones of which may become dominant at different times, producing major institutional change. (See also the studies collected in Morgan, Whitley, and Moen 2005.)

Streeck and Thelen (2005) and Thelen (2004) consider various ways in which a succession of gradual changes, each of which in turn lies well within the bounds of performance of a particular form of institution, can gradually render the case unrecognizable; we can rarely be certain whether change has taken place within a system or has changed the character of a system. By combining already existing elements the Schumpeterian entrepreneur makes something new, thereby creating change. Such change can be contrasted with what Lévi-Strauss (1962) called *bricolage*. He considered that people in simple societies would approach new technical problems by putting old, familiar tools together in new combinations. But these combinations remained no more than the sum of their existing parts, which were dismantled at the end of the task to resume their familiar shape. No new tools developed. There is a difference between Lévi-Straussian and Schumpeterian new combinations: the one remains static; the other creates a new entity. Campbell (2004) in fact uses the idea of *bricolage* with this implication. We can tell if the latter process has happened if a new combination then becomes a new unit that itself becomes a component for further new combinations. In that case, quite radical change can eventually result, transforming the original situation, even if the original components were all present within the system. In real life, exogenous components may also be available, as we have seen; but Thelen's accretions of small changes can work even with solely endogenous initial components. This can be the case, provided that the initial components are capable of change of some type.

This demonstrates again the importance of characterizations of national, or indeed local, or sectoral, contexts that are alert to some, even minor, diversity, as this can be the seed of major system change. There is a further point here. One of the ways in which empirical cases differ may be in their capacity to contain diversity. In a tightly coupled national or other case, there may be so much congruence among component parts, that they allow no scope for new combinations. Others, more loosely coupled, may easily entertain diversity. This formal characteristic of the degree of possible diversity may be more important than the substantive character of the institutions concerned. For example, there may be two systems that each contain extensive free markets; but in the former the market mechanism exists alongside others, while in the latter the market order is rigorously enforced, such that no other institutional form is permitted.

For the basic building blocks of such complexities, Crouch (2005) uses the concept of different types of governance developed by Rogers Hollingsworth and other neo-institutionalists (Campbell, Hollingsworth, and Lindberg 1991; Hollingsworth and Boyer 1997; Hollingsworth, Schmitter, and Streeck 1994; Hollingsworth, Müller, and Hollingsworth 2002). Governance comprises those mechanisms that maintain the stability of institutions, and are therefore at the heart of institutional determinism. A number of different governance modes can be identified, including the state (as both government and a system of law), the market, the hierarchical internal authority of the corporation, formal associations, and a number of less former institutions ranging from networks to communities. Different modes are likely to produce institutions with different forms of behaviour. Again, however, an empirical case may contain a combination of two or more of these mechanisms. The balance of these combinations may change, producing changes in the institutions themselves (Crouch 2005: ch 5). Recent developments by writers in the French *régulationiste* school, which used to insist on a rather rigid characterization of forms or stages of capitalism, have similarly led to far more variegated analyses. This enables writers in this school to identify a complex variety of forms of capitalism, though still tending to be limited to national types (Amable 2003; Boyer 2004*a*, *b*).

In these different ways, various contributors to the neo-institutionalist tradition have shown how it is possible to cope with diversity and major change while retaining the concept of institutional constraint. There is no claim to predict the kinds of changes and innovations that will be undertaken: this literature is an actor-centred institutionalism (Scharpf 1997) that provides scope for agents. But they are not completely free agents, their range of initiative being bounded somehow by their institutional starting point: the random walk.

By looking at local cases and specific sectors, we are here better able to explore the potentiality for variation and change around a strong institutional core that lies in the hands of key actors than is the case with the national accounts that dominate the literature (for other local and sectoral approaches, see Crouch et al. 2001, 2004; Hollingsworth et al. 1994;

Swann et al. 1998). By considering particular sectors in particular localities we are able to identify more clearly a particular institutional configuration than if we look for signs of change within a generalized and amalgamated national case. We can then examine to what extent that localized sector corresponds to the account usually given in the literature of the national institutional structure.

Therefore for us an initial question is: *Do governance structures of the local economies conform to the national innovation regime of their country, in which they are 'embedded', or do local economies institutionally diverge?* In order to answer this, it will be necessary to specify national innovation and production regimes, differentiated by institutional sectors (corporate financing, corporate governance, industrial relations, vocational and further training, inter-firm cooperation, national innovation modes), on the basis of existing literature in this field. In a second step, local economies will be analysed on the basis of our own empirical research (statistical calculations and in-depth interviews), in order to give an overview of the particularities in the governance of the selected case studies. These are the fundamental means by which the profile of the national innovation regime can be distinguished from the governance of the selected local economies.

A second question is: *Can it be shown that particularities in the governance of local economies contribute to the economic success of these entities?* If departure from national systems is found only in failing local economies, the hypothesis of the priority of national systems would be supported rather than refuted.

Finally: *Does the divergence of local economies from structural patterns of the national innovation and production system enable us to suggest in which institutional sectors local economies may successfully diverge from the national model and in which not?* If local and sectoral departures from national innovation and production regimes can be demonstrated, new insights will be provided for the relevance of complementary orders and incoherences between institutional sectors of these regimes. Do the governance structures of similar local economic branches in different countries show similarities, which would hint at a dominance of sectoral particularities, prevailing in all cases regardless of country patterns or national innovation and production models? The varieties of capitalism literature itself argues that there may be branch-specific governance requirements, but usually assumes that an ability to provide appropriate governance for a branch will depend on the national system in place.

These questions lead us in particular to look for the following forms of departure from apparent national institutional orders:

1. There may be characteristics of local institutions and infrastructure that support forms of economic organization that differ from and may even 'defy' the overall national architecture.

2. In a stronger version of 1, there may actually be creative incoherences at work, rather than confusion and handicap, in the difference between national and local, whereby local institutional entrepreneurs are able to produce innovative outcomes, working between the contradictory incentives of national and local institutions.
3. Firms may at times be less bounded by national institutions than theory about the national base of types of capitalism usually assumes.

The Cases

The above arguments have led us to a methodology of microanalysis and case studies. Only in that way can we identify the details of easily ignored diversity that may produce major change, or the cases that show how and why activities considered to be impossible within a nation state of a certain classified type may in fact thrive. Of course, as we have already stressed, case studies can demonstrate only that something can possibly exist in a certain context. They cannot demonstrate relative importance or typicality. It is therefore important to be careful in the interpretation of case-study evidence. For example, if a study shows that dedicated banking arrangements specializing in a particular sector can develop at local level in the UK, it does not disprove overall characterizations of British banking as arm's-length and market-driven. Nor does it demonstrate that British banks can easily slip into this different mode, let alone that in general they are changing towards it. It does, however, refute the contention that British banks would find such behaviour impossible; it may lead us to explanations of how it was possible in the case in hand; it draws our attention to a possible productive incoherence and an unexpected local-level complementarity; and just possibly it may alert us to steps in progress towards more significant change. Case studies can demonstrate possibilities, and they can lead to speculation about possible more general developments, suggesting hypotheses for further research; that is all. These are therefore the only ambitions of our project.

The cases to be studied cover different forms in the evolution of production in the industrial and post-industrial economy: a craft industry (furniture-making); the paradigmatic mass-production industry (motor car manufacture); an advanced, high-science and high-tech industry (biopharmaceuticals); and a high-tech services activity (television film-making). Our studies attempt to answer our questions through a series of paired comparisons, each taking a German case and one from another national context. As already noted, Germany is the country on which the idea of a coordinated market economy has been most directly based. According to this concept, German firms should do well in twentieth-century industries requiring highly skilled manual labour, stable banking capital, and constant fine adaptations to improve existing ranges of products, but should not succeed in sectors requiring radical, science-based innovation with rapidly changing knowledge, and highly flexible capital. They are also regarded as being unlikely to succeed in services as opposed to manufacturing. Among our four sectors, we should therefore expect German firms to be successful in furniture-making and motor-manufacture, but less successful in biopharmaceuticals and television.

Furniture-Making

Furniture-making exists also in non-industrial societies. Its production processes were transformed by mechanization, but many of its products do not depend on mechanization for either their design or their existence. It has historically been a craft industry, dependent on high levels of manual skill and small firms, and this usually remains the case at the expensive and high added-value end of the range. But fully mechanized production on Fordist principles in large corporations has also developed strongly in the sector. Given that this is a light industry, with portable products, with pre-industrial roots but easily subject to mass production, it is easily susceptible to globalization for low-priced mass-market products. But some production continues in high-wage industrialized countries. This gives rise to obvious questions: under what circumstances is this survival possible? In what parts of the market are furniture firms in rich countries operating? Are they thriving? And, most important, what institutional arrangements are associated with their success and in which countries is it possible to find these arrangements?

For this industry we compare the traditional district Ostwestfalen-Lippe in north-eastern Nordrhein-Westfalen with a similar traditional case in Småland and Västra Götaland in southern Sweden. Germany is known as a country in which smaller enterprises can thrive; they are well organized, and law and fiscal regime are favourable to them and to family-based business in general. Establishing a strong *Mittelstand* was fundamental to Christian Democratic policies for avoiding what was seen as the massification of society represented by both communism and Nazism, the two nightmares with which mid-twentieth-century Germany had been confronted. Sweden, in contrast, is an economy of large firms consolidated around an even smaller group of holding companies. This pattern dates back to the aristocratic character of early Swedish industrialization, but it was also favoured by the social democratic and trade union forces that have dominated the polity since the 1930s. Organized labour was suspicious of small enterprises, where it was always more difficult to establish trade unions; and was reluctant to facilitate the inter-generational transfers of wealth needed for the maintenance of independent family firms. Although there are of course many small firms in Sweden, the Swedish economy therefore developed most strongly in sectors dominated by large corporations: mining, motor vehicles, traditional pharmaceuticals, and telecommunications. Further, it was the strategy of Swedish labour to encourage the mechanization and even robotization of industry in order to increase the productivity of relatively unskilled labour. It was not interested in low-technology craft sectors likely to pay low wages. We should therefore predict a very poor outlook for an SME-based furniture industry in Sweden, certainly much poorer than in Germany. However, if an SME sector in Sweden manages to be successful, we should see some divergence from the national model, whereas this should not be necessary in Germany, whose institutional structure should cater well to the needs of small-scale furniture companies.

Motor-Vehicle Manufacture

Motor-vehicle manufacture has been the classic industry of the mass-production age, and was a major contributor to manufacturing output in many industrial countries in the second half of the twentieth century. It too has been challenged by globalization. European and North American producers were challenged first by Japan, then by Korea. In addition, Western European and US firms have located a growing share of their production outside their core region. Most recently, there has been a shift to the post-communist economies of Central and Eastern Europe, and also to China. Although famously subjected to Taylorist techniques during the early twentieth century, which enabled it to employ low-skilled labour, motor manufacturing was transformed in the last third of that century to become far more demanding on its labour force, suppliers, and institutional infrastructure. In Germany and Japan in particular there were major developments in both advanced machinery and labour skill that made possible more efficient production and greater sophistication as well as variety of products. These combined with developments originating in Japan, which improved the efficiency and quality of relations between the core manufacturing firms and their suppliers that depended on both high skills and high levels of organization. It also became an industry in which constant improvements in design and product performance and variety became major instruments of competition. Consequently, the automobile industry is seen as one of the core sectors for incremental innovation. Therefore, here the key questions relate mainly to the institutional requirements of the shift in production away from the core countries. What does a new production area require if it is to compete at these sophisticated levels?

The accidents of history here make possible an exceptional experiment. German motor manufacturing firms have invested heavily in production in the countries of Central Europe, which, having thrown off most of the institutional legacy of their Soviet period, may be considered to have generally weak national institutions and therefore not to have acquired their own distinctive national forms of capitalism. But one among them, the German Democratic Republic, was allowed to unite itself to the western Federal Republic of Germany almost directly after the fall of communism, and in theory immediately inherited all West German institutions, an entire *acquis nationale*. The other central European countries had both the obligation and the opportunity to construct, or to import, new institutional structures, possibly in continuity with some survivals from the past. We here therefore compare the plant established by the Volkswagen-Audi group in Zwickau, Saxony, in Eastern Germany, with that in Győr in North-western Hungary. Neo-institutionalist theory would predict that, provided the West German institutions had been appropriately transferred, an East German region would soon start to operate as part of a coordinated economy, and would therefore succeed at the motor industry. It is not clear that the various schools of capitalist diversity have much to say about Hungary, as their protagonists have not yet classified the former communist countries. Have Eastern German *Länder* simply inherited West German institutions, or has the transfer embodied deviations that might contain innovative possibilities? Hungary we see as a meeting point of many institutional fragments: some national historical residues; some path-independent new approaches; some regional specificities; institutional borrowings; and not least the organizational preferences of VW-Audi itself—which may or may not be simple transfers of their practices in Germany and other Western European economies. Indeed, the conduct of VW-Audi in Zwickau also raises questions whether individual enterprises follow national policy in taking former West German institutions into the *neue Länder*; while the Hungarian case raises questions concerning which constraints of the German model are adhered to only because they are imposed, and which firms would follow even without that pressure.

Biopharmaceuticals

Biotechnology, and in particular biopharmaceuticals, are becoming as emblematic of the early twenty-first century as motor vehicles were of the late twentieth century. The sector applies very advanced science and strong links between universities and the rest of the public research base on the one hand, with flexible and sophisticated firms on the other. It has distinctive and high requirements for skills, financial arrangements, corporate governance, and legislative framework. Since it is concerned with human health, it is subjected to intensive regulation, with intervals of several years between setting the objective to attempt a new product and its arrival in the market. The question that arises is: given the preciseness of these requirements, is this sector one that can thrive only in certain institutional contexts, as anticipated by Stephen Casper (Casper 2000, 2002; Casper and Kettler 2001; Casper, Jong, and Murray 2004; Casper, Lehrer, and Soskice 1999) who considers that liberal markets of the British and US kind are particularly adapted to favour high-risk entrepreneurial activities in new sectors.

The strongest biopharmaceuticals district in Germany is that around Munich, the capital of Bavaria. If varieties of capitalism and neo-classical theory are correct, this sector should be weak and lacking a conducive institutional environment. If the sector has strengths, according to our theory these should be explained either through local specificities of the region or sectoral specificities that shield it from national institutions, or through previously unrecognized elements in the national institutional structure. Within Europe the UK is usually seen as the closest to a liberal market economy and the first successful biotechnology and high-tech region is usually considered to be that around the city of Cambridge (Casper and Kettler 2001). We shall therefore compare Munich with this district, and also examine the relationship of the Cambridge area to the national British institutional structure.

Television Film-Making

Having considered cases from three phases of industrialization, for our last we turn to the post-industrial economy, towards a services sector that uses the products of advanced technology. Television film-making has been transformed in recent years by both technological and organizational changes. First, developments in camera and lighting technology have transformed the skills needed by camera teams and reduced the numbers of personnel needed in a team. Second, the break-up of public monopoly television programme providers produced a major growth of very small enterprises. The question arises whether one can identify institutional contexts more and less likely to respond positively to these changes. In other words: what institutional framework is used by modern TV production firms and which, if any, national model does it resemble?

We here again use a comparison between Germany and the UK. In both countries national broadcasting monopolies were required to down-size their in-house production activities and purchase programmes from independent producers. In both cases a large number of very small, project-based firms developed, and in both, anxieties were expressed that some important collective goods provided for the sector by the public producer—in particular workforce training—would be at risk. Both countries were equally affected by the changes taking place in camera and other film technology, which were also seen to have implications for training. The British industry is focused on the national capital, London, though in reality it is concentrated on a very small part of that city, the area known as Soho that has long been a centre for the film and entertainment industry. In Germany it is concentrated on Cologne in Nordrhein-Westfalen, close to the previous capital of the Western Republic, Bonn. Neo-institutional theory would expect the British liberal-market economy to be better able to respond to the changes, because of its flexibility.

The Changing National Contexts

Before embarking on these comparative studies it is necessary to consider the basic characterizations that emerge from the existing literature of the national economies with which we are here concerned: Germany, Sweden, Hungary, and the UK. We shall not do this in a static and stereotypical way, but by attempting to recognize that these are all economies that have undergone major institutional change during the past two decades. These national 'portraits' therefore have to be 'moving images'. This enables authors of the case study chapters to relate their local findings, not to an outdated national account but to one as contemporary as their own research. Not to do this would risk presenting as a comparison between local and national something that was in effect a comparison over time. We present these national accounts in the following two chapters. One is devoted to Germany, as this is the country at the centre of the study; the other deals more briefly with the other three.

2

Rule-Breaking and Freedom of Rules in National Production Models: How German Capitalism Departs from the 'Rhenish Equilibrium'

ULRICH GLASSMANN*

Accounts of the German socio-economic 'model' frequently start from an image of how that economy and its institutions operated in the 1980s and early 1990s. Not only has this become out of date, but the fact that this is a system undergoing continuing change means that it is difficult to depict German institutions in a state of equilibrium. They have to be presented, not only very differently from the outdated accounts but also as institutions undergoing change. This becomes clear at a number of points in the following chapters, as, for example, when Keune, Piotti, Tóth, and Crouch (Chapter 5) compare the situation in the eastern part of Germany with the western, and repeatedly need to point out that the latter is changing. In this present chapter I try to give an account of this 'moving image', rather than a 'snapshot' of contemporary German capitalism, to provide a base for the appraisal of the regional and sectoral variants of that economy that appears in later chapters.

How the German Model Used to Work

While local and sectoral differences of the kinds that are discussed in subsequent chapters have long existed in Germany, certain peculiar features of the general national system have been well known: for instance financial institutions supporting industry through a *Hausbanken* relationship. This special connection between the world of finance and industry involves the ownership of a large amount of German enterprise shares by credit institutions, which combine their own interest with those of the company by lending money to firms, especially in times of economic crisis. As a result of this, national firms

* For their valuable support in gathering data I would like to thank Natalie Ruppert and Jan Sauermann.

always received particular support from banks, allowing them to finance and stimulate new innovation processes in established product markets.

At the same time, corporate governance structures have been rather stakeholder oriented and not very transparent. Consequently, the capital market was attractive to institutional investors like banks or state organizations, but rather unattractive to small shareholders and foreign private investors. As the representatives of financial institutions occupied seats on the corporate boards of large enterprises, banks could easily influence long-term firm strategies; so could trade unions, which were guaranteed rights of co-determination through the same institutional mechanism. This institutional interplay created a consensus-driven behaviour of actors on the capital and labour front, often supported by associational bargaining and state mediation. Thus, hostile takeovers of large enterprises by other firms were rather rare. In general, firms survived economic downturns with relatively cheap credits from their *Hausbanken*, while small- and medium-sized companies (SMEs) often turned to regional public sector banks in order to capitalize.

The dual system of industrial relations enabled capital and labour to ensure social peace. As it allows firm-specific measures to be negotiated on many issues, while wage determination is delegated to the autonomous system of free-collective bargaining on the associational level, strike rates have been rather low. Nevertheless, the German production model was tied to a high-wage economy in which professionally skilled workers operated very autonomously on the shop floor, thus contributing to the high quality of manufactured goods.

One of the most important institutions that supported this path of production can clearly be seen in the dual system of vocational training, which served as a model for many other countries and provided workers with certified training according to formalized vocational profiles. Drop-out rates in this system could be kept at a very low level (Münch 1995). The same can be stated for wage differentials, which illustrated the capacity of formal institutions in German capitalism to prevent the rise of a dual labour market (Streeck 1997).

Many of these developments date back to the reconstruction of the economy in the Bonn Republic after the Second World War. The German economy became a strongly embedded world of high-quality production (Streeck 1991), with export-oriented industries, generating advanced knowledge in the car market, machinery manufacturing, electronics, and industries alike. However, this model came under pressure many times, certainly during and after the oil price crisis in the 1970s when it became difficult to contain inflation and unemployment rates increased (Scharpf 2000).It also suffered from the deregulation of financial markets and the following events in the 1980s, and many of its original institutional arrangements were transformed as a result of German unification, the Treaty of Maastricht, and the establishment of the single European market in the 1990s (Schmidt 2002). Despite all that, many observers of the German political economy are undecided whether these events have caused any real changes inside the above-mentioned institutions, or whether we just witness slight adaptations by which this model is maintained with its core functions, thus only revising some of its internal processes in order to achieve the same results. This chapter seeks to answer the following question: if and how the institutions of German capitalism have changed.

The German Model Today

We shall here limit our attention to the institutional sectors identified in Chapter 1 as central to the current study: the financial sector, companies, and their internal governance structure, the system of industrial relations, the vocational training system, the management of inter-firm relations, and the national innovation system. These will be examined in turn in an inter-temporal perspective. Use will be made of indicators often employed to show whether those features, which have always been regarded as being typ-ical for the German production system, still exist, and if they do, to what extent they have changed. Evidence from various case studies will also be used.

Enterprise Financing

As mentioned above, larger German banks like Deutsche Bank or Dresdner Bank have maintained close relationships to German industry and tradition-ally supported German enterprises with credits. Historically, this is because industrialists founded many of the larger German banks in order to capitalize large-firm entrepreneurial activity (Lütz 2000). The whole financial sector was shaped by a self-regulatory regime, involving banks, industry, and associa-tions. This arrangement allowed every actor to control the strategies of the others. For instance, banks were able to control enterprise strategies through their influence on the corporate board of directors, which was important for them as large moneylenders and institutional shareholders. Firms could rely on large financing institutions when markets turned down, because banks wanted to gain revenues from these enterprises. In order to make sure that German firms could deal with economic downturns, banks actively engaged in credits to support innovations, which are generally inevitable in times of crisis, but increasingly difficult to finance.

Associations, especially the unions, supported the *Hausbankenprinzip*, because they were guaranteed some influence on the regulation of the finan-cial sector. More precisely, they gained influence through co-determination, but more importantly they preferred a system in which institutional investors stabilized national enterprises. As a result of this, major layoffs became less likely than in economies with shareholder-oriented financing systems which

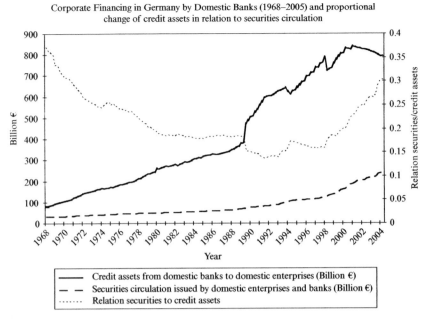

FIGURE 2.1. Corporate financing in Germany by domestic banks (1968–2005)

Source: Deutsche Bundesbank: Zeitreihen-Datenbank.

Note: Securities include stock market shares of domestic enterprises and industry bonds.

promoted such measures indirectly. The *Hausbankenprinzip* therefore protected the clientele of the unions and increased their credibility in public.

In sum, every group of actors concerned with business, financing, and labour took impressive benefits from this system. The arrangement may be depicted as an equilibrium. At the same time, this analysis raises the question why any of the involved actors should have wished to depart from it. First of all, it can be shown by Fig. 2.1 that banks did indeed do so. The two indicators used are the amount of credit assets given from domestic banks to domestic enterprises and second the amount of securities circulation issued by domestic banks and domestic enterprises. Moreover, the specific relation between the two indicators is of importance, because if enterprise-financing institutions would not have changed, the relation between the two indicators should not have changed as well. The first indicator represents the more or less classic activity German banks performed when giving credits to domestic enterprises. The second represents activities on the comparatively underemployed private capital market. We witness a clear trend reversal between the two indicators. Although credit business by banks has increased enormously in absolute terms, financing institutions did not simply reinforce their traditional money-lending strategy. Quite in contrast, securities circulation issued by domestic banks and enterprises has also increased.

As can be inferred from Fig. 2.1, the unification process has contributed to the increase of credit business. Thus, higher amounts of credit assets cannot be interpreted as a reinforcement of enterprise support by banks. They are simply an expression of new market opportunities in East Germany, now being included as 'domestic credit business'. The relation between credit assets and securities circulation, however, changes dramatically from 1999 onwards. So far, we do not witness a higher importance of private capital markets in contrast to credit business, but an extreme and continuous trend reversal over the last six years.

What happened? Why should banks and domestic enterprises behave differently now and why should they depart from the Rhenish equilibrium? The deregulation of capital markets and an increasing internationalization of national economies from the 1980s onwards have changed incentive structures, both for German banks and for German companies. In an environment of increased international competition the Rhenish equilibrium caused some major problems. One could imagine that cooperation could have been maintained, had not both companies and banks come under stress more or less at the same time. While German companies relied on banks as important institutional investors, open capital markets offered many alternative investment options for German financing institutions. However, the universal banking system was not designed to provide adequate support for investment banking in the first place. Because of this, some banks began to restructure their business and merged with investment banks from abroad. For instance, Deutsche Bank merged with Morgan Grenfell and later with Bankers Trust, while Dresdner Bank merged with Kleinwort Benson (Lütz 2000). But these new players followed different rules and were not bound to principles of national solidarity. Quite in contrast, investment bankers even earn commissions if they succeed in organizing hostile takeovers. Although this paradigm shift was clearly intended by the respective national banks, the consequences were probably less understood, at least by the public. Because of this, even employees of the traditional banks reacted with outrage when it was revealed in 1997 that Krupp had organized a hostile takeover of its most renowned German competitor in steel production, Thyssen, with the deliberate support of Deutsche Bank (Beyer and Höpner 2003). More precisely, the deal was initiated by the investment bank Deutsche Morgan Grenfell. Although the hostile takeover did not materialize—because both companies agreed to talk amicably about synergies in steel production, and because the unions protested against the large numbers of layoffs which would have been unavoidable—this event certainly made clear how outdated the *Hausbankenprinzip* was becoming. Lütz (2000: 17) observes that '[d]omestically, the big banks are deliberately *disengaging themselves from industry* ... in an effort to improve their international reputation as security traders and business consultants'.

This has had two important consequences: first, German banks withdrew more and more from risky credit business, even if national enterprises ran into trouble financing their innovation measures in times of crisis, and second, they reduced their shareholding in national enterprises in order to avoid conflicts of interests.

German firms have thus experienced a twofold problem in the 1990s: they tended to lose their most important investors, and they could no longer rely on cheap credits when times were hard. And times became incredibly hard in the 1990s, with a recession in 1992 and 1993 that hit the most established industrial sectors, the car industry and the machinery industry among others experiencing the most dramatic challenges (Crouch 2004). In a reaction to this development, large firms restructured considerably in the mid-1990s. Car manufacturers quickly understood that in the new era of international competition, firms needed to be present in foreign markets in order to aggressively displace competitors, who formerly satisfied regional demand. Large firms needed fresh capital in order to reposition themselves in the international market environment, while at the same time conditions for private shareholding were anything but transparent and institutional investors withdrew. At this moment, the Rhenish equilibrium was beyond the pale for the second group of players: large firms.

The *Hausbankenprinzip* clearly deteriorated generally over the past decade. If this is found in case studies, it should not be treated as an exceptional characteristic of a local economy. In earlier work on the German machinery industry (Glassmann 2004) we found leaders of SMEs in the Stuttgart region explaining that their *Hausbanken* had stopped supporting industry after the famous Maho-Deckel machinery firm had had to declare bankruptcy. The withdrawal of banks certainly reinforced the recession of the early 1990s. Furthermore, these SMEs did not hint at alternative ways of enterprise financing apart from self-financing through family money. It has also been difficult for innovative concepts of enterprise financing to emerge. As an evaluation of the federal government in 2004 revealed the following:

The worldwide collapse of start-up financing in the recent years has hit Germany in a disproportionate manner. Due to this, technology-oriented start-ups are hampered in Germany and young research-intensive enterprises are endangered ... in the very early phase of research and development based start-ups the market for venture capital in Germany has almost completely run dry (Bundesministerium für Wirtschaft und Arbeit/Bundesministerium für Bildung und Forschung 2004: 7).

As a result, the federal government has started to promote new forms of enterprise financing, especially directed at *Mittelstand* firms, thus expanding entrepreneurial capacities for innovation. With a particular concern for the access of venture capital, it has offered resources financed through equity funds from the European Recovery Programme (originating from the

Marshall Plan), the European Investment Fund, and private capital in order to foster initial research and development (R&D) initiatives.

Corporate Governance Structures

As mentioned above, a second group of players departed from the Rhenish equilibrium in the 1990s: large companies. One of the fundamental problems for large firms was that they had to buy markets and were in need of large amounts of financial resources in order to stay competitive, while the German model mainly provided such resources through declining arrangements of institutional shareholding. Managers of the larger firms like Daimler-Benz started to restructure (Töpfer 1998) and increased the firms' attractiveness to private shareholders (Beyer and Höpner 2003: 180). This opening was directed at attracting financial resources from the private capital market and included several different measures. Among these was the option to get listed at the New York Stock Exchange. In order to do this, firms had to adopt American accounting standards. Enterprise profit and spending strategies needed to become more transparent. On the legal side this process was supported by the new corporate sector supervision and transparency act (KonTraG) in 1998. This law changed many provisions under commercial and stock corporation law. For instance, the liability of the board of directors, consultancy firms, and managing boards has been increased. Moreover, it introduced innovative forms of risk management, now implemented by large corporations. In particular, financial institutions take their profit from these innovations. New forms of transparency, like firm ratings, entail risk management by which investment profitability is evaluated. This turns out to be an important instrument for banks to develop indicators for their investment strategies. Thus, KonTraG changed the corporate world in Germany.

Many larger companies concentrated on core competences, in order to make way for the reallocation of investments in one particular sector, like car production. At the end of this process larger firms started to merge with foreign companies of the same sector in order to complement their product line and distribution network. This aim was pursued for instance by Daimler and Chrysler.

The downside of all this was the rapid sale of subsidiaries, the closure of plant sections, and the creation of major redundancies. In the face of high non-wage labour costs, employment became a mere 'cost issue' that needed to be dealt with. Tax avoidance became an imperative on the strategy agenda of the managing boards of large companies. In short, more or less within a decade, many large enterprises, which were renowned for their responsible interaction with labour, finance, and cooperating firms, constituting truly social institutions, transformed into primarily market-oriented production structures. These are steered by new crews of managers who see themselves confronted with totally different incentive structures and opportunities. In response, they depart from old rules, moving their activities to the global scale. This development certainly contains a destructive force which is not primarily driven by entrepreneurial creativity. These changes have probably been underestimated, because they were not first of all driven by inventions but by restructuring processes. Economic activity itself has changed, not its physical production outcome. The process involved a repositioning of the most powerful actors in the world of business and finance. The dissolution of formerly established interlocking contacts is quite impressive. Thus, Beyer and Höpner (2003: 184) wrote the following:

Until the mid-1980s, the extent of interlocking directorates between the 100 biggest German companies was stable; starting in 1984, it began to decline from 12% of all possible interlocks to less than seven% by 1998. . . . Between 1996 and 2000, the number of capital ties between the 100 biggest German companies declined from 169 to 80.

Institutional structures have changed enormously, which is why *The Economist* (2005: 9) commented as follows:

Germany's surprising economy: . . . Germany's big companies have restructured and cut their bloated cost base. . . . Given this corporate turnaround and strong export performance, it is not surprising that both profits and the stock market have been rising sharply.

However, the process did not seem to increase the employability of workers, or job opportunities in creative industries. Company and bank management just restructured what was already there, causing exclusion among older and less qualified workers on the labour market. There remains also a lack of exchange of innovative ideas and truly entrepreneurial activity beyond the mere restructuring processes of large firms and finance.

German corporate governance structures have therefore changed enormously. Thus, if in our case studies we find shareholder-oriented companies, which try to acquire financial resources through private capital market institutions, this should not be regarded as completely unorthodox behaviour. As with financial institutions, corporate governance structures have changed, but this transformation has also damaged the economy. In particular, it has affected employment opportunities and worsened the survival rate of smaller supplier firms.

Industrial Relations: Alive or Eroding?

While it has long been assumed that associations, the third player supporting the Rhenish equilibrium, would rather keep their institutional structures and would probably remain a more constant factor among the institutions of German capitalism, Anke Hassel (1999) has shown that industrial relations in Germany tend to erode. First of all, the coverage of the system is declining,

TABLE 2.1. Collective agreements vs. company agreements (1989–2004)

	West Germany		East Germany		Germany	
	Number of collective agreements	Company agreements as % of total agreements	Number of collective agreements	Company agreements as % of total agreements	Number of collective agreements	Company agreements as % of total agreements
1989	32,000	25	—	—	32,000	25
1990	33,449	26	670	64	34,119	27
1991	35,295	28	2,372	64	37,667	30
1992	36,123	28	3,368	49	39,491	30
1993	37,179	29	4,548	48	41,727	31
1994	37,933	30	5,233	48	43,166	32
1995	37,747	32	5,891	49	43,638	34
1996	38,508	32	6,640	47	45,148	34
1997	40,066	33	7,268	46	47,334	35
1998	41,828	34	7,712	46	49,540	35
1999	43,517	36	8,051	48	51,568	37
2000	46,277	37	8,663	48	54,940	39
2001	48,669	38	8,926	50	57,595	40
2002	48,176	41	9,153	50	57,329	42
2003	49,589	43	10,047	49	59,636	44
2004	51,095	44	10,677	50	61,772	45

Sources: Hassel (1999: 494, Table 6); Bundesministerium für Wirtschaft und Arbeit (1998–2004).

affecting both works councils and wage agreements. Second, collective agreements appear to be more and more decentralized. Decentralization, it is argued, destabilizes the balanced division of labour between company-level activities and associational bargaining. Social peace, it was assumed in the past, has been successfully ensured because industrial relations were organized in the form of a dual system. Wage bargaining was delegated to the associational level and only firm-specific measures were left to the works councils (Jacobi, Keller, and Müller-Jentsch 1998). Unlike many other countries, Germany could resist a process of decentralization in the 1980s (Hassel 1999), due to the capabilities of the industrial relations system to introduce flexible measures through firm-level representation of labour. Exactly this division of labour was at stake in the 1990s (Table 2.1).

As customer firms have begun to squeeze their suppliers in order to make them produce for lower costs, while non-wage labour costs are generally high and have been rising, firms could no longer accept sectoral and nationwide agreements which narrowed their scope for competitive offers or just did not suit counter-cyclical developments at firm level. Because of this, during the 1990s firms started to resign from employers' associations. An interesting empirical account for this development in the machinery industry is given by Schroeder (1997). As a result, collective wage agreements no longer cover the same proportion of firms and workers. Hassel (2002: 312) noted that between 1995 and 1998 the coverage rates of West German plants shrank from 53.4 to 47.7 per cent. In East Germany the share fell from 27.6 to 25.8 per cent between 1996 and 1998. The same trend can be shown for the coverage rates of employees by collective agreements. In West Germany coverage declined from 72.2 to 67.8 per cent in the years between 1995 and 1998 and in Eastern Germany from 56.2 to 50.5 per cent in the same period of time (ibid.).

The erosion thesis has been contested by Thomas Klikauer (2002), who argues that the works council system is of continuing importance, that shop stewards should be taken into account as a significant resource of the unions to solve problems on the plant level, that regional-level bargaining is stable and 'tripartite arrangements are still flourishing' (Klikauer 2002: 296). Although he raises interesting objections, Hassel replied that Klikauer's interpretation of the accessible data is rather obscure (Hassel 2002). Do the indicators used give any evidence of a real erosion of the system? Could the transformation of the industrial relations system instead preserve a certain strength of the unions? Although it is true that some legal provisions like co-determination rights were strengthened under the SPD/Greens government, and that these provisions help further to install the unions as powerful veto players, their base of legitimacy and their capability for centralized action is definitely in decline. What remains for them is not a positive influence on the coming shape of modern workplaces and payment, but a veto power resting on a declining mandate. Because of this, indicators like centralization, density, and coverage are indeed important, because they show to what extent unions' activities are designed to solve labour conflicts without damaging the national or local economy.

Hassel argues that the most important indicator is the relation between company-level representation and associational bargaining, since the particular balance of these two spheres in the industrial relations system was claimed to be responsible for '... social equality, industrial peace and economic performance' in Germany (ibid. 309 f.). Table 2.1 shows to what extent the system decentralized its organizational structures between 1989 and 2004 in West and East Germany. Company-level agreements continuously increased as a share of total agreements from 25 per cent up to 45 per cent between 1989 and 2004 in all Germany.

However, if we differentiate between East and West, it can easily be seen that the main paradigm shift occurred in the West where the number of company-level agreements used to be rather low in 1989, but show a continuous increase of almost 20 per cent until 2004. In the East the whole system was much more decentralized from reunification onwards and quickly stabilized at around 50 per cent of company-level agreements after a short phase of centralization from 1990 to 1992. Thus, although today the two systems

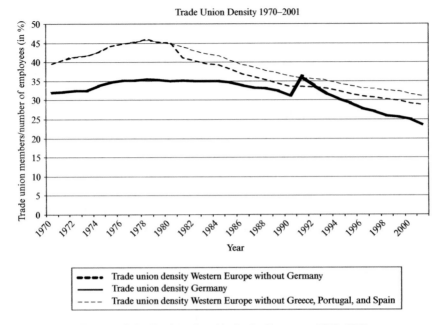

FIGURE 2.2. Trade union density in Germany, 1970–2001

Source: OECD (2003): Labour Force Statistics: Corporate Data Environment.

almost converge, one should not infer from this that industrial relations in the East are identical to those in the West. Institutional transfer has attempted to achieve similar features, but delegates from Western associations were rarely accepted as coequal partners to fight for the interests of workers in declining firms and industries. The decentralized structure in the East therefore remained in its place. Unions do not always receive strong support in East Germany, because their organizational structure and staff is still generally associated with Western interests.

There is also clear evidence of union membership decline. It shrank to 25 per cent in 2001 and seems to be declining more quickly than the Western European average, as can be inferred from Fig. 2.2. After reunification, membership rates went up due to the high numbers of membership in East Germany, but this proved to be temporary. The disproportionate loss of members in the East during this time influenced the overall decline, but density rates in the West are unstable as well: 'While membership in the East was halved during the first six years after unification, about a quarter of trade union members were lost in the West' (Hassel 2002: 314).

One could still claim that all these profound transformations have had little effect on outcomes of the industrial relations system, for instance income differentials. These used to be rather low and stable in the German economy. However, as Fig. 2.3 shows, even this is no longer the case. In both parts

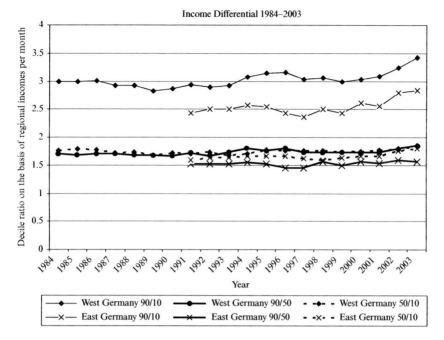

FIGURE 2.3.   Income differentials in Germany, 1984–2003
Source: DIW 2004, SOEP-Monitor.

of Germany income differentials between the top and bottom deciles started to increase since around 2000. With respect to wages Kitschelt and Streeck (2004: 18) concede that '… Germany is one of the more egalitarian countries'. In addition, however, German workers have accepted longer working hours and even wage cuts. *The Economist* (2005: 9) summed up the result of this changing world of work:

Thanks in part to this new flexibility, unit labour costs, a benchmark for competitiveness, have fallen sharply relative to other countries. In the past five years Germany, long the most costly place in Europe in which to do business, has won a new competitive edge over France, Italy, the Netherlands and even Britain. That is a big reason why, last year, it regained its position as the world's biggest exporter.

Another interesting observation can be made of Fig. 2.3. It again shows that the political economy of Germany integrates two worlds of production and industrial relations. While the data depicting income differentials for West Germany (90/50) and (50/10) more or less converge on the same decile ratio, those for East Germany do not. Here the (50/10) ratio shows a higher decile ratio than the (90/50), which means that the differential between middle and low incomes in the East is higher than the differential between high and middle incomes. As a result we see true winner and loser groups emerging: high-income groups in the West versus low-income groups in the East, the latter suffering the most from transformation. It was in the East that unions lost members disproportionately, the system remained decentralized, and coverage is much lower. The industrial relations system has become fragile, because it still supports an insider–outsider labour market. Unions may thus be seen as strong players, and in fact they still are strong, but their base is eroding as well as their influence on social peace and egalitarian politics.

The Vocational Training System

The vocational training system has been much debated over since the mid-1990s (Crouch, Finegold, and Sako 1999; Kern and Sabel 1994). Originally it was seen as the most important pillar for high-quality production and worker integration. Drop-out rates could be kept at a very low level in international comparison (Münch 1995); certified skills, especially for manufacturing jobs, were mediated in theory (public vocational schools) and practice (firms) at a high educational level. Distinguished formal vocational profiles secured the social status of the worker and a high level of qualification yielded high incomes. Apprentices obtain their formal certification from chambers of industry and commerce, armed for the external labour market. Originally emerging from craft industries, the formal vocational profiles of the dual system could not always keep pace with industrial development, though it was usually able eventually to adapt new technologies. (For example, CNC-turning machines demanded a different set of skills than older technologies which relied much more on the craft-component, even in industrial production. New vocational profiles were created, demand and supply became more balanced again, and the system seemed to recover.)

In the 1990s the same scenario recurred, first in the metal-manufacturing industry, because machinery design and electrical engineering increasingly grew together. But the vocational schools, which maintained the division of labour, demanding specialization either in machinery or in electrical engineering, did not bring together these skills in one vocational profile (Bahnmüller 1997). At the same time lean production and team work were on the strategy agenda of many firm managers, trying to absorb Japanese organizational structures into German corporate culture (Streeck 1996). It was always assumed that the dual training system, because it maintained a high degree of vocational specialization, and because it supported further qualification up to the *Meister*, had the effect of creating relatively strong hierarchies in German firms, preventing the establishment of loosely coupled teams on the shop-floor. So far this did not cause any concern, but the recession in 1992–3 made managers consider whether these structures provided adequate scope for flexible skill creation and worker assignment. This was a particular worry for the new emerging industries like information technology and media production, because the skills demanded could be taught only through completely new

Annually Signed Vocational Training Contracts in Germany (1978–2003)*
and Annual Percentage Change of Applicants Not Placed in an Apprenticeship

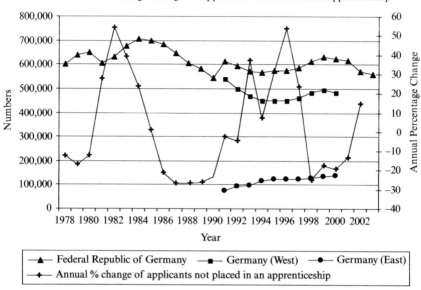

FIGURE 2.4. Vocational training contracts in Germany, 1978–2003

Source: Bundesinstitut für Berufliche Building: Graue Papiere (1978–2003) der Bundesagentur für Arbeit; * New contracts, evaluated end of September.

profiles. Moreover, demand sometimes included knowledge and skills very close to artistic abilities. The formal training system was not designed to teach such kind of creativity, because even if craft skills often demanded this component as well, it was directed at a defined work stage. If there is anything new about the new economy, it is indeed the artistic and 'playful' element of production in the new growth sectors, driven by either the natural sciences and engineering or the entertainment industry.

The old economy did not immediately yield to the new, but asserted its position as Germany's economic backbone. Interviews with machinery firms in 1999 demonstrated that firms were still reliant on the dual system of vocational training and preferred it to alternative training options (Glassmann 2004). Figure 2.4 shows that annually signed vocational training contracts in West Germany have declined over time. This alone does not demonstrate a linear decline of the system, but is strongly associated with a cyclical decline of offer of training contracts by enterprises because of the economic situation.

Growth in the services sectors and in cutting-edge technologies produce more significant problems, as these tend to require employees who are either more or less qualified than the products of the training system; there is demand for both employees with degrees and for those with low skills. There are shortages of graduate engineers, natural scientists, and highly trained employees for Internet and telecommunications businesses (BMBF 2005). At the same time the system is still extremely rigid. There is little counselling available at the federal employment office for persons who have obtained a particular occupational profile, but need to reorient at age 30. The system is designed for lifetime employment paths, while demand on the labour market is rapidly changing.

Meanwhile, many who have obtained a formal qualification but cannot find a job start to work on the basis of so-called *Minijob* or *Midijob* contracts. Here the worker, even if he has obtained vocational training in a different sector, only gets paid up to €400 or €800 a month. As a result of the Hartz-laws of the SPD/Green government, workers on such contracts contribute to social insurance progressively according to their salary, but as payment for these jobs lies below the poverty-threshold, they need to combine several of them or apply for social assistance.

Further, the training system does not deal easily with creativity. It assumes hierarchical enterprise structures, in which apprentices have little autonomy. If Richard Florida (2002, 2005a,b) is right that we witness 'The Rise of the Creative Class', and that creative industries provide important opportunities for growth and employment, then Germany is ill prepared for the workplaces of the future.

Inter-Firm Relations

Inter-firm relations have been characterized as cooperative in the orthodox perspective on the German model of capitalism. This was due either to a process of coordinated specialization in local economies, where firms engaged in similar sub-sectoral activities (Herrigel 1996), or to the fact that German enterprises have been embedded into encompassing institutions which coordinated and supported cooperative management. Financial institutions pursuing long-term investment strategies and supplier firms serving as a local production-base profited from this cooperation. The model of *soziale Marktwirtschaft*, in particular its social implications, was dependent on this structure, and it appeared rational for firms to contain predominantly competitive behaviour.

Again, this mode of production has changed in ways about which it is difficult to generalize, because the development of inter-firm relations does not follow a one-dimensional logic. Large firms very often work as flagship enterprises for local production systems, whether these are the large pharmaceutical plants near Cologne, steel plants in the Ruhr area, car plants in Stuttgart, or enterprises in other sectors and regions. Large firms have been important due to their innovating capacities. They also operated as customer firms for the entrepreneurial *Mittelstand*. Larger plants often transfer collective competition goods, such as R&D, to medium-sized enterprises. Vertical relations between flagship enterprises and the local production base form an essential part of the German political economy. In many cases, these relations are well established. They rest on formal as well as informal contacts and can be characterized as long-term, also because supplier firms offer niche products that cannot easily be acquired elsewhere.

Whether the local production base can be regarded as similarly cooperative has been much debated. The cooperative engagement in south-western Germany has been overestimated by the literature in the past (Piore and Sabel 1984). Nevertheless, vertical inter-firm relations have been of major importance to the German economy.

Major changes occurred in the 1990s. As large firms restructured to cut their cost base, they also reassessed supplier relations. If local suppliers wanted to stay in the production chain, they had to produce for ever lower costs. This led medium-sized firms to analyse their potential in order to form alliances with larger companies, in particular when they wanted to produce abroad. First-tier supplier firms received massive support from large enterprises, in particular for R&D, in order to enhance their role as highly competent and specialized system partners, relying on outsourcing strategies to produce whole systems, which were then assembled on the line at the larger firm. Together larger enterprises and first-tier suppliers began to squeeze lower-tier suppliers, creating new conflicts with unions and bankruptcies.

The German *Mittelstand* was crushed by this new kind of competitive behaviour. In particular, the new cost margins, often calculated on the basis of East European labour and production costs, completely overstrained management in SMEs in the early 1990s. Large financial institutions had begun to pressure smaller firms on access to credit. Larger firms pressured smaller ones with respect to production costs. Rising unemployment was one result.

The mode in which innovations were introduced no longer rested on cooperative initiatives but became a matter of self-help. Interestingly, new forms of cooperation emerged among many smaller companies in local economies, which could not self-finance and develop what was needed for them to stay competitive. This was reinforced by the fact that the restructuring process of large firms coincided with the pressure imposed by European Monetary Union on the budgets of public institutions, reducing public services available to enterprises, in particular those provided by federal and *Land* governments for fostering cooperation.

Later some larger firms returned to a moderate mode of cooperation after experiencing the downsides of working with foreign suppliers, especially from Eastern Europe. As our studies in following chapters show, today there is considerable variety among sectors and regions in the extent and nature of change. Some local production systems have actually increased cooperation; others have not. Some firms became closer allies to larger firms; others not.

38 *Ulrich Glassmann*

Innovation

According to the varieties of capitalism literature, German firms produce mainly incremental innovations in established product markets, while firms in liberal market economies have been able to introduce radical innovation and establish whole new product markets. All the above mentioned features of the German model—interlocking contacts between firms, between banks and firms, the stakeholder orientation of the latter, and so on—facilitate this path and hinder German enterprises from engaging in radical innovation.

Restructuring in the second half of the 1990s was connected to an increase in research and development, spending rising to more than 7 per cent of GDP in German manufacturing. Germany thus maintained its position as one of the most R&D-driven economies in Europe, coming close to the US economy, which in contrast shows declining shares of R&D expenditure in manufacturing (Figure 2.5). The changes analysed above should not be misinterpreted as a withdrawal from innovative firm strategies. There was also a rise in patents during the 1990s, Germany now leading with patents among European countries (Eurostat 2001), though in terms of patents per million wage-earners Finland, Sweden, the Netherlands, and Switzerland ranked higher than Germany in 2002 (BMBF 2005).

Has Germany become more attractive for innovative activity in technological fields that have been rather difficult to establish in the past? The answer is yes and no, depending on sectors and regions. In biotechnology the number of enterprises rose from around 200 in 1995 to almost 600 in 2003. Between

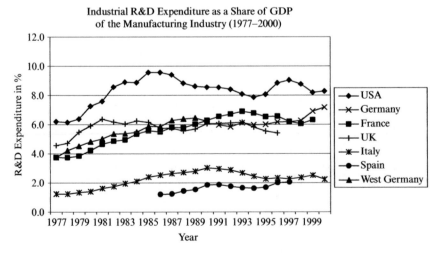

FIGURE 2.5. Industrial R&D expenditure, Germany, 1977–2000

Source: OECD: National Accounts; OECD: R&D Expenditure in Industry, div. Vol., own calculations, own depiction.

1998 and 2003 the Federal Ministry for Education and Research invested around €1.03 bn into support for biotechnology. Of this, €281 mn has been directly used by private enterprises for their research. While the government concedes that the firms' ability to market such innovations are still under-developed, research capacities as such have certainly increased (BMBF 2004).

In information and communication technology Germany expanded its R&D activities between 1995 and 2000, but could not catch up with average expansion of OECD countries in this sector, and more importantly could not eliminate some major weaknesses. There is still a lack of qualified personnel, as well as infrastructural shortcomings: broadband access is not facilitated through television cable wire, but mainly rests on DSL-technology. Deutsche Telekom remains a quasi-monopolist in the broadband market, which is why charges remain rather high (BMBF 2005).

In the service sector Germany again expanded its R&D activities between 1995 and 2000, though again remaining well behind the general development in OECD countries. It caught up with leading nations in the value added that knowledge-intensive service activities create, but not in employment in the sector. It seems that knowledge-intensive services are produced in-house by enterprises already engaged in R&D-driven manufacturing. Service-only firms have not emerged. Germany has outsourced some research activities to the USA (for instance in the pharmaceutical industry), while the growth of its economy rests on R&D-intensive export goods. Therefore if innovation is taken into account today, Germany has become not less, but even more dependent on the automotive industry.

It can be inferred from this that Germany has not yet turned its innovative profile upside-down. The most important fields of innovation and export sectors of the past remain the same today and determine to some extent what innovative activity can be found in the country. On the other hand, production and innovation in these traditional industries has changed, and many new markets have emerged. Interestingly, when asked why they do not innovate, technology has been the last issue that manufacturing firms have mentioned, listing instead finance, customer acceptance, laws, qualified personnel, and market information (ibid.). Meanwhile, the German state actively stimulates innovations in such new technological fields as nanotechnology and biotechnology, though employment effects in these industries are rather low compared with those in traditional industries.

Conclusions

In recent years the German economy has witnessed a tremendous process of institutional change. In enterprise financing the private capital market has become much more important compared to the past. A clear trend reversal can be observed in the relation between credits given by German banks to domestic enterprises (credit assets) and securities circulation. Banks withdraw more and more from being long-term money lenders, while reducing shareholding in German enterprises. They want to catch up in investment banking, and therefore need to restructure, reallocate their investments, and change their attitude as long-term financing institutions for German enterprises.

Corporate governance structures are changing likewise. As corporations need to reposition themselves in an international market environment, their demand for a fresh capital influx has been rising. Because credit business is more difficult than in the past and institutional investors withdraw, rescue only seems to come from the private capital market. Consequently, large firms restructured extensively. They started to adopt American accounting standards, increased transparency, and fostered shareholder orientation. In order to be successful with the last, they accelerated the dissolution of networks between domestic enterprises and started to pressure smaller firms.

As a result, many firms, especially SMEs, needed to operate according to new cost margins and to increase flexibility in the production process. This led many to opt-out of employers' confederations in order to side-step collective agreements. The industrial relations system started to erode, furthering a process of decentralization that created an imbalance between the associational bargaining level and that of plant representation. In West and in East alike, membership rates decreased (though much more in the latter) and coverage shrank. What is left to the unions is a strong veto power representing labour market insiders. While the 35-hour week has long been on the unions' agenda, working hours have now started to rise over 40. Wage differentials have increased, showing clear winner and loser groups. Germany is losing its social homogeneity. This economic development is mirrored by the transformation into a more pluralist party system and the success of extremist parties, in particular in the peripheral regions of East Germany. On the other hand, the German economy starts to catch up again with international competitors. Unit labour costs have declined relative to other countries.

New vocational profiles have been successfully created for emerging industries like the new media sector, but the traditional system remains in place for much of manufacturing. This system has started to develop some socio-economically disintegrating effects. Since younger cohorts have a lower level of education than older ones and the general education system has defects, access to apprenticeship becomes increasingly difficult for some, while reorientation at a later age is almost impossible. Meanwhile the system also imposes standards which ignore creativity and talent, especially in the service industry.

Inter-firm relations changed in the 1990s as a result of the repositioning of larger firms. Since they needed to cut their cost base, lower-tier suppliers have been squeezed with incommensurable cost and quality standards. This development crushed the German *Mittelstand*, while some first-tier suppliers formed strategic alliances with larger firms. In some cases, the local production base was completely wiped out; in others larger firms later returned to a more moderate mode of interaction. It has also been observed that smaller firms increased cooperation among themselves as a result of these pressures from banks and larger firms. This is an ambivalent development, very much dependent on sectors and regions.

Indicators for innovative activity in Germany show that the restructuring processes of larger firms and SMEs have not just been measures taken to reduce labour costs. R&D-driven innovation has been clearly extended, even in services as well as information technology and telecommunications. However, the general appearance of the German economy has not been altered. It still lacks appropriate initiatives in cutting-edge technologies and venture capital. The dependence of innovative activity based on developments in the automotive industry has even increased.

Thus, German capitalism has changed, but it has not transformed into a liberal market economy. It has not adopted opposite features in contrast to its past characteristics of a coordinated market economy. However, it definitely has changed some fundamental rules, which determine how the game can be played with a good prospect of being successful. In order to explain this, one must keep in mind that the post-war Rhenish equilibrium was not the result of a functional best practice logic, but simply a compromise between political, economic, and societal actors to ensure social peace while exploiting the positive consequences of a capitalist system. However, economic actors are not always coequal partners as often assumed in economic models. They were actors furthering economic development by making use of their respective power resources. These power relations could be contained as long as the international environment was more or less stable, at least not offering ample opportunities for alternative modes of production and innovation. This changed with the deregulation of financial markets, the end of the cold war, the establishment of a single European market and monetary union, and the rise of new technologies. In a changing international system, all make use of their respective power resources to maintain their status and displace competitors. Economic development, which was confined by national laws and compromises, now shows its original dynamic: creative destruction. Germans may have forgotten the inherent logic of capitalism, because for so long it seemed as if the *Rhenish equilibrium* was an optimal point of outcome at the system level, from which none of the above-mentioned actors could have wished to depart. However, economic development always means to depart from such steady positions. Benefits seem to increase now if the rules are broken.

The prospect for the German economy is ambivalent. Spatial incoherence of the production model will be inevitable, as the support of growth and employment in the creative industries appears to be an imperative for regional development. However, the positive effects of this process will be unevenly distributed among territories and classes. With this the old problem of German politics returns on the agenda: *die soziale Frage*. But this study is not designed to deal with welfare politics. It rather seeks to answer the question how regions can win this game. Actors may have found arrangements on the local level by which they are able to substitute old rules of the German model of capitalism, and this might be the beginning of a new diversity.

3

Three Cases of Changing Capitalism: Sweden, Hungary, and the United Kingdom

COLIN CROUCH, MAARTEN KEUNE, PERNILLA S. RAFIQUI, ÖRJAN SJÖBERG, AND ANDRÁS TÓTH

In the previous chapter Glassmann has demonstrated the error of treating Germany as a static exemplar of a formal model, but has depicted it instead as a system in the process of change. This is essential if we are to appraise whether local institutional innovators are following or running counter to a presumed national system in their entrepreneurship. The same approach therefore has to be followed for the other three countries being considered in the cases presented in this study. This will be done below, though not in as much detail as for Germany, the country at the centre of our concerns.

Sweden

Sweden is normally depicted in the literature as a highly homogenous society and economy. Also, the lengthy, until recently only occasionally interrupted, political dominance of social democracy has led to a particular emphasis in characterizations of Sweden on its strong and extensive welfare state and its powerful trade unions. However, another major feature of this economy is its domination by a small number of large corporations. Given the small size of the Swedish population, the number of major multinational firms based originally in the country is remarkable. This aspect of Sweden exists in a paradoxical relationship with social democracy. On the one hand, the corporations form the major alternative to social democracy and exist in some antagonism with it; on the other hand, social democratic policies have favoured their growth. A more nuanced and complex account is needed than is usually provided. This has been even more true in recent years as Sweden, like all other advanced economies, has undergone considerable change.

Enterprise Finance

Broadly speaking, Sweden is more closely related to the historic German model of the provision of credit than it is to a stock-market-based system. In fact, it is only during the last few decades that the stock exchange has emerged as something other than a minority venue to access finance for investment purposes, and to this day it is dominated by the industrial giants of the country (Henrekson and Jakobsson 2002*a*, *b*, 2005; Högfeldt 2003). Venture capital is a still more novel feature of the national financial landscape. However, it does not simply replicate the *Hausbank* system. Although there are several similarities to other bank-based systems, as Reiter (2003: 106–9) notes, there are also important points of divergence that have a considerable impact. These include a limited role for state-owned financial institutions (including banks); the 'historical compromise' between state, trade unions, and business as a basis for institutional change and economic policymaking to which also banks were made subject; a selective protectionism under which interventions in the financial sector were engineered with a view to supporting strong (and indeed few) owners within manufacturing; and, finally, holding companies controlling banks rather than the other way round. Thus, the major commercial banks of the country—and after successive waves of consolidation early on they were reduced to just a handful—have had a *Hausbank* function to the major industrial groupings within the country. Indeed, because of the manner in which the economy evolved during the early decades of the twentieth century, banks themselves became important owners of industrial stocks. In particular, during the 1920s banks emerged as important owners of equity, often as a result of a transfer of ownership when stringent lending and repayment conditions were enforced on ailing or only modestly solid firms. These stocks were transferred to a number of industrial holding companies, the two largest of which still control a sizeable part of Sweden's large multinational companies. Thus, 'Investor', the vehicle of the Wallenberg family, has a close association with the bank that emerged from a string of mergers and acquisitions—many of which not only involved banks owned by the family but indeed were engineered by them—to form today's SEB. The other major holding company, Industrivärlden, for its part has a close association with Handelsbanken.

Smaller firms have had far more difficulty in securing access to the resources of these banks. That the structure and *modus operandi* might pose a problem is made clear by the observation that the tax system prevailing throughout much of the post-war period, including after the tax reform of the early 1990s, made debt a much preferred means of finance for large and small firms alike (Davis and Henrekson 1999: 65; Henrekson and Sanandaji 2004: 76). Instead, when the main commercial banks have not been present, able, or willing to supply the credit needed, the system of savings banks has often catered to the needs of small firms. Also the bank of the agrarian movement, Föreningsbanken, which subsequently merged with the dominant network of savings banks to form Föreningssparbanken, served this function, as did Sveriges Kreditbank and Postsparbanken, both controlled and directly or indirectly almost entirely owned by the government (and subsequently, in the 1970s, merged to form PKBanken, the Swedish origin of today's Nordic giant Nordea). All in all, however, credit has often proven hard to come by.

As the structure of the financial system has created problems for start-ups and small- and medium-sized firms (SMEs) alike, private savings and retained earnings have figured prominently. However, although the general direction and trajectory was established early on, in particular following the turn taken by Sweden during the 1970s, the taxation system has forcefully intervened to reduce the importance of this route. Larger firms have at times had to comply with mandatory investment funds that served the dual purpose of reinforcing the basic Keynesian system of macro-economic management and of maintaining high levels of investments in those sectors that formed the backbone of Swedish industry. Others, although not operating under this particular constraint and the incentive structure that it provides, have found it difficult to accumulate substantial private capital through savings so as to build funds that could be used for investment purposes. As a result, and possibly already by the 1950s, new firm formation has been low (Braunerhjelm and Carlsson 1993), and those firms that have been established have remained small and typically confined to industries with low entry barriers. Services and handicrafts, not to speak of firms that serve as vehicles for tax mitigation (typically in the form of one-man operations) rather than production units, have seen a fair number of start-ups. In manufacturing, and except during the 1990s, such ventures have been almost entirely confined to a limited number of metal-, plastic-, or wood-based industries. Today, corporate profit taxes at least nominally compare quite favourably with other industrialized countries; though this is not true of capital gains, dividend, personal wealth, and income taxes (see, e.g. Henrekson and Jakobsson 2002*b*).

Corporate Governance

Some of the difficulties created by the taxation system can be handled by setting up an *aktiebolag* (abbreviated AB), that is, a limited share company. This implies that a rather substantial amount of money needs to be set aside as basic equity capital—neither access to venture capital nor IPOs on the stock exchange are an option outside the high-tech sector and/or the ranks of relatively well-established firms. Also, a certain level of activity has to be secured, not to speak of the requirements with respect to book keeping, auditing, and reporting that are more stringent than is the case with less ambitious forms of incorporation. (Forms supported by current legislation include *enskild firma*, *handelsbolag*, and *kommanditbolag*, here listed in order of not only increasing requirements but also increasing levels of protection from personal risk taking.)

In fact, secondary sector firms tend to opt for a limited liability share company, with most of the stocks held in the hands of the original entrepreneur, his or her family, and a few other individuals who are in one sense or another close to the entrepreneur or the family in control. Such family-owned companies also dominate within the furniture industry. In recent years, or so it is claimed, ownership by outsiders has become more common also in the segments of industry where family ownership once reigned supreme. Reasons for this include the taxes levied on inheritance or gifts (these taxes were removed in 2005, however). As a result, owners often found it more profitable to sell to non-family members, with the result that even in the country's few industrial districts non-local, including foreign, ownership has become a common phenomenon (Gummesson 1997).

Should bank credits not be available to the extent needed, family firms of course face the traditional trade-off of expansion and diluting ownership or stagnation but staying firmly in control. Inviting outside capital also implies inviting outside co-owners and outside interests. This might be a most welcome input, but often it appears to be seen as a potential threat rather than a possibility. This is especially so, Henrekson and Sanandaji (2004: 66–8) argue, as pecuniary incentives to growth are effectively eroded by the current system of personal income and wealth taxes (cf. Berggren, Olofsson, and Silver 2000). Larger companies have often availed themselves of the possibilities afforded by national legislation regulating ownership and corporate governance; smaller firms typically do not have the same number of options or freedom of manoeuvre. As in most other systems, differentiation of voting rights across share owners is an option also in Sweden. Hence, A-shares typically weigh much more heavily than do B-shares, sometimes by a factor of 10,000 or so. Trade in the former, however, suggests a considerable rebate on shares that come with strong voting rights. This very arrangement presupposes public listing. Similarly, some tax concession that may allow owners of family firms to avoid public listing are available, but again size is an issue as this is an option only open to the very largest (such as H&M, the garment retailer).

In short, the system of corporate governance, like the prevailing system of corporate finance, has privileged the larger firms or those that are part of the pyramid-like structure set-up under large holding companies (Högfeldt 2003; Reiter 2003) in a system that in a sense was geared to creating capitalism without capitalists (Johansson and Magnusson 1998: 121). Independent small-, and above all medium-sized, firms are at a disadvantage in both these respects. This is also seen in the resulting structure of industry, including the one under consideration in Chapter 4 (furniture). The composition of firms in terms of size, age, type of activities, degree of vertical integration, and so forth, is indicative of the processes and structure of incentives at work. We shall return to the issue of the structure of the industry as we look at the differences and similarities across our three chosen cases of local economies where furniture production has (or has had) a dominant position. Suffice it to note at this point that nationally the size composition is one of predominantly very small facilities, as many as about two-thirds of them one-man operations. The number of plants with more than 200 employees comes to no more than 14, with another 215 falling within the range 20 to 199.

Industrial Relations

Research on industrial relations can often be pigeonholed as belonging to either of the following four perspectives or approaches: the discourse on corporatism, human resource development, institutional economics, or comparisons of labour market regimes (Elvander 2000). Each combines elements from mid-range theories drawn from two or more different disciplines. Although Sweden has been characterized as an example of corporatism (e.g. Lindbeck 1997), we find, as in a recently published study of Swedish wage negotiations (Lundh 2003: 14), that the latter two are the ones most relevant here.

We may then note that the twentieth century was marked by an increasing importance attached to bilateral negotiations between trade unions and employers' associations, as codified in the so-called Saltsjöbaden agreement of 1938. From this point, non-adversarial industrial relations were to prevail for several decades to come. Generally speaking, industrial interests and unions have tried to settle their differences at the negotiation table rather than through legislation. The government, which has been active in the sphere of industrial relations, has also favoured negotiations and bilateral or at times trilateral agreements over direct intervention by means of regulation and legal provisions. This said, it should be noted that such labour market legislation as exists provides strong protection of incumbents; indeed, it comes as no surprise that the insider–outsider theory of labour market economics has seen substantial Swedish input (Lindbeck and Snower 1989). The overall effect has been to increase the risk of recruitment and employment. On the other hand, it has often been claimed that it has proven beneficial in terms of investment in those employed.

Another important implication of the Saltsjöbaden agreement can be found in the area of wage policies. During the period up to the mid-1970s wage negotiations for industrial workers were increasingly centralized, usually concluded between Landsorganisationen (LO), the national union of trade unions, and Svenska Arbetsgivarföreningen (SAF), the national employers' federation. From that point on, these negotiations were again decentralized, typically being held at the industry level.

Between 1956 and 1975, wage talks were set against the background of a wage policy that favoured not only the same pay for the same work (by

occupation and industry), but also in practice fostered industrial restructuring; this was the Rehn-Meidner model which set out to combine active
labour market policies with a restrained form of Keynesianism (LO 1951).
By imposing the same wage scales on all firms irrespective of their ability
to pay, low-productivity firms were simply made to shut down, labour and
other resources being reallocated to more productive units. This worked
quite well as long as there was a high level of demand for labour in most
manufacturing industries, a situation that had changed rather dramatically by
the first half of the 1970s. Also, under this wage regime, which subsequently
was formalized in the so-called EFO model (Edgren, Faxén, and Odhner
1970), productivity levels in exporting and import-competing industry set
the upper bound on the combined tolerated wage raises, with employees
in domestically oriented and protected industries and in the public sector
following the lead of those employed in the outward-oriented industries. This
formula was to make a considerable imprint on wage negotiations well after
its formal demise at the hands of the world-wide period of 'stagflation' during
the 1970s. In fact, it is still supposed to provide the benchmark for the public
sector.

One reason for the relatively benign outcome of these arrangements was
the realization of both unions and the employers' federation that negotiations were much to be preferred over legislation. Similarly, while the unions
recognized the need for, indeed benefit of, free trade and continuous rationalization, employers were quite prepared to accept—in fact, at the beginning
were instrumental in pushing for—centralized negotiations as a means to
implement the equalitarian wage policies. This helped them pursue rationalization without attracting opposition from labour, while at the same time
avoiding competition among employers for labour. Both the experiences of
the 1920s in particular, the low point as far as peaceful industrial relations
in Sweden are concerned (Johansson 1989; Lundberg 1985), and the early
realization—evidently well ahead of the so-called golden years during the late
1950s and early 1960s—that labour would be in short supply contributed to
this outcome.

After the 1970s, as already noted, conditions changed rather dramatically,
but in the short term the problem of rapidly increasing unemployment was
'solved' thanks to an expansion of public employment (especially for women)
and a series of competitive devaluations of the Swedish currency. By the mid-
1980s, liberalization of the credit market and the capital account injected
considerable amounts of capital, resulting in high growth and improved levels
of employment, up to that point always the main preoccupation of Swedish
post-war governments. However, as this could only postpone the inevitable
structural problems that had built up over the years, the economy collapsed
during the first half of the 1990s. In particular, the public sector shed labour
while exporting industries found some consolation in a rapidly depreciating
currency. At this point, increases in wages were held back by the slack in

the labour market, a new and consistent focus on inflation abatement and industry-level agreements between labour and employers.

Vocational Training

The willingness on the part of LO to accept free trade and policies designed to induce or at least allow for structural change in part hinged on the other part of the deal, that labour should be supported by unemployment benefits, above all being able to find new jobs if laid off. Towards this end active labour market policies were pursued, an integral part of which was training. Thus, in addition to implementing regional policies based on micro-economic instruments, including support for the geographical relocation of unemployed workers, upgrading of skills, or complete retraining was offered. Typically vocational or practical in orientation, such training was often supplied through government agencies but also the formal education system.

This must not be taken to imply that vocational training weighed heavily in the latter. On the contrary, secondary institutions of education, although turned into comprehensive schools which did include all secondary-level education and training, saw a step-wise shift towards subjects and skills needed for university entrance—also in those programmes primarily catering to the needs of youth who had no intention to continue at the tertiary level. A process that began in the early 1960s, it reached its peak towards the end of the closing decade of the twentieth century. In parallel, the network of schools and programmes focusing on vocational skills was closed, integrated into the traditional structure of secondary education identified by the label *läroverk*, now renamed *gymnasium*. The three national schools that provided highly specialized vocational training across a selection of occupations within the handicrafts or with manufacturing in mind were also closed down.

Thus, as the restructuring of secondary education beginning in the 1960s provided for vocational programmes, albeit within a setting that traditionally had catered for the needs of those destined for tertiary education, vocational training as such lost whatever similarity it may have had to its German counterpart (which arguably was not all that much). During the 1990s, however, and in part inspired by the German system and the debate in neighbouring countries such as Denmark, industry involvement once again became much more pronounced and programmes more clearly designed to cater to industry needs were established, even to the point of industrial firms giving financial or in-kind support to training programmes. Indeed, as the market for both primary and secondary education was opened to non-public actors—public support of individual pupils being transferable also to approved not-for-profit private sector establishments—a few larger manufacturers set up their own *gymnasium*-level schools with a view to training specialists in their own field of operation (ABB being one of these firms).

Another tangible result is that there is now a national programme for advanced vocational training, *kvalificerad yrkesutbildning*, supervised by the Swedish Agency of Advanced Vocational Education (*Myndigheten för kvalificerad yrkesutbildning*), the latter being established in October 2002. Financing and overseeing post-secondary-level training programmes, the duration of which might be anything between one and three years, the Agency was established once a pilot programme begun in 1996 had run its course. Also, beginning in 2003, two-year tertiary-level programmes were launched, leading on to a diploma, *yrkeshögskoleexamen*. Entry requirements include a school-leaving certificate from a two- or three-year secondary school programme with an appropriate profile plus, for those who have not completed three years of secondary training, at least four years of work experience within the selected field. Unlike many vocationally oriented secondary and post-secondary programmes and courses, the focus here shifts towards theory and production methods. These new *yrkeshögskolor* have initially been established within existing universities and university colleges. Even so, it should be said that despite these efforts, vocational programmes are still something of the stepchild of Swedish secondary- and post-secondary-level educational establishments.

Relations between Firms

The Swedish economic landscape has long been dominated by a small number of large corporations. Many of these were established during the inter-war period or earlier. They have accounted for a very high share of employment, exports, and R&D, but have also traditionally relied on a large network of subcontractors. In particular this has been the case in manufacturing, especially the production of vehicles and transportation equipment. In these hierarchically structured networks, relations have typically been rather smooth, stable, and mutually beneficial, albeit neither necessarily cordial nor neutral to size. One reason for this state of affairs has been the rather low level of competition in both intermediate and final good markets in Sweden—competition, such as it has been, has for the most part expressed itself through imports—and an ability of larger firms to exploit export markets. Subcontractors, on the other hand, at least in industries such as vehicles and transport equipment, have not been excessively dependent on one customer, thereby reducing risk and downward pressure on the prices of their products. However, cartel-like arrangements are not unheard of, and both for historical reasons and for reasons of a small domestic market and/or relatively weak regulatory authorities, oligopolies are a frequent occurrence.

More recently, this has changed. Not only have larger firms in times of distress tried to make subcontractors absorb a disproportionate share of any cuts in prices and profit margins, but entire networks of subcontractors have been restructured in the manner seen elsewhere (including Germany), the car industry being a good case in point. The pressures of globalization have led to substantial outsourcing, which to an extent has meant new local firms being created or solicited to provide non-core inputs and services. Outsourcing has also implied that jobs have relocated to low-cost locations outside Sweden. What is new here is that SMEs, starting in the early 1990s, have also begun to imitate the behaviour of the largest firms. Thus sourcing and investment abroad has grown by leaps and bounds also for this category. This need not imply a fragmentation of the fabric of industrial production in Sweden; one reason for small- and medium-sized manufacturers and service providers to relocate to Asia or Central and Eastern Europe has been a need to follow their major customers. Thus, 'defensive expansion' has been of some significance as has the need to keep up with the cost advantages of the competition from abroad.

Beyond such structurally influenced relations between firms, and although the environment can be said to be quite cooperative, very little of the network of firms seen in some other countries exists. Except at the local level, informal networks are of little consequence outside the circles of owners and managers of large enterprises. There are no formal arrangements that would be the equivalent of Japanese *keiretsu*, but thanks to the manner in which industrial relations have been managed and wage negotiations have long been conducted, SAF, the employers' federation served as a focal point throughout much of the post-war period. SAF merged with Sveriges Industriförbund (Federation of Swedish Industries) in 2001 to form Svenskt Näringsliv (Confederation of Swedish Enterprise). It is indicative that it is still trying to define its role while at the same time having been criticized for not properly serving the needs of business. On the other hand, national industry associations are active and, although not compulsory, enjoy high levels of membership.

Whether they have been able to use SAF and its successor for their own ends need not detain us here, but Sweden's large manufacturing firms have at times been able to set the agenda politically, or at least to enable solutions that were less damaging for them than for smaller firms. This includes a willingness to go along with the policy of 'capitalism without capitalists' and an ability to shield themselves from the high wage, high tax policies favoured by a long succession of social democratic governments. It comes as no surprise then that smaller firms do not tend to see the industrial giants of the country as a champion for their cause; their main advocate, the organization Företagarna which claims about 80,000 members, often assumes a different stance from Svenskt Näringsliv.

Conclusion

Despite the changes that have taken place in the Swedish economy and welfare state in recent years, it remains a system based around large enterprises. In fact, rather over-generalizing, one could argue that Sweden has moved from an economy based on large firms in engineering and motor manufacture to one based on large firms in various high-tech activities. Both corporate finance and corporate governance favour large enterprises and provide little scope for SMEs. The industrial relations system remains one based on a high level of organization of both sides of industry, but it has undergone two major changes. First, it has become considerably more decentralized at sectoral and corporate level. Second, it has adapted sectorally more than most, accommodating the private tertiary sectors that often remain outside national systems. The VET system remains one in which state schools and large corporations are dominant, though there has been some growth of apprenticeship-like patterns. Inter-firm relations remain dominated by major features already discussed: a strong level of formal associations and domination by large corporations and their supplier networks.

Hungary

From the 1970s on Hungary became noted as the Soviet bloc country that developed most autonomy from Moscow. There was a gradual decentralization of economic decision-making and responsibility for performance from the centre to the enterprise level, strengthening the autonomy of enterprise managers; the legalization of certain forms of private economic activities; and the beginning of borrowing on international markets to finance growth and consumption (Crouch and Keune 2005; Keune (with Kiss and Tóth) 2004). The country started to import western technology, and stepped up exports to western countries. It did so to a much greater extent than most other state-socialist countries. These reforms were, however, gradual and they took place within a state-socialist context. Indeed, they were attempts to prop up a slowly stagnating economic system instead of attempts at changing the system itself.

While in some respects therefore the country experienced fewer shocks of institutional change than other CEE countries after 1990, it did not continue on the path of 'reform communism', but faced a much more dramatic process of institutional innovation. This innovation has not necessarily produced surprising or original institutions, but as elsewhere in CEE has depended strongly on imitation and importation of existing western practices. The renewed (but not always new) national political elite embarked on a quest to build 'western-style capitalism', posing privatization, macro-economic stabilization, and liberalization of prices and trade as policy priorities. Also, all post-socialist Hungarian governments, whatever their political persuasion, have posed foreign direct investment (FDI) as the main economic policy tool to restructure and modernize the national economy. In addition, the 1990s saw an accelerated appreciation of the role of local and regional institutions and policymaking, following from attempts at political, administrative, and fiscal decentralization, often explicitly modelled on practices in the European Union (Keune and Tóth 2001).

After 1989 there was no doubt that Hungary would abandon the state-socialist system, establish political democracy and a market-based, capitalist economy. However, much debate has taken place in Hungarian society as to what 'type of capitalism' would be appropriate. The debate has largely evolved around the (very simplified) notion of a choice between the 'Rhenish' and the 'Anglo-Saxon' model. This 'model search' is a subject of intense political debate and conflict, and innovations pointing in either direction have been made over the years, representing different (domestic and external) ideas and interests.

Those who push more in the direction of the Rhenish model would retain many characteristics of the former regime (heavily institutionalized system, overall importance of the state, widespread universal welfare services, dense network of catch-all institutions). They point to the impact of neighbouring Austria and Germany, the European discourse on the European social model, as well as the related components of the *acquis communautaire*. The population on the whole seems to prefer a continental European-style welfare model: its stability, security and relative income equality, and an important role for the state to ensure the provisions of such a welfare state. Many large state-owned business organizations and domestic entrepreneurs who are well interconnected to local political elites with somewhat paternalistic attitudes also prefer a long-term-based model which ensures security and stability.

Other factors are pushing rather towards a more liberal, Anglo-American capitalist model. One is that the weak administrative capacity of the state, weak unions, and weak employers' associations mean that the actors required to build up and enforce the institutions of a Rhenish model are not readily available. Also, the lack of strong domestic companies in the all-important export-oriented manufacturing sectors means that the economy is dependent on strategic foreign investors and on FDI in general for investment and economic modernization. Intense competition among other countries in Central and Eastern Europe and beyond for investment forces government to adopt policies akin to an Anglo-American model. Part of this regime-competition is the race for lower and lower taxes, which put important constraints on public expenditure. The liberal model is also pushed by the powerful international financial institutions, as well as by the European Union through its Stability and Growth Pact, competition policy, and other market-oriented policies.

As a result, at present, the 'Hungarian model' cannot simply be classified as either one of these alternatives. Institutional innovations have not been conforming to one model or the other. In addition, profound institutional change continues to be on the agenda and no clear equilibrium has been achieved. As a result, the Hungarian model is hard to fit into one of the two boxes of the varieties of capitalism framework and it is clearly on the move.

There have been a number of quite undisputed elements in the Hungarian 'model search'. For example, ultimate priority was given to accession to the European Union. Joining the EU became so important to Hungary that '... the legitimacy of the transition itself depends on the success of EU accession' (Andor 2000: 2). Hungary became a member of the EU in May 2004. Also consistent, and important for the present discussion, is the fact that post-1989 developments in Hungary have been very uneven in geographical terms (Fazekas and Ozsvald 1998; Keune and Nemes Nagy 2001). This disparate performance can be explained by a number of factors, some more and others less directly related to FDI. They include the sectoral structure inherited from the state-socialist era; the embeddedness of enterprises in the local economy; geographical location; infrastructure; historically developed industrial culture, education, and skills; historically developed contacts with the West and western producers; and the character of local development strategies followed by local actors, including their attempts to attract FDI (Fazekas and Ozsvald 1998; Keune and Nemes Nagy 2001; Keune et al. 2004). These factors result in differing regional material and institutional contexts for economic activity. They influenced both the destruction of state-owned enterprises and employment inherited from state socialism and the creation of new enterprises and employment after 1989, including the inflow and growth of FDI projects.

Enterprise Finance

During the state-socialist period there was of course no stock exchange, and banks played only a small role in funding investment. State enterprises received funding allocations based on their part in national economic plans. However, and like firms in the capitalist world, enterprises could retain part of their trading surpluses and could use these to finance autonomous investment. Following the collapse of the state-organized economy, there have been changes. The state's role in funding has passed to the banks, which therefore play something of a *Hausbank* role. There is a stock exchange, but it is still small. Already before the fall of communism, a new important source of finance had become inward investment by Austrian, German, and other foreign multinationals. This activity has grown steadily since the 1990s, and can now be regarded as the most important source of new investment for major projects.

For all post-1989 governments, regardless of their political colour, attraction of FDI has been the main tool to restructure the Hungarian economy. On the one hand, this stems from the country's high foreign debt inherited from state-socialist times and the respective need for foreign currency. On the other hand, FDI has been considered the major instrument of economic modernization because it can provide new employment, access to western markets, modern technologies, as well as up-to-date know-how and work practices. As a result, many facilities have been offered to FDI companies, including extensive tax holidays. Such facilities were offered not only by the state but also by local governments interested to attract FDI to their towns and cities (Keune and Nemes Nagy 2001). As a result, throughout the 1990s Hungary was the main FDI destination in CEE, surpassed only after the millennium by the Czech Republic and Poland. The Audi plant that forms the centre of analysis in Chapter 5 has been the major post-1989 FDI project in Hungary.

As such, inward investment must be considered part of the emerging national model. It introduces a sharp distinction between existing Hungarian firms and the newcomers, and generates major debate about the extent to which it would be relevant to ensure the growth of a national Hungarian capitalism based on Hungarian enterprises. While national capital resources remain low, inward investment remains a highly attractive source of economic dynamism and growth. Hungary, and indeed the CEE countries in general, are not alone in having this sharp division between domestic and foreign capital. It is the case in virtually all countries where local capital is able to support little more than SMEs. This phenomenon brings with it requirements and characteristics that differ from the other forms of finance discussed more widely in the neo-institutionalist literature.

Corporate Governance

As in some other CEE countries, the privatization process in Hungary allowed managers often to take control of the businesses in which they worked. This has enabled the firms concerned, if they so desired, to pursue strategies free from pressures for rapid profits that would have followed from importation of a pure neo-classical shareholder-driven form of capitalism. In the absence of access to much venture capital, this has probably been fundamental in providing some stability to Hungarian enterprises.

Industrial Relations

During the state-socialist period trade unions and employers' associations that were more or less state-controlled played a prominent part in a form of authoritarian corporatism. Although the unions were generally regarded as having been complicit with the state-socialist regime, some elements had made important contributions to dissident movements. As elsewhere in CEE, they were therefore able to continue in existence following the fall of the regime, and to maintain the major assets that had been built up during the state-socialist period. Alongside them grew up a plethora of new, highly divided, and fragmented organizations. During the early 1990s the initially high membership of the old official unions collapsed, but this was not compensated by much growth in the new ones. Employers remained similarly disorganized. Available to these during the state-socialist period had been only the state-dominated official structures, and they now did little to create new structures. The prevailing climate of liberalized labour markets did not encourage co-ordinated action; Hungarian firms were usually too small to be able to support membership of associations that would bring them few tangible benefits; and foreign multinationals had little interest in developing Hungarian associations.

Despite the dominant neo-liberalism, there has been a paradoxical national policy of encouraging social pacts and producing collective bargaining law that seems to contradict both the reality on the ground and the dominant aims of labour-market policy (Keune and Tóth 2006). This is explained partly by the non-economic functions of industrial relations institutions: they may play a part in generating national solidarity beyond the scope of economic policy. Second, by the end of the 1990s, as Hungarian policymakers began to turn their attention to entry into the European Union, they confronted the same paradox within the *acquis communautaire*: a simultaneous encouragement of liberalized labour markets and strong industrial relations institutions. Therefore, the authoritarian corporatism of state socialism was not replaced by the liberal variety. Instead, the labour market more or less resembles an asymmetrical free market. The high level of national unemployment means that it is a buyer's market.

The system is highly decentralized and, as mentioned earlier, the trade unions and employers' associations are fragmented. There are six national trade union confederations, divided along political cleavages. In the metal sector, two major unions belonging to different confederations compete with each other. According to the law, it is up to employees working at a non-unionized company whether they set up a union to represent their interests. Such a union has the right to join any sectoral, regional, or national trade union associations, or to maintain its independence as a company union. Legal regulations compel management to inform, consult, or negotiate with company unions. Employees also have the right to elect works councils. Statutory works councils primarily function as bodies for information and consultation; they do not have co-determination rights.

Union density has fallen from 100 per cent during state-socialist times to about 20 per cent. In manufacturing industries and private services union density is even lower. Employers' organizations are in a similar situation: there are nine associations and their coverage is low. Collective bargaining coverage is around 30 per cent. Collective agreements are made almost exclusively at company level. Sectoral agreements cover only some 11 per cent of the employed and their coverage is constantly decreasing. In addition, since the Labour Code in some instances allows for the setting of more flexible working conditions by collective agreements, especially where working time is concerned, frequently the employers' interest in collective bargaining is driven by the wish to make use of these regulations.

Finally, it is important to mention the informal sector as a major characteristic of the Hungarian version of post-socialist capitalism. Although there are enormous difficulties in its definition and measurement, comparative studies agree that the informal sector in Hungary is among the largest in CEE. Schneider (2002) estimated its size to be 24.4 per cent in 2000–1, and claimed that of the population aged 16–65, 20.9 per cent were active in the informal sector. This means that an important part of the Hungarian economy is not, or not totally, governed by the constellation of formal institutions.

Vocational Training

Before the Second World War, vocational education and training in Hungary shared many characteristics with the Austrian and German dual system, combining school-based and enterprise-based learning. In the state-socialist period, both the school and vocational training system and the economy were nationalized. The link between state enterprises and vocational training schools then became even closer. Although most vocational schools were formally independent from the state enterprises, they often catered to specific groups of companies. Also, often, after two years of school-based training, a year of enterprise-based training followed, and trainees would be employed in the same enterprise afterwards. In smaller towns, where one state enterprise provided most employment, the local vocational school was basically run by this same enterprise. Consequently, the vocational training system was based on strong institutionalized links between schools and enterprises, including channels for enterprise-based training facilitating the school-to-work transition. However, even though institutional links between enterprises and schools were strong, the central state defined most of the curriculum of the schools, leaving little room for flexibility and local adaptation in this respect.

After the early 1990s the vocational school system experienced profound changes. The two most important features were the disruption of the state-socialist enterprise-based economic model and the reform of vocational education to provide more up-to-date and flexible training.

The disruption of the state-socialist enterprise model practically ended close linkages between vocational training schools and enterprises. Training facilities in companies were closed, the school–company relationship was disrupted, and the school-to-work transition became more problematic: at present only some 30 per cent of vocational students participate in an enterprise apprentice shop or a practical workplace experience, compared to some 70 per cent in 1989. Vocational training hence has become more school-based. The end of the dual school–company training system is especially accentuated in manufacturing, and today the majority of apprenticeship arrangements can be found in services.

At the same time, reforms of the vocational training system tried to adapt both the training organizations and their curricula to the new exigencies of the market economy. Political and economic actors shared the view that a general reform of the vocational training system was necessary. As indeed in Germany, the skills provided by the 'old' system were deemed obsolete and not corresponding to a 'modern' market economy. Also, the way curricula were defined was judged too inflexible for the adaptation to sectoral and technological change and to the short-term requirements of changing and new enterprises. In addition, curricula were seen to be too narrowly focused on production skills and lacking more general skills important for continuous skill acquisition, 'life-long learning', and flexibility on the side of employees. The need for reform was further underlined by the downsizing or bankruptcy of many traditional state enterprises, the growing importance of multinationals as well as SMEs, and new human resource strategies.

Today, local governments largely own the Hungarian vocational training system, which comprises two main types of school. The vocational training schools are rather narrowly focused on the acquisition of specific skills for specific professions providing a three-year curriculum, and vocational secondary schools, providing a four-year curriculum, give a broader education which also serves as an entry to higher education. Vocational training schools have seen the decline of student numbers by almost 40 per cent since the early 1990s, while vocational secondary schools have rapidly increased participation.

The central state does not impose detailed curricula anymore. Rather, the Ministry of Education defines a frame curriculum, providing for the local definition of actual curricula. It also maintains the National Vocational Qualifications Register, a framework of state-recognized qualifications which provides the basis for the development of common training profiles for both initial and continuing vocational education. The Development and Training Fund, financed by a specific enterprise contribution (called the Vocational Training Contribution at the rate of 1.5% of wage costs), is a sub-fund of the Labour Market Fund, and is used to finance both the vocational training school system and the training of the employed. Nonetheless, enterprises have the right to directly finance particular vocational schools instead of paying the levy to the central Development and Training Fund.

Inter-Firm Relations

During the Austro-Hungarian period Hungarian enterprises were organized in *Kammern* of the typical Austrian kind. This system was dismantled, or rather incorporated into the communist model, during the state-socialist period. As already noted, there has been little interest in re-establishing an associative model in the new Hungary, and there is little evidence of informal inter-firm relations among Hungarian SMEs, except to the extent that this is implied by the black economy. This means that vertical networks of customer–supplier chains around certain foreign MNCs become the main form of inter-firm relations available to Hungarian firms. This pattern is of course limited to those regions where inward investors developing local supply chains exist.

Innovation

Although the state-socialist system produced high levels of skill in certain sectors and certain kinds of industrial infrastructure, it had a poor record for innovation. There is little or no legacy of centres and institutes assisting firms with innovation. Those Hungarian firms that became entrepreneurial in the later decades of the former system largely did so through their links with Austrian and German enterprises. Little has been done subsequently to change this situation. The main national policy approach has been to expose Hungarian firms to foreign markets and to inward-investing MNCs, to encourage a transfer of western practices at the corporate level.

Conclusion

It emerges from the above discussion that economic governance in contemporary Hungary can best be characterized as exogenously driven by the corporate hierarchies of inward-investing MNCs. The national contribution to governance has been mainly limited to providing a market economy with which the inward investors will feel comfortable. Beyond that an extensive black economy enables firms to evade taxation and regulation. This intensifies the country's existing competitive advantage of being a low-cost producer of cheap goods.

The case on which we concentrate in this book, the Audi development in the region of Győr, occupies a particular place in this context, enabling us to observe an inward investor with maximum scope for making use of local resources. This region, starting from an already strong base, has managed a process of adaptation in a relatively successful way in the past 15 years or so in comparison with most other Hungarian regions as well as the rest of CEE. Hence, it does not constitute an example of a general Hungarian (or CEE) low-value-added experience, but an example of inward-investment with its own, corporate-led dynamics. This implies a segmented economy, with a low-cost, not particularly innovative, domestic sector, and an inward-investing sector, in which innovation may occur and spread to Hungarian firms—if it is the policy of the various multinationals so to do. We should expect to find diversity among firms in this respect. Some may be using Hungary solely as a base for cheap labour; others may be using the combination of low costs and certain legacies of skill and infrastructure from the state-socialist period to produce competitive combinations of high value added and relatively low cost.

Certainly some national developments assisted the process (Crouch and Keune 2005). One has been the central importance given to foreign investment by the national governments during the 1990s, the strategy referred to above. Second is the process of political and administrative decentralization taking place as part of the transformation of the country's political economy, making local governments and local public institutions more important players in economic development. Third was the process of economic decentralization during the 1970s and 1980s, as well as the way the privatization process was regulated in the early 1990s, which (as mentioned above) opened the possibility for enterprise managers to control the privatization of 'their' enterprises and personally benefit from this process. However, as early as the 1960s the region had become increasingly and unusually involved in the Western, particularly Austrian, capitalist economy. The abandonment of state socialism in favour of capitalism did not present a similarly profound problem to this coalition as it has to those in other regions in Hungary and around CEE that have attempted similar innovations in local development policy.

The United Kingdom

The UK is today sometimes depicted as an adjunct to the US economy, which is itself in turn often presented as a real-world representation of an economics text-book. In reality the British case (even more the American one) is more complicated than that. It is a political economy with various layers of different forms, reflecting social compromises that took place at different times, affecting different sectors differentially. Further, this is a process that continues as it adapts to further change. At least as much as Germany, it is a 'case in movement' rather than the embodiment of a theoretical model. This complexity has provided considerable scope to institutional entrepreneurs, though British institutions also present various blockages to some kinds of innovation, the nature of these blockages changing over time.

Corporate Finance

Although the London stock exchange has long been one of the biggest and most international in the world, this very internationalization, dating back to the earliest days of industrialization, meant that it played only a small part in the financing of British industrial and other economic activity. As in most stock-exchange-based systems, firms relied very heavily on retained earnings to finance new investment. This continues today (Corbett and Jenkinson

1997). Banks typically provided only short-term lending. Entrepreneurial ventures long had considerable difficulty in this climate. Small firms, lacking access to the stock market and their own existing capital, found banks unwilling to support innovative activities. There has been a long history of British innovators having to move to the USA for substantial development of their projects. By the 1970s, the role of the City of London (as the British financial sector is called) within the wider economy had become so small that its value was seriously debated, particularly as it was believed that its international orientation might be inhibiting access to capital by British firms. (This was in the period before global financial liberalization.) Indeed, the Labour government of the day appointed the immediate past Prime Minister, Harold Wilson, to chair an enquiry into the role of the City in the British economy (UK Government 1977). Industrial firms, which had been expected to take this opportunity to criticize the financial sector, rallied to its defence; the ability it provided to them to liquidize assets and move out of unprofitable sectors more than offset any funding problems with which it might be associated.

The sector had also long enjoyed a privileged relationship to government, being an exception to the general British pattern of distance between government and private firms. The Bank of England, itself located within the City, was closely linked to the leading banks and other financial institutions, and it obviously enjoyed a special relationship to the Treasury (the British finance ministry). The Treasury was thus a virtual sponsoring ministry to the sector. This from time to time became important over such issues as a potential devaluation of the currency, which might be in the interests of export industries, but which, by threatening the pound sterling in its then role as a reserve currency, was perceived to damage the interests of financial sector firms.

Many aspects of this basic picture, though not the political importance of the City, changed radically in the mid-1980s, until today the stock exchange and the financial sector in general play a leading part in the economy in their own right in the creation of wealth, as employers of labour, in the provision of services, and in export earnings. The earnings of the sector are important in stabilizing the country's external accounts, which would otherwise be in deep difficulty as a result of its continuing large deficits in traded goods. The financial sector has become the leading sector of the economy.

The UK was one of the very first to liberalize its financial sector and to introduce advanced information technology to the operations of stock markets in 1986, in an operation known as 'the Big Bang'. British financial firms were therefore in a strong position to take advantage of the subsequent global liberalization, reinforcing the international role that had played for a far longer period. The UK stock market, which had become far smaller than those in New York and Tokyo, now ranks alongside them as one of the largest and most active in the world. Vast funds can be raised through it, and though new stock issues continue to play a far smaller role than retained earnings in the funding of new investment, the City plays a major role in corporate affairs through the ability of corporate raiders to use it to mount hostile takeover bids. It also enables investors to have the confidence to make risky investments, as they can use highly flexible share markets and the mass of financial products that entrepreneurial City firms create to withdraw their funds and to hedge their bets. At the time of writing the very success of this model of highly creative risk trading is experiencing considerable crisis in the wake of its involvement in the US sub-prime mortgage crisis, but in the preceding years it undoubtedly played a major role in sustaining investor confidence in a manner that was not matched in other EU countries or Japan.

There is a particularly large role for institutional investors, including insurance and pensions firms. It should be noted that these do not conform to the model of short-term capital invested in the spot market as is assumed by models of a pure liberal market economy. Their holdings in individual firms are often so large that their purchase and sale of shares would directly affect the price. They are therefore likely to make longer-term commitments, which require them to monitor firms directly and become involved in their management. In this sense they may behave not unlike a German *Hausbank*. This form of finance is particularly important in the UK, as the British pension system includes a large private component that is routed through these firms. In recent years an increasing number of private investors have placed their funds with these intermediaries rather than investing directly in enterprises. This further strengthens their role within the economy. Investment and pension funds now own about 44.6 per cent of all shareholdings in the UK. This is considerably less than in the USA (71.5%), but more than in Germany (2.8%) or France (8.4%) (Windolf 2002: 39). Insurance firms own a further 18.8 per cent (5.7% in the USA, 10.6% in Germany, 10.5% in France) (ibid.). Fewer British firms are consequently owned by individuals and families (10.1%) than in Germany (18.9%) or France (18.0%), though this is considerably higher than in the USA (only 1.8%) (ibid.). The proportion of firms actually owned by banks in the UK (10.2%) is very similar to that in Germany (10.8%), both being, perhaps surprisingly, considerably less than in the USA (20.4%) (ibid.).

In recent years a lively venture capital market has also developed in the UK. Venture capitalists too take a longer-term interest in the firms in which they invest than is implied by the stock-exchange model of capitalism. The proportion of venture capitalists who become dedicated specialists in particular sectors is probably lower than in the US high-tech industries, which may account for continuing difficulties for UK firms in getting support for major innovative projects (see Chapter 6 for the case of pharmaceuticals). Outside these particularly dynamic sectors of the economy, SMEs continue to rely primarily on bank overdrafts for their investments.

Corporate Governance

The standard form of British corporate governance in larger firms comprises single-tiered boards dominated by institutional shareholders. Shareholder dominance has become important over the past 20 years, following the rise in importance of stock-exchange capitalism. However, some management-dominated large firms exist, as do many small, privately owned firms which are not quoted on the stock exchange.

Following a series of scandals about insider trading and other problems of the conduct of boards, City institutions sponsored an enquiry into corporate governance under the chairmanship of a leading corporate director, Sir Adrian Cadbury. The Cadbury Report (1992) set new standards for corporate governance, transparency, the role of non-executive directors, and the priority of shareholder interests. These are, however, without legal force and are ignored by some major enterprises. Government legislation has followed similar priorities. The 'Big Bang' had already begun to initiate a period of more carefully regulated banking and other operations. Lütz (2003) has explained the paradox of how, in both Germany and the UK, liberalization and globalization came to imply more formal, statutory regulation at the level of the nation state than in the past. Earlier regulation of the City had taken the form of informal deals and understandings, an example of network governance, not a pure market. International investors needed transparency, known rules, and guarantees that they would not be treated as outsiders. They therefore sought a legal form of regulation, produced and enforced at national level, but to acceptable international standards. The UK government established in 1986 the Securities and Investment Board (SIB), the first time that the regulation of the City had been placed on a clear legal basis.

Problems have continued with behaviour in the sector, the most recent being, as noted, the involvement of British banks in the US sub-prime mortgage crisis. At various points government has strengthened requirements for transparency and responsibility, and in 1997 it extended the role of the SIB to have a more general supervisory position over the whole financial sector, renaming it the Financial Services Authority (FSA). (The current sets of rules from various sources, governing the sector, are found at FSA 2003.) A central aim of successive change by government has been to strengthen shareholder power as the main guarantor of corporate efficiency, by ensuring strong information flows to shareholders and a lively stock market with scope for hostile takeovers of non-maximizing firms. Partly in response to this development, and partly as a result of certain unintended consequences of the corporate taxation system, many British companies have joined the general international trend towards ownership by private equity capital. Private equity funds purchase a firm's shares and, for a period of years, remove it from the stock market. This affords a period of protection from the threat of hostile takeover while a firm remedies problems with its business model.

It is also withdrawn from the requirements for disclosure and transparency in relation to shareholders to which a publicly quoted company is subject. The flexibility of the British financial system is therefore capable of both providing mechanisms for exposing managers to the rigours of shareholder maximization and providing them means of temporary shielding from its pressures.

British corporate governance is today less characterized by interlocking directorships than in its own past or in Germany (Windolf 2002: ch 3). If there is 'co-ordination' among British firms, it is conducted through the investments of financial institutions, in particular pensions and insurance funds, discussed above. A small number of these have holdings in large numbers of firms, thereby constituting constellations of interests not so different from those produced by bank holdings in Germany or Sweden. A relatively small number of institutional shareholders are today the principal owners of shares in British firms, and they dominate capital markets (Scott 1997: 83–5). Although banks do not engage in much direct ownership of firms, they frequently manage the assets of the pension funds (ibid. 88). Linkages across the UK economy are also produced through mergers and acquisitions: a firm that is absorbed by another normally loses its separate legal identity, while in Germany it retains it. Linkages in Germany are more likely to take the form of mutual representation on company boards. Shareholdings are far less concentrated in the UK, reducing the power that any particular shareholding may have (Windolf 2002: 61–75).

Industrial Relations

For much of twentieth century, the UK maintained a primarily voluntaristic system of industrial relations based on strong craft-based unions in manufacturing, with a gradually growing role of general and unskilled unions. This suited both the economic liberal preferences of employers and, more surprisingly, those of unions. British unions considered that they could establish better positions for themselves through exercising collective power within the market than through relying on law in a system where judges' perspectives were strongly shaped by collective law traditions of aversion to interference with trade (Davies and Freedland 1993). British unions were seen as among the most powerful and autonomous in the world. These preferences of employers and unions alike also produced aversion to the disciplines and restraints of neo-corporatist arrangements. Except in wartime, bargaining parties insisted on their freedom to bargain without constraint from either government or overall national framework agreements. This system developed in a context of primarily branch-level bargaining, but at various periods, particularly in the 1960s and 1970s, it fragmented to highly disaggregated levels, with bargaining in individual plants. In a context of low unemployment more or less guaranteed by Keynesian economic policy, the system became associated with high inflation and general instability. There were frequent pressures, mainly from government, to adapt the model in a neo-corporatist direction (Crouch 1977). These enjoyed at best temporary success. The structures of the organizations concerned and the traditions of state practice did not support corporatist arrangements.

In the final quarter of the twentieth century, two major departures took place. First, the centre of gravity of union organization shifted to public and some private services (e.g. banks) as deindustrialization set in and the superior organizational levels of public employees began to affect the structure of the union movement. Second, following a series of major political confrontations, government and social partners abandoned the search for neo-corporatist institutions. Governments moved to a more formal, law-based system of regulating both collective and individual relations, distancing themselves from direct engagement with organizations of labour and capital. This latter meant a move away from neo-corporatism towards reliance on free markets. Keynesian demand management was being abandoned at the same time, so workers were left more exposed to the consequences of their bargaining demands.

Employers' organizations more or less collapsed, and trade associations have also become weak, as large firms see little point in collective organization for bargaining and prefer to lobby government directly for their trade concerns. Unions lost members, but have retained more organizational and bargaining capacity than employers (European Commission 2004). Outside the public services they primarily negotiate with individual firms. The large firm has in general become the basic operating unit for business politics of all kinds. Meanwhile, a large area of employment completely unregulated by industrial relations institutions exists in the private services sector (apart from the mainly unionized banking and insurance industries), where employees are not permitted by their employers to join unions. Some of this employment exists in the shadow economy and low-paid, low-skilled sectors, but others in contrast in high-science areas where unions are rarely important to highly skilled workers who can depend on their individual labour-market power. At the same time, and particularly following the election of a Labour government in 1997, the move to a more law-based system has brought some new employee rights as well as constraints on unions. There is today a minimum wage in the UK, and the government partly abandoned the former British practice of opting out of European regulation of some elements of the labour contract (Davies and Freedland 2007).

In general, the British industrial relations' situation is more complex today than at almost any previous time. With the exception of neo-corporatism, which is entirely absent, almost every form of industrial relations can be found somewhere. There is still tough negotiating situations in heavily unionized sectors, especially public services and some oligopolistic industries; legally regulated rather than bargained relations in many sectors; union-free and virtually unregulated situations in many low-paid services, extending to a shadow economy.

Vocational Training

The historical British pattern was of a wide diversity of apprenticeship and certification programmes in the recognized manual and technical skills. Outside the range of what is normally considered to be the terrain of vocational education, a small proportion of the population completed an academic education or prepared for the professions. This left a clear majority of young people entering the work force with only basic education and no recognized skills at all. This situation has long been seen as unsatisfactory by policymakers, and there have been many attempts to address it. There has, however, been little stability in policy, and frequent changes of direction.

National structures for supervising apprenticeship and similar programmes have been frequently changed as this form of education moves in and out of fashion. After vigorous attempts to revive various kinds of dual-system training in the 1980s, the concept was then abandoned. It has recently come back into favour with government and some employers. The system of further education colleges and their associated qualification structures have similarly been subject to frequent change. The changes are governed primarily by a drive to privatize provision and expose the remaining public institutions to competitive pressure. The major emphasis today, however, is on changing the university system from an elite to a mass model. Once very low, the proportion of school leavers moving on to university has now reached levels of over 30 per cent, and the government's target is 50 per cent. In the process the concept of university study is changing to include more vocationally relevant courses.

It is difficult to describe a given set of institutions as constituting a British 'system', as they change so frequently, but it is possible to discern particular fairly consistent trends in policy and institutional development (Crouch, Finegold, and Sako 1999). First, there are complex approaches to the tension between general and vocational education. Historically the former has always held much more prestige than the latter, and has also been supported by those wanting education to be more than job training. On the other hand, there has long been a perception that the UK lagged behind competitor countries in some, particularly technical, fields because it lacked professionally qualified workers. Recent changes in the economy seem to have offered a resolution of this dilemma, justifying a policy of concentrating on vocationally relevant education, but permitting this to be defined more broadly than the older concept of acquiring craft skills and techniques. It is argued that economic development today tends to happen in service sectors where specific technical knowledge is not required, but where employees need to have certain 'social skills'. This makes possible the launch of forms of qualification which, while oriented towards working life, concentrate on vocationally relevant general skills rather than technical ones. This approach is embodied in the current system of National Vocational Qualifications, which at its lower levels avoids too much technical specificity.

There is a pronounced oscillation around localist and centralist approaches to the delivery of vocationally relevant courses, but with a strong overall trend towards centralization. Until the 1980s these tended to be provided by institutions governed by local educational authorities in conjunction with national professional accreditation bodies. LEAs lost this role during the 1980s, colleges being given increased autonomy within a more market-based system of making courses available. Meanwhile, responsibility for developing employment-related training was passed to new appointed local bodies, Training and Enterprise Councils (TECs) (Crouch et al. 1999: 183–92). At the beginning of the new century these last were abolished and replaced by a regional structure. Over this was a new national framework, which took over supervision of the previously local further education colleges. Within this framework, a diversity of individual approaches has developed in different sectors. In some cases, there has been the return of traditional apprenticeship models mentioned above; in other cases, there has been a collapse of any employer participation in vocational education.

During the past 30 years, the old system, whereby very few young people outside the top 40 per cent of the ability range acquired qualifications when they completed education, has changed considerably. Not only has there been a big rise in the proportion going on to higher education, but there have also been developments at the lower end, enabling certification of quite moderate achievements. These include the NVQ system, which is to some extent a part of the overall picture that contradicts the logic of some other parts. This has enabled the breakdown of vocationally relevant skills into very small components, with students of below-average ability able to put together some combinations of recognized skills. As these build up to higher levels they become flexible units that can be put together in a diversity of ways to match emerging skill sets for particular groups of occupations. This has proved particularly useful in fields where new occupations are emerging (as discussed in Chapter 7). There is, however, some debate about the value of the skills being certified at the lower end of the range.

Inter-Firm Relations

In general, British firms do not engage in close relations with each other, except for some supplier/customer corporate links. There was in the past an elaborate network of both trade and employer associations, as well as voluntary chambers of commerce representing firms in a particular city or area. These different forms have had divergent experiences over the past years. During the 1980s the chambers of commerce, which had historically played

a minor role in relations with local government, acquired a national promi-
nence. There were government plans for them to become centrally involved
in the delivery of the new training agenda, some ministers in the Conservative government of the time admiring the German approach to corporate
organization. However, when the TECs were abolished, the chambers lost
their role in this and have returned to their former position. As noted above,
employer associations experienced major decline during the 1980s and 1990s,
when relations between employers and unions either collapsed or moved to
firm level only. Several collapsed completely, or changed their character into
providers of consultancy services. The decline of trade associations has been
less dramatic, as lobbying either the British government or (increasingly) the
European Commission over trade issues remains important. However, large
corporations are likely to prefer to lobby on behalf of their own interests alone
rather than for a whole industry. Here too there has been a shift to associations taking on a consultancy role rather than one in the representation of
interests.

Relations between large customer firms and their suppliers in the UK have
traditionally been 'arms-length' contractual ones. There was some departure
from that model during the 1980s, when Japan was perceived to be the
most dynamic economy, and there was widespread imitation of its methods.
Particularly in the motor industry, government encouraged Japanese firms
to set up plants in Britain, with the hope that they would develop typical
Japanese long-term tutelary relations with local suppliers, thereby spreading
Japanese approaches deep into the British economy. There was some success
in this process, but by the mid-1990s perceptions of the Japanese economy
had become negative, and there was little interest in learning from it.

Innovation

For much of the twentieth century, the UK had a reputation for fine basic
science that then had difficulty finding capital to turn the results of science
into innovative products. British research was typically brought to development and to the market in the USA. While there is still evidence of this taking
place, two different factors seem to have improved the situation. First, the
development of venture capital markets based in London, combined with
the global deregulation of capital movements, has made it easier for British
entrepreneurs to find capital without leaving the UK. There has been no
shortage of capital, and the highly developed nature of financial markets in
risk management has been helpful to firms with risky new ventures. Second,
the shift of a good deal of innovation from manufacturing to services has been
more attractive to British investors, the country having long-term weaknesses
in most manufacturing industries, but with a strong record in several services
sectors, especially financial services.

Conclusions

Although the British economy does not conform fully to the stereotype of a liberal market economy, it has moved closer to that type over the past quarter century. Its systems of corporate finance and government, industrial relations, and innovation have certainly moved in that direction. Or, more accurately, one should perhaps say that the globalization of markets has enabled British firms to access capital and other factors of production not necessarily available within the UK alone. This is the case with corporate finance and venture capital. It can also apply to the highly imperfect 'market for institutions'. Although the period of Japanese imitation in the UK was brief, it did demonstrate a potential capacity for reaching out to approaches not easily found within the country but perhaps useful to its firms. At the present time British political and economic institutions are primarily interested in imitating the USA, which is leading to a greater similarity between those countries' institutions than at any time in the past.

It is difficult to fit the British approach to skills into a simple neo-liberal frame, unless frequent institutional change and instability is seen as essential to neo-liberalism. Policy here has been strongly determined by central government policy, and the frequent policy changes correspond to changed views within government rather than to any demonstrable market adjustment. It is useful to a market-based system if skills can be generic and flexible, as this makes it possible to leave short-term adjustments to employers signalling changed demands to a labour market that can quite quickly respond. Where skills are needed that are more specific and take some time to acquire, a free-market model for their acquisition does not work so well.

4

The Furniture Industry in Ostwestfalen-Lippe and Southern Sweden

PERNILLA S. RAFIQUI, MARTIN SCHRÖDER, ÖRJAN
SJÖBERG, HELMUT VOELZKOW, AND COLIN CROUCH*

The areas around Ostwestfalen-Lippe in the German Bundesland of Nordrhein-Westfalen and in Småland and Västergötland in southern Sweden both have long histories of specialization in small-firm furniture-making. In both cases, our research, in addition to documentary work, included extensive interviews with personnel in organizations relevant to the sector in the areas. There is a disparity in the sizes of the areas studied, the German example covering a wide region while the Swedish one comprises three clusters confined to small towns, and the Swedish study considers a longer historical perspective.[1]

The Two Districts

Ostwestfalen-Lippe

In 2006, 196 of the 1,114 companies in the German furniture industry were located in Ostwestfalen-Lippe. In all, 23,229 of the industry's 121,334 employees work there and the region's furniture producers account for 24.6 per cent of all German turnover in furniture production, mostly growing at a faster (or shrinking at a lower) pace than the rest of German furniture production; in 2006 turnover grew by 11.8 per cent compared to 7.2 per cent nationally.[2] Nowhere else in Europe can an area with such a dense concentration of furniture producing companies be found (Goller 2001: 6). The firms offer a broad range of products: kitchens and kitchen furniture, bureau furnishing from bookshelves to writing cabinets to chairs, cupboards and upholstery, as well as store equipment. They were able to keep their share of employment in the German furniture industry constant throughout the 1990s, but until recently they shared in the general retrenchment of the German economy.

* Rafiqui and Sjöberg worked on the Swedish research, Schröder and Voelzkow on the German, Crouch integrated the studies. Fuller details of the Swedish case will be found in Sjöberg and Rafiqui (2006) and of the German case in Voelzkow and Schröder (2006).

After the economic opening of Eastern Europe in the early 1990s, the German furniture industry had to face tough rivalry from the newly emerging competitors. With the advantage of lower labour costs, Eastern European countries, most of them now having joined the EU, are producing furniture designated to be exported to Western Europe. The bigger German furniture companies have in turn established branch production sites in Eastern Europe, thereby increasing import pressure on the domestic market. In addition, there are now 30 furniture-buying cooperatives, whose main demands are lower prices, shorter delivery times, and increased flexibility of production. Companies complain that uniform demands from these cooperatives reduce the variety of products by exerting price pressure that only the most profitable products can bear. Turnover in the industry in Ostwestfalen-Lippe declined by 10 per cent between 1995 and 2003. It was an open secret that as much as half the companies might go bankrupt before consolidation can occur (interview at the University of Applied Sciences Lippe/Höxter, 15 June 2004). But there are also some positive developments, as the furniture industry in Ostwestfalen-Lippe was able considerably to increase foreign turnover in the most recent years, rising from 10 per cent of total turnover in the middle of the 1990s to 30 per cent in 2007. Due to this, together with domestic demand that is slowly picking up, the situation has since improved. However, not only external circumstances have contributed to this. From 2003 to 2007, every employer accounts for 30 per cent more turnover. However, companies now only spend 16 per cent of turnover on wages, 30 per cent less than 10 years ago (information obtained from IG Metall).

The companies are found at opposite ends of the market: those with low-cost products, which—despite high wage-related costs and competition from Eastern European producers—are still able to compete using high-productivity mass-production; and those competing on quality rather than price. The middle price segment is of minor and decreasing importance. Small- and medium-sized companies (SMEs) specialize in flexible supply of high-quality parts and customer-specific production, demonstrating the continued viability of 'diversified quality production'. Within the sector a particularly strong role is played by kitchen furniture, accounting for 60 per cent of turnover in German kitchen production in 2006, and possibly for 20 per cent of all Western European kitchens. Nine of the 10 biggest kitchen producers of Germany are situated in the region, six being situated in a perimeter of 10 km around the city of Herford (Pfeifer 2000: 6, 9).

The kitchen furniture industry displays some peculiarities: production is more automated than in the rest of the furniture industry. The share of labour costs, 25 per cent, is relatively low, and the sub-sector has a particularly high export trade, while imports play only a minor role. Kitchen producers in Ostwestfalen-Lippe were not affected by a decline in turnover to the same extent as those in other regions of Germany, declining by 5.5 per cent between 1995 and 2002 against a national decline of 11.8 per cent. In turn, when turnover picked up in 2006, it grew at a rate of 13.5 per cent against 10.1 per cent nationally. Employment similarly declined by 'only' 11.2 per cent against 29 per cent for the sub-sector nationally and then started picking up by 0.1 per cent in 2006, when it kept declining in Germany as a whole by 3.2 per cent.[3]

Småland and Västergötland

Forestry-based industries are an important feature of the Swedish industrial landscape. Pulp and paper alone account for about one-tenth of Swedish exports, and sawn timber and various wooden products provide substantial further income. To this could be added related industries, such as machinery and intermediate goods, which have developed in response to local demand as the use of Sweden's plentiful forestry resources has expanded. Along with sawmills, the arguably most widely dispersed part of the forestry-based industry is production of wooden furniture. This makes the furniture industry an interesting candidate when investigating national and local institutional arrangements.

It is an industry dominated by small firms; in 2004, 73 per cent of the country's 3,100 furniture enterprises were one-man operations and 91 per cent had less than 10 employees.[4] Total number of employees in the industry reached almost 25,000 in the years 1999 and 2000, but then returned to the normal level of around 20,000. Notably, only two firms with more than 500 employees existed in 2004 compared to five in 1995. Overall Sweden is a net importer of furniture. Its firms are, like those of Denmark, concentrated at the upper end of the quality market, both countries being important exponents of the style labelled 'Scandinavian modern'. The traditional characterization of the industry in Sweden is that it is mature, fragmented and consists mostly of SMEs that are family owned or run as partnerships (e.g. Larsson and Malmberg 1997). Although agreeing with this description at an aggregated level, a study funded by Vinnova (Authority for Innovation Systems) argues that this image misses a few but important points about the industry. Brege, Milewski, and Berglund (2001) show that the industry structure is significantly more centralized in terms of turnover and profitability. They identified nine strategic groups within the sector,[5] and estimated that some 10 per cent of the furniture firms account for 60 per cent of the sector's turnover. Most of them are found in what they refer to as the 'IKEA cluster', that is large volume producers and suppliers to IKEA, and among enterprises producing office furniture. About one-third of the enterprises in the study reported a financial position weak enough to render them the epithet 'crisis enterprises'. The majority of these were found within the strategic groups 'traditional home furniture makers' and 'carpentry shops'.

The historical geography of the industry shows that it has long been concentrated in particular regions, especially in Småland and in neighbouring

Västergötland, with a propensity to cluster in certain small urban areas. Ålund (1946) listed Bjärnum, Bodafors, Malmbäck, Nybro, Nässjö, Tibro, Tranås, Vaggeryd, Vetlanda, Virserum, and Värnamo as important furniture producing localities in the 1940s, and a modern version of such a list would not look much different. Indeed, Brege et al. (2001) largely confirm that the location pattern has been remarkably stable despite radical changes in technology, materials, and the manner in which production is organized. In this study we concentrate on Tibro, Virserum, and Älmhult. The first two represent clusters of traditional producers of home furniture, and share a history as two of the country's most successful locations for furniture production. However, only Tibro has been able to hold on to that position while Virserum has virtually disappeared from the map in terms of furniture production. Älmhult was the birthplace of the global furniture giant IKEA. This is a location that has the potential of constituting a 'leading firm cluster' (Markusen 1999), though we find that in practice IKEA is the centre of its own non-geographical corporate cluster, which happens to have the historical furniture town of Älmhult as its base.

Tibro urban area is located in the Skaraborg part of Västergötland, in the *kommun* (municipality) of Tibro in which it is the main urban area. In 2002, the urban centre of Tibro had just above 9,000 inhabitants. The same year, about 50 per cent of the working age population of the *kommun* was employed within manufacturing, an unusually high number by Swedish standards, the largest sector within which was furniture making. Virserum is located in the very centre of Småland where the three counties of Jönköping, Kronoberg, and Kalmar meet, on the Kalmar side of the border. The second largest urban area in the *kommun* of Hultsfred, Virserum had just below 2,000 inhabitants in 2002. Since the peak of its furniture era in the 1940s, Virserum parish has lost not only most of its employment opportunities within manufacturing but also half of its population.

At the end of the Second World War, Tibro and Virserum stood out as particularly important localities for furniture making in Sweden (Bohman 1997: 35, 71). Today, only two small furniture firms are located in Virserum, while Tibro remains an important cluster, with some 47 furniture producers employing around 780 people. In addition, there are a number of furniture agencies, two flooring companies, one kitchen producer, one producer of machinery and equipment, and one firm that specializes in maintenance of wood-cutting machines. In other words, Tibro can still live up to its logo 'Tibro—The Furniture Centre of Sweden'.

The *kommun* of Älmhult, finally, has about 15,000 inhabitants of whom some 8,000 are found in the main urban area, also called Älmhult. It is located in the county of Kronoberg in southern Småland, some 125 km south-west of Virserum. Lewis (2005: 64) describes Älmhult as 'an old, remote farming town, with two main streets and a railway station; it is an odd place, in hindsight, for a revolution in domestic design'. The founder of IKEA, Ingvar

Kamprad, comes from a small village outside of Älmhult. It is remarkable that this small location has continued to play a major role for the firm, even after it has grown into a global conglomerate.[6] Staying close to its roots is a core strategy of IKEA (Salzer 1994) and the values it credits itself to promote via its product design and price setting (Torekull 2003). In line with this, a considerable part of IKEA's operations are still located in Älmhult, even though Kamprad as well as the headquarters left Sweden already in the 1970s. No less than 10 companies within the conglomerate are located in the town. In turn, IKEA is the main private sector employer in Älmhult; in 2004, some 3,050 people worked in its 10 units, constituting almost 40 per cent of the *kommun* workforce. The firm also contributes considerably to the *kommun*'s revenues. However, the presence of IKEA has not fostered a wider furniture production sector in the area. Hence, the so-called 'IKEA cluster' of suppliers producing for IKEA that is mentioned in reports and evaluations of the Swedish furniture industry is not located in Älmhult. Is it even a geographical cluster? This is somewhat difficult to answer as IKEA has a policy of not releasing any information about its suppliers, including their location. The literature indicates, however, that for all practical purposes the 'IKEA cluster' (Brege et al. 2001) is a functional and not a geographical one.

Corporate Governance and Finance

Ostwestfalen-Lippe

The kitchen furniture cluster of Ostwestfalen-Lippe is one of SMEs (Abelshauser 2000: 20). The share of family-owned companies is estimated at about 70 per cent, while 85 per cent of all companies employ less than 200 employees. Most are administered by their owners; sometimes business management is conducted on a dual basis, so that a member of the owning family and an economically educated managing director share responsibilities, the latter being responsible for the commercial part of business management.[7] Some have completely handed over control to professional managers. There is however a diversity of size, with one company, Nobilia Werke J. Stickling GmbH & Co. KG in Verl, having a turnover of €7.8 million in 2006 and about 1,760 employees. It is among the biggest kitchen producers in Europe, producing more than 380,000 kitchens a year (interview with VHK, Westfalen-Lippe, 19 September 2003). However, even that company remains family-owned.

Capital ties between companies are rare (Pfeifer, Kremer, and Schorn 1997: 8). However, there are some very significant exceptions among the larger firms. What was for a long time the biggest firm and is now the second biggest, the 'Casawell-Gruppe', with more than 2,500 employees, now belongs to Alno AG (a stock company). With this spectacular merger, one of the biggest kitchen producers in the world was founded, the aim being to offer the whole range of furniture products, including the entire price range.

More than 12 well-known companies belong to the Nobia-Group, which has its headquarters in Sweden. Finally, Rational Einbauküchen GmbH, with its main seat in Melle in southern Lower Saxony, bordering on Ostwestfalen-Lippe, has evolved from an artisan company to an internationally recognized enterprise with about 320 employees. Since 1993, the company has belonged to the Italian Snaider group, the fifth-biggest producer of kitchens in Europe.[8] German conglomerates that once held an interest in kitchen-producing companies are now disentangling their subsidiaries. In this manner, AEG lost Alno and Miele, changed its kitchen-producing subdivision into a self-standing company, and sold it to a Swiss stock-exchange quoted company. Further moves towards concentration cannot be ruled out; particularly where these are accompanied by insolvencies.[9] Even though the juridical framework of companies has not changed, it is probable that trends towards a shareholder value orientation will be reinforced in future.

The Alno case is one of only two instances of German kitchen furniture enterprises seeking stock-exchange quotations. The other, Kruse & Meinert, was an Ostwestfalen-Lippe firm. In the former the result was widespread redundancies; in the latter, bankruptcy. Typically of the German economy, most companies in our cluster have relied on regional banks and the locally rooted savings banks (*Sparkassen*) for finance. However, they find themselves affected by new policies for granting credit under the so-called Basel II agreement (interview with the metalworkers union IG Metall, 9 September 2004). This agreement among the large central banks and supervisory authorities of the financial sector has made procuring credit more difficult for SMEs. The aim is to protect banks from lending too much money to bad debtors. Banks are supposed to be able to issue credit with more favourable conditions, on the condition that the debtor is good; more equity capital has to be provided if the credit risk is higher. Additional funds, which banks need for 'bad debtors' with higher risks, have to be paid by the applicants for the credit. Riskier credits become more expensive, and borrowers have to be 'rated'.

Large-scale enterprises tend to be ranked more highly, reducing their credit costs, while these are rising for SMEs. This is affecting the traditional relationship between banks and furniture SMEs in Ostwestfalen-Lippe (interview with VHK, Westfalen-Lippe, 19 September 2003). Generally, the financial buffer of most companies is very thin, most of them only having very limited supply of equity capital (cf. Blumenreich 2002: 14). Due to Basel II, low demand and structural problems of the industry, companies are encountering more and more problems in acquiring needed capital at 'their' banks (interview with IG Metall, 9 September 2004). The new guidelines of Basel II erode the personal relations based on trust, which up to now have dominated the company–bank nexus. The new way of issuing credit especially creates problems for companies of the furniture industry, since traditional

Mittelständler are reluctant to present data that banks need to evaluate credit-worthiness. The actual financing problem of the furniture industry therefore is partially rooted in a problem of mentality, since entrepreneurs now have to explain their prospects of production, deliver data about the market in which they operate, give an overview about ownership conditions and their system of distribution as well as their strategy for public relations. Also, they have to give information about possible successors, in case the proprietor of the company retires. All of this information then makes up the rating, which determines how much interest rate has to be paid for a credit. In family-owned enterprises, in which the owner is involved with its personal capital, these new criteria for openness and transparency are seen as an intrusion into privacy (interview with VHK, Westfalen-Lippe, 19 September 2003).

Småland and Västergötland

Similar changes are taking place in Sweden. While, as was explained in Chapter 3, Swedish financial institutions have not generally favoured SMEs, the low entry barriers enjoyed in furniture production have made it easier to circumvent these hindrances. Credits obtained from banks and suppliers have been the dominant mode of finance. Should the stock market be available to them more easily than what now appears to be the case, family firms of course would face the traditional trade-off of expansion and diluting ownership, or stagnation but staying firmly in control. In our interviews, furniture makers come across as no exception in this regard, treating the involvement of external co-owners and outside interests as more of a threat than an opportunity.

Top-end Swedish manufacturers, specializing in design furniture, have to some extent been able to attract funding from venture capital or outside investors, often also geographically located at some removefrom the production facilities used (Brege et al. 2001). However, it appears that such funding has been accessed thanks to the contacts, reputation, and the generally high profile of designers rather than manufacturers, the services of the latter often having been solicited on a contract basis or through other arm's length arrangements.

Family-owned businesses mostly in the form of *aktiebolag* (limited liability company) have been predominant within all three of our Swedish case-study areas, in all three locations—IKEA still being a non-listed family enterprise (T. Sjöberg 1998; Torekull 2003). The option of listing on the stock exchange was discussed in the mid-1970s, but Kamprad convinced the board that too much stress would be put on instant profits and fast expansion, with little room left for building up large financial reserves that allowed for 'grand and bold decisions' (Torekull 2003: 145). As a rule, IKEA has relied on retained earnings to fund its activities, including most of its expansion worldwide. One of Sweden's main commercial banks is indirectly mentioned as a bank the firm uses, but funding is for most parts discussed in terms of own capital, usually combined with deals with local authorities or foreign nation states. The first of these deals was indeed with Älmhult *kommun*, and it was Kamprad's experience there that led to such arrangements becoming a core part of IKEA's location and expansion strategy since.

Family ownership was also the norm in Tibro and Virserum. Most firms started out as partnerships but were turned into *aktiebolag* over time. Today, even the smallest firms employing a handful of people are usually run in this form. The fact that they are family owned and run, defines a rather specific set of problems. In Virserum, problems arising in connection with takeover by the next generation are often given as an important reason for the decline of the cluster—a problem also experienced in Ostwestfalen-Lippe. This includes the financial burden the tax structure puts on the heirs, and hence the company, in connection with the takeover, but also a lack of interest from the next generation to take over a company in the first place. The generation which were to take over in the 1970s and 1980s had completed their education away from home and often been encouraged to seek employment in other sectors of the economy. As a result, one may detect a pattern that links firm closure with generational shifts in the Virserum data. The vast majority of firms survived for two generations, only one making it into the third.

However, this pattern is not found in Tibro. Although generational shifts until now have been difficult from a taxation perspective, they are not commonly mentioned as a problem. Instead, firms have been inherited or sold, traditionally to new local owners but recently more often to external investors. Currently, almost 15 per cent of the stock of firms within the furniture industry and connected sectors are owned by external capital, in the form of national or international investment funds, holding companies, or business groups (interview IUC Tibro, August 2005).

In both Tibro and Virserum, financial resources have typically been limited to bank loans and retained earnings, as well as making use of suppliers' credits. This last category is not often mentioned in the literature but remains one of the largest sources of funding and cash flow management for firms in Sweden, in particularly small firms. As a result, firms became linked to others via an intricate system of 'cross debts' that served both as a means of helping out in times of distress, but also allowed entrepreneurs a hold on each other for future potential needs. Bank capital rather than equity capital has been the main source of external funding in Tibro. More recently, national or regional initiatives in the building and financing of new or expanding firms, through government entities such as NUTEK and Almi Företagspartner as well as bank-owned investment funds have become more visible, though in general such initiatives have seen more application within the service and retail sectors, including the establishment of a large-scale factory outlet, Fabrik 19, which offers locally produced furniture as well as imports.

Contrary to IKEA, furniture producers in Tibro have in general low levels of retained earnings and own capital: borrowed capital from local banks constitute the main part of the debts side of the balance sheet. Naturally, this gives heads of local banks a particularly strong bargaining position vis-à-vis the firms, but—as in Germany—also provides an incentive for close ties between the two and representatives of the industry are commonly found on the board of local banks. The relatively low level of own capital in combination with low solidity proved particularly harmful in the aftermath of the financial crisis of the 1980s when small firms were not admitted temporary exemption from the rule of claiming interest losses within the same fiscal year as they occurred. Hence, an external shock and an institutional constraint brought many firms into, or on the verge of, bankruptcy, which demanded local banks to stretch their resources as far as possible in order to avoid massive firm closure and joblessness in Tibro.

After supplier's credits, bank loans stand out as particularly important also for firms in Virserum. In general, banks had little problem with failing loans as they always asked for guarantees of personal collateral from entrepreneurs and were highly ranked among debtors in case of bankruptcy. At times subsidized loans or guarantees from the local *kommun* assumed some importance, as did the financial services and loans provided by regional and national support agencies that were predecessors of today's Företagarna and Företagspartner.[10] Further support included the industrial board of the *kommun*, which not only provided loan guarantees but also engaged in securing subsidized industrial land and in training activities. In fact, in Virserum local authorities often stepped in to supply land at discount value, as well as providing factory facilities and direct support to troubled enterprises. By the 1980s one can detect an 'externalization' of investments also in Virserum as a virtual wave of restructuring efforts were launched to save its furniture firms. Most new owners (individuals or firms) came from outside the cluster, from various parts of the country. With one main exemption, W-Möbler—the only firm still producing furniture in Virserum—these restructuring attempts failed.

In sum, it appears as if, apart from the issue of small firm size, both Virserum and Tibro fit the national system of corporate governance and finance: in both locations firms operate within a financial system built on bank loans and supplier credits, which may be classified as stakeholder rather than shareholder based. There are however two instructive differences between the two. First, even though supplier credits have been an important form of working capital sourcing in both locations, the resulting network of financial reciprocity was mostly internal to the cluster in Tibro while it for the most part was external in Virserum. Hence, the presence of bank loans combined with bills of exchange within a local system of production (discussed below), ensured that all dimensions of coordination (information, monitoring, sanctioning, and deliberation) were present within the Tibro furniture cluster, but to a much lesser degree in Virserum. Still, this is driven by features of the system of organization of production, and, hence, constitutes no deviation from the national system of corporate governance and financing per se.

A second difference is that although generational shifts offered the same legal and financial challenge to heirs who wanted to take over the business in both Tibro and Virserum, this did not turn into firm closures in the former to the degree that it did in the latter. The reasons are somewhat difficult to pinpoint, but there is so far no evidence that firms in Tibro had invented or adopted strategies to circumvent the problems by having, for example, discovered and made use of loopholes or options offered by the regulatory system (most probably under guidance of local auditing firms or banks). Hence, there are no indications of departures from the national model in this regard either.

Älmhult, on the other hand, offers a break with the national system of corporate finance and governance, driven by strategies of the firms within the IKEA conglomerate located there. IKEA, though a large firm and in that sense typically Swedish, has chosen to remain family owned and to stay out of the stock market and it has relied heavily on retained earnings to finance its operations, including its global expansion. Although having all options of the Swedish hybrid system open to it, IKEA in effect constitutes an outsider to it, as well as to both the shareholder versus stakeholder models of governance and banks versus equity models of financing. One goal of IKEA is to have a financial position strong enough to ensure that it is in full control of its future. Insulating itself from potential demands from banks, shareholders and stakeholders alike appear as an important element of this strategy.

Industrial Relations

Ostwestfalen-Lippe

Both trade unions and employers' associations in the German furniture industry have been involved in mergers in recent years. The Gewerkschaft Holz und Kunststoff (Wood and Plastic Trade Union) organized employees of the furniture industry until 1999, when it joined the much bigger IG Metall (Metal Industry Trade Union), having lost almost half of its members between 1991 and 1999. Employers' interests are represented locally by the Verband der Holzindustrie und Kunststoffverarbeitung (VHK, Association of Furniture Industry and Plastic Processing) Westfalen-Lippe, which has its headquarters in the middle of Ostwestfalen-Lippe (Herford). This association resulted from a merger of earlier associations, which were divided in the district of Westfalen and Lippe. About 80 per cent of relevant companies are members of the associations. In addition a new employer association which also has its headquarters in Herford has been founded, representing furniture, machine, and system-producers. A network of work councils has also been founded, comprising 46 work councils from 30 companies, to try to solve the common problems of firms in the local sector (Winkelmann 2001: 140 ff.).

The *Flächentarifverträge* (collective pay agreements) negotiated between trade unions and employers' associations have started including more flexible working arrangements. That which is in force from October 2005 to October 2008 incorporates as its main changes more flexible working time and grants employers more rights to vary payment of workers according to the financial situation of the firm. Lately, however, there are also more and more exceptions to the rule of *Flächentarifverträge*, especially in crisis-ridden enterprises. Among supplier companies there is a trend to sub-contract work-intensive and low-qualified occupations to companies that are not bound by collective agreements (Pfeifer et al. 1997: 24). As described in Chapter 2, a softening of the system of centralized, industry-level pay agreements is taking place in many sectors in Germany. The furniture clusters seem to be fully part of this change taking place in the German model.

Småland and Västergötland

The Swedish system of centralized wage negotiations described in Chapter 3 may have contributed to the undermining of the cluster at Virserum, while Tibro withstood its consequences. Neither location experienced any pronounced unemployment among employees of the furniture industry during the early phases of rationalization. Those who lost their jobs in Virserum could often move to other furniture makers or to other manufacturing industries. Also, certain categories of workers moved to Virserum when demand was high, only to move out again when technologies shifted and demand of their services decreased, which was the case, for instance, in upholstery. However, importantly, Virserum hosted a number of metal manufacturing firms that served as an alternative source of employment as job openings and wage levels in furniture making started to fall behind. Somewhat ironically, then, a system of industrial relations typically credited with an ability to prevent poaching of workers and job-hopping '[b]y equalizing wages at equivalent wage levels across an industry' and ensuring that workers '[receive] the highest feasible rates of pay in return for the deep commitments they are making to firms' (Hall and Soskice 2001a: 25), appears to have contributed to the decline of the dominant industry at Virserum. Timing and the shifts resulting from an increasingly internationally oriented economy did contribute, but unless combined with the existence of more attractive employment in other industries locally it would not quite explain why Virserum failed when Tibro did not.

It is not the case that Tibro was immune to challenging developments linked to technology, market demand, and demography. However, there are a few features of Tibro that potentially helped to insulate it from the most severe effects of these events. First, the furniture industry in Tibro was never, and is still not, exposed to a competing manufacturing sector of any significant scale locally. In fact, local furniture entrepreneurs appear to have been hostile to the establishment of other manufacturing activities in the *kommun* and at times actively have lobbied against it. A second feature was the relatively smaller size of firms and the higher share of one-man units operating in Tibro than in Virserum, meaning that a relatively larger share of those occupied in furniture production were self-employed or working in partnerships. Hence, even though furniture wages were falling behind those of other manufacturing industries, more of those active in furniture production were influenced by other incentives than merely income differentials when choosing their occupation.

In sum, although industrial relations in Sweden appear to be an institutional sphere in which the national system—in this case centred on industry-level wage negotiations—offers very little room for local institutional variation, this does not imply that outcomes will be similar across space. On the contrary, our chosen case studies illustrate how local differences of a non-institutional kind have the potential to influence local outcomes of national institutional arrangements.

Vocational Training

Ostwestfalen-Lippe

The conventional image of the well-trained German workforce is one that can be observed in the furniture industry of Ostwestfalen-Lippe. A good supply of broadly skilled workers and entrepreneurs is frequently mentioned (Abelshauser 2000: 20), though there is some lack of high qualifications. As in other industrial sectors, employees can be split into three groups: the first consists of workers without any qualification, which traditionally make up a high share in the furniture industry, in this case accounting for about 30 per cent. However, their importance is decreasing due to growing demand for qualified workers. The second group are employees with qualifications obtained through the 'dual system'. The third group are those with a university degree. They are of increasing importance, though only 1.5 per cent of employees in the cluster have such qualifications (Pfeifer et al. 1997: 35).

The regional University of Applied Sciences has initiated new academic courses suited to the qualification needs of the furniture industry. The duration of training is shortened by combining carpentry vocational training with studies in economics of furniture production in a four-year course of study. Otherwise, it would take seven years to complete a traditional vocational training and a course of study one after the other. Part of the training takes place directly in companies, while another part is taught in the University. The course is financed by local companies and the Ministerium für Arbeit und Wirtschaft (Ministry of Economics and Work) of North Rhine Westphalia. The project is embedded in the Zukunftsinitiative der Möbelindustrie 'ZiMit' (Future Initiative for the Furniture Industry). As a further reaction to the intensified demands for qualification, a state-approved, private *Berufsakademie* (profession academy) has been founded in the city of Melle. Twenty regional companies of the furniture industry, the city itself, and the district of Osnabrück are supporters of this semi-university, which trains 24 students 'dually' every year. A course of study at the *Berufsakademie* is combined with work in companies, so that *Abiturienten* (secondary school graduates) are able to acquire the theoretical and practical knowledge that is closely linked to the needs of local companies.

These different initiatives in vocational training show that companies, in collaboration with institutions of higher education, are making an effort to build up the necessary human capital needed for diversified quality production. Similarly typical for the evolution of the German model, non- and semi-qualified employees are of decreasing importance. Both in the dual system of vocational qualifications, and in the University of Applied Sciences, prerequisites to raise the overall level of qualifications in the sector are being established. The close cooperation of the 'social partners', the workers, and business associations is also typical. Finally, the fact that training is conducted by companies and the state, giving the role of coordinating the nexus to the social partners, largely conforms to the German model.

Småland and Västergötland

In Sweden, about 40 secondary schools provide vocational courses for those wanting to work in high-quality furniture production. Advanced training in furniture production or related crafts are also offered on a number of locations across the country. There is the high-profile Capellagården (located in Öland, Kalmar county), originally set up by one of the most well-known furniture designers ever to emerge from Sweden, Carl Malmsten. Here furniture making is a craft, not an industrial trade or profession. Other similar establishments exist nationwide, many of which also cater to the aspirations from those who engage in the craft purely or predominantly as a hobby, rather than professional reasons. Within our Swedish clusters, we again see a difference between Virserum and Tibro. In the former there had been talk of establishing a furniture-making school on at least two occasions, first in collaboration with some local enterprises and later within the new school system at a secondary school level in 1968. Still nothing materialized and the town received no secondary school under the new system—an indication of its weak position relative to Hultsfred, the new *kommun*'s primary urban centre. Virserum's single pan-industrial local business association and the local municipality did lobby for the establishment of a secondary school in

Virserum, including vocational training in metal manufacturing as well as furniture making. They failed on both accounts. The dual industrial structure and the local system of industrial organization that did not favour local cooperation, which we will return to below, may have contributed to this. This is in marked contrast to Tibro, where the local secondary school, Fågelviksgymnasiet, has for some 20 years offered a three-year basic education programme within wood production and techniques, which may be complemented with an additional one-year programme focusing exclusively on wood furniture making. This final year is offered under the umbrella of the Swedish adult education programme, *komvux*, and students are offered to take the *gesäll* (journeyman) test on their way to earn the title of *mästare* (master). Education is focused mainly on modern furniture production, but recently the school started collaboration with Hantverkscentrum i Tibro and offers a special educational programme for traditional and artisan-based furniture production including upholstery, renovation of antique furniture, wood carving, and so forth. All these programmes attract students nationwide.

Again, it is noticeable how local contexts and contingencies have a bearing on local outcomes of national systems.

Inter-Firm Relations and Business Associations

Ostwestfalen-Lippe

In both countries informal day-to-day cooperation among firms is difficult to achieve, because furniture designs are so vulnerable to copying. Inter-firm cooperation does however exist, through the medium of formal associations. In Ostwestfalen-Lippe a number of these, representing different sections of the industry, are active, and in 1996 came together to found the 'house of furniture', a common building for all associations of the industry in the region. A German furniture museum was established in Herford in 2001. The various associations offer their members help with vocational and further training, research and development, and the advancement of exports.

With respect to R&D, the typical German pattern of a well-developed infrastructure at Land level (Bundesländer) is found in the furniture industry in Ostwestfalen-Lippe: of particular importance is the University of Applied Sciences Lippe-Höxter, offering its services in the fields of research and development as well as for technology diffusion. In addition, it provides a course of study in wood engineering and techniques of wood processing.[11] In the framework of this course, three laboratories have been created for wood-processing machines and technologies; furniture construction and development; and material and production technology. The university also tries to support the industry through a number of practical research projects, such as 'Environment-Friendly Furniture—Design, Production and Marketing', aiming to support 'regional furniture companies in supplying furniture for the future'.[12] There is also a jointly organized furniture design competition and a professorship established, and initially funded, by the local industry and by a foundation to promote Lippe as a furniture production site.

Another collaborative project is the 'Kitchen Mile', a joint project of 24 companies, all situated on the Autobahn A30. These companies give their fairs at the same time, thus lowering transaction costs for interested customers. In addition, sectoral coalitions such as the work group 'The Modern Kitchen' are important as producers of collective competition goods. This association represents the common interests of kitchen producers, most of which have been engaged in the association for more than 40 years. In addition, there are association networks, which companies join to develop their economic potential by exchange of information.

There is a divide between bigger and smaller companies in the use of such cooperation projects as fairs. While bigger companies fear losing their identity, smaller firms see the fairs as a means to strengthen their contacts with buying cooperatives and the trade (cf. Pfeifer et al. 1997: 28). Tougher competition, however, triggered by the economic crisis and intensified by companies offering similar designs and products, is putting a strain on efforts to cooperate. Tough price pressure is also being exerted by buying cooperatives, which almost have a monopoly on furniture demand (interview with VHK, Westfalen-Lippe, 19 September 2003). Ironically, it is by stronger cooperation that one way of countering the crisis could be found, but associations have to engage in laborious persuasion to get companies to work together.

Småland and Västergötland

A number of voluntary business associations and formal networks also exist within the Swedish furniture industry. There are also several examples of cooperation across furniture firms, at both national and local levels, outside the scope of these associations. These traditions seem to have been particularly strong in Tibro, where for various historical reasons (Ålund 1946; Ståhlberg 1942) furniture entrepreneurs early on made collective use of the few factories with modern equipment that existed and tended to specialize in particular parts of the production line. With a brief interlude in the 1930 when factory owners wanted to 'be on their own' (Larsson 1989: 29) and refrained from cooperating with other firms in this manner, the system has essentially survived. In 1987, some 60 per cent of all furniture producers located there were suppliers of intermediary goods, mostly to firms within the cluster. In effect, Tibro has been characterized by a fluid local production system based on horizontal linkages, and informal or formalized local cooperation. As such, Tibro is an abnormality in the industry as well as with the national system at large (see Chapter 3 this book). Importantly, in the latter half of the twentieth century, this structure was complemented by a number of larger scale companies that all functioned as important leading firms in various phases and segments of the development of the cluster.

In Virserum, units were larger and industrialization more rapid. This was due to firms working with oak—a hard and very heavy raw material that invites faster mechanization and larger scale production. Hence, a local system of industrial organization based on separate and vertically integrated units emerged already from early stages in the evolution of Virserum's furniture cluster. It appears as if this in turn fostered or at least further enhanced a local tradition and attitude that was not conducive to collaboration between firms. All production steps were usually done in-house, and during certain time periods, firms or owners of firms would include forestland in their lists of assets in order to secure supply of raw materials. They made far less use of collaboration along or across the production line. This pattern has persisted and been reinforced until the current period. While several associations are active in Tibro, very little associative action took place in Virserum.

Finally, inter-firm relations within the furniture industry in Älmhult largely became an internal affair to the IKEA conglomerate. IKEA firms participate, on the other hand, in local development networks, such as Växande Älmhult. IKEA is in fact at the core of the only innovation system identified within the industry; however, this is international rather than national or local in nature (Brege and Pihlqvist 2004).

Conclusions

The purpose of this chapter has been to juxtapose governance of the furniture industry in Ostwestfalen-Lippe and southern Sweden to the characteristics of the German and Swedish 'models', respectively, in order to determine whether these regional sectors have been typical of their national cases; and, if not, whether any deviance from a model can be seen to have embodied a *productive* incoherence.

Ostwestfalen-Lippe emerges as a typical German SME sector. The local specialism can be explained, not as a case standing outside the national model, but in terms of a concentration of attributes characteristic of the national model in which it is embedded. It is an example of what Amin and Thrift (1995) have termed 'institutional thickness'. Numerous external mechanisms (associations, universities of applied sciences, the works council network, etc.) provide collective competition goods for companies (vocational and further training, diffusion of technology, export promotion, etc.), which are not available in other regions of Germany in comparable quantity and quality. However, it is important to note that the 'German model' of which the district is an example is not the static stereotype based on the 1980s and deemed to be on a path dependency incapable of change. Instead, the regional cluster is undergoing the same process of change as the embedding national model (see Glassmann Chapter 2 in this book). These changes could be seen in corporate governance and finance, industrial relations, and vocational training. There was less change in the role of business associations.

Our account of the Swedish cases made possible a within-country comparison on variables of importance to our overall project. The two older ones (Tibro and Virserum), which shared several similarities including that of being based on SMEs, have experienced divergent outcomes. In the case of Virserum, we found a cluster that had not been able to reap the benefits that the Swedish model of a coordinated market economy has to offer in terms of strategic coordination of actors, long-term financing, and cooperative labour relations. There were attempts to adjust and fit in, but perhaps because of the predominance of SMEs—for which the Swedish model is not well designed—companies in the cluster found it hard to do so. Indeed, because of the presence of other manufacturing industries in this small community, industries that were better adapted to the emerging Swedish model, furniture makers may have lost out in the competition for labour and other resources. Virserum firms did not try to develop a common strategy and did not consciously build a local environment that was conducive to its needs. Instead it comes across as being quite passive in this regard, seemingly comfortable with local authorities and general business associations taking strategic initiatives—of which there were few, and then not necessarily in favour of furniture making but rather other lines of manufacturing—and fighting the rearguard action once the decline set in. Today, Virserum is but a shadow of its former self. A contingent factor that may have contributed to this was the fact that the industry's crisis of the 1970s occurred at the same time as a local government reform in which Virserum was merged with Hultsfred and became 'demoted' to a secondary town within the new administrative unit. Furniture production was not big in Hultsfred, and one may wonder how this influenced the balance and competition between furniture and other manufacturing firms in Virserum.

Tibro urban area was not affected by this reform, and maintained its primary status. The furniture industry there has been not only much more successful but also more proactive. It offers more of an example of a productive deviation from a national model, as firms have not accepted the national institutional setting as given, but have used a distinctive local institutional infrastructure to gain competitive advantage. Local initiatives to further the interests of the industry, and to build coalitions within it and with other stakeholders, have been a common theme, as has the pattern of industrial organization established early on. The latter, known in the industry as the 'Tibro model', has favoured fragmented rather than integrated vertical production chains, allowing for more competition in markets for components and final output. Yet, stories of cooperation, in addition to that at the community level, along both vertical (suppliers–customers) and horizontal (across similar producers) lines, abound. The bottom line, then, appears to be that while Virserum did try to fit in, but was not particularly successful over the long haul, Tibro made use of the opportunities that the institutional setting provided both by commission and by omission. At the same time, Tibro's departure from a Swedish national model does not fit the dualistic division of all economies into 'coordinated' and 'liberal', as it confronted the national approach to coordination (which itself differs considerably from the German one) with a further different form of coordination. At the same time, the products it offers still conform to a model of incremental rather than radical innovation.

Finally, in the third case, that of Älmhult, patterns become still more complex. IKEA might at first sight look like a rather typical exponent of the Swedish 'big firm' model of coordinated capitalism. It is large, it is heavily engaged in cross-border activities, and owes a thing or two to the traditional resource pool of Sweden. Home-grown innovations are similarly part of the story, as is the long-term view taken on investments under a system where debt finance is typically the most attractive form of corporate finance across all size classes of firms. It has also at times taken a serious interest in cooperating with local and national authorities, to the point that it has tried to influence outcomes that are beneficial to itself and, at times, the industry. Yet, it can be seen as a deviant case. Not only is it primarily a retailer that has occasionally integrated upstream into production; also, early on it broke with a number of traditional traits of the Swedish manner of conducting and organizing business. IKEA's complicated legal structure, the lack of transparency, and its move abroad are all divergent, as are the pioneering forays into low-cost global outsourcing of components and final products. It has also made a strong point about using its own funds to support expansion and all manner of investments. Compared to other major Swedish multinational companies it does not have a particularly close relation to any part of the national banking system without therefore allowing itself to risk exposure to fickle stock markets. If anything, it betrays a propensity to try to insulate itself from the Swedish regulatory environment, while at the same time trying to profit from what it sees as good, as for example the traditional values provided by that environment.

Overall, the Swedish furniture industry is rather different from its counterpart in Germany, where incoherences appeared to be a disadvantage, while success included an ability to make use of the national institutional infrastructure. It might well be then, that the key to success for the German cluster, consists in shielding itself from erosion of aspects of the German model, which are taking place at the national level. In the Swedish case, it is quite evident that national institutions and institutional arrangements alone cannot possibly account for the rather different experiences, be it success or failure, which our chosen industry has been subject to at different locations. As such, these differences might of course be due to context in the sense that nationally uniform institutions are played out in different local circumstances. Yet, it appears that local patterns of operation matter. This includes both the result of locally devised solutions to problems experienced and local responses to opportunities that have presented themselves. Although not always possible to trace to local institutional arrangements, such deviations from the national pattern may indeed make a difference when local actors go about their business.

In this connection, two further points need to be underlined. The first is the realization that local deviations from a national template, the success of Tibro and IKEA notwithstanding, need not be beneficial. Local circumstances, inducing local institutions, might be either supportive or destructive, as the case of Virserum illustrates. The other point is that there are few signs of some inevitable path or trajectory that an industry has to follow because of the national institutional environment within which developments are set. This is not only a comment on the notion of path dependence, which often has been applied in a rather deterministic fashion. It is also to suggest that the varieties of capitalism approach runs the risk of pitching the analysis at too high a level of abstraction; the categories it identifies, which as a set may well be ideally suited to accommodate differences across countries, provide little by way of help in understanding either intra-national variation (as in the Swedish cases) or intra-model change (as in the German case).

Notes

1. The fact that the account below tends to find a higher degree of complexity in the latter may be a methodological consequence of the ability of research to pick up more detail at a low level of aggregation—an argument that of course lies at the heart of our whole project.

2. Data from the Chambers of Industry and Commerce of Bielefeld and Detmold; Landesamt für Datenverarbeitung und Statistik NRW; Statistisches Bundesamt.

3. Ibid.

4. The notion 'one-man' seems appropriate in the case of furniture making where most employees and owners of firms traditionally have been, and still are, men.

5. A strategic group consists of a number of companies within the same industry that follow similar business strategies in terms of a number of specified variables. In their study, Brege et al. (2001) used the following variables: market, production technique, degree of value added in production, degree of design content, and type of product. The groups were (1) large-volume producers; (2) traditional producers of home furniture; (3) traditional producers of furniture for private and public businesses; (4) design-oriented producers of home furniture; (5) design-oriented producers of furniture for private and public businesses; (6) producers of beds; (7) full-range producers of office furniture; (8) carpentry shops focusing on interior design; (9) suppliers of wooden and metal parts, waxes and other surface products, and foams.

6. IKEA began as an eclectic one-man enterprise in 1943 and started to sell furniture on mail order in 1948. Today it is a global conglomerate with some 200 furniture stores in about 25 countries; some 1,500 suppliers in 55 countries; nearly 84,000 employees worldwide; and a turnover of more than €12 milliard (approximately SEK 117 milliard) in 2004 (IKEA 2004).The IKEA story is almost impossible to detangle from that of its founder and their intertwined lives have been the subject of numerous articles and three books (Björk 1998; T. Sjöberg 1998; Torekull 2003). At home, Kamprad has become the mega entrepreneur personified, which has made him the country's perhaps most known and respected self-made man.

7. http://www.nrw.de/01_land_nrw/11_land_und_leute/113_nrw_lexikon/lexmoebel.htm (15 June 2004).

8. www.rationalde/deu/unternehmen/unternehmensdaten.html (5 March 2005).

9. In all Germany, the number of companies in the kitchen industry declined from 139 to 113 between 1998 and 2004. In Ostwestfalen-Lippe, shutting down of companies could also be observed. 'Goldreif', for example, an enterprise belonging to the Swedish Nobia-Group had to close. Another example is the furniture producer 'RBK Möbelwerke GmbH' (former 'Gruco Möbelwerke'). In mid-2003, the insolvent company had to declare that it was unable to find an investor and therefore had to lay off its 202 employees (http://www.internationalde/cgibin/forum/printnews2.pl?ID=3997 (11 March 2005).

10. Between 1967 and 1989 Sveriges Investeringsbank AB (Investment Bank Sweden), a state-owned bank, had the mandate of assisting in the ongoing restructuring of the Swedish business sectors. The means were loans and equity to long-term and particularly risky projects. From the mid-1970s, the bank took a special interest in small- and medium-scale enterprise

development and backed up organizations like Företagarföreningen and Utvecklingsfonden at the regional levels.

11. http://www.fh-luh.de/fb7/laboure/labour_holz_stosch.html (22 September 2004).

12. http://www.fh-hoexter.de/fachbereiche/fb8/fachgebiete/chemie/umwelt/ moebelprojekt/ (22 September 2004).

5

Testing the West German Model in East Germany and Hungary: The Motor Industry in Zwickau and Győr

MAARTEN KEUNE, GENY PIOTTI,
ANDRÁS TÓTH, AND COLIN CROUCH*

In this chapter we consider the development of two car-manufacturing plants, both of the VW-Audi group, in two areas that had been parts of the former Soviet bloc: Zwickau and Győr. There is however a major difference, in that Zwickau is in the former German Democratic Republic and therefore in that part of the former Soviet territories that rapidly after 1989 became part of the Federal Republic of Germany, while Győr is in Hungary. The comparison therefore enables us to consider, not only which formerly West German institutions VW-Audi takes with it when it establishes plants in areas which might be considered to have weak institutional legacies of their own, but also how this differed depending on whether these and other West German institutions were also being transferred by other means. Our research involved, in addition to documentary work, extensive interviews with personnel in the VW-Audi plants in the two locations, as well as actors involved in public policy.

The process of German reunification was characterized by an extension of the West German constitution and institutions of the social market economy to the east. So far few neo-institutionalist studies have included the process of transformation in East Germany and their consequences for the German model in their analytical scheme. Even in cases in which East Germany has been considered—for instance in the field of industrial relations—the perspective has mainly been that of western firms investing in the eastern part, thus neglecting the problems related to the processes of institutional transfer and specificity of East German phenomena (Thelen 2000). Other more critical contributions (Wiesenthal 2004) pointed out possible consequences of reunification for the tenability of the German model, but the main argument was constructed around the fault of politics in choosing a shock therapy and in

---

* Keune and Tóth worked on the Hungarian research, Piotti on the German, Crouch integrated the studies. Fuller details of the Hungarian case will be found in Keune and Tóth (2006) and of the German case in Piotti (2006).

the very quick transfer of already obsolete institutions in a contest in which basic premises were lacking. Far less attention has been devoted to concrete processes themselves and to the net contribution of East German actors and pre-existing institutions.

In most studies, attention has mainly been drawn to the processes of privatization and their consequences in terms of 'colonization' of the East German economy by western investors (Grabher 1996; Grabher and Stark 1997*a*). In this view, the dominance of external investments led to the creation of so-called 'cathedrals in the desert', that is, industrial plants that do not rely on local suppliers but on firms' existing external networks. Second, the dismantling of the *Kombinaten* and the privatization of their cores (*Stamm- betriebe*) to external entrepreneurs had as a consequence the destruction of existing inter-firm and intra-firm networks. This would contribute to create a desert around the privatized plants or at best to a lack of synergy if not to the separation between the productive activities of the external and local entrepreneurs. As losers of the battle for the best parts of the privatized firms (the so-called *Filetstücke*), local entrepreneurs were not considered to play a relevant role. With the exception of cooperative networks, the dom- inance of western firms might therefore have permitted an unproblematic transfer of consolidated German institutions. Furthermore, the processes of privatization have been considered not only as a turning point but also as the beginning of a coherent path-dependent (non-)development that differed from that of other east European countries, leading ultimately to continuing unsatisfactory economic performance in East Germany (Stark and Bruszt 1998).

However, western entrepreneurs are not the only actors in the East German economy. If analysis is not restricted to privatization but extended to other concurrent forms of investment incentives, the role of West German investors certainly remains important, but at least in regions with an existing industrial tradition, the role of local entrepreneurship has probably been underesti- mated (Bluhm 1999; Koch and Thomas 1997). The presence of both local and non-German actors—neither of whom had experience of the West German model and had little interest in pursuing it—could have contributed to make the transfer less automatic. Lehmbruch (1994) similarly argues that the top- down institutional transfer from west to east was not really a case of passive implementation, particularly since the West German model itself had already been fragmenting since the 1970s.

The institutional transfer to the east indeed shows a differentiation among policy domains (*Sektoren*) that can be imputed to the degree of technical compatibility and of public as opposed to market regulation, to the strategies and interests of corporate actors, as well as to the unintended effects of their strategic action. Furthermore, windows of institutional change might differ according to the influence of interests and organizations (in both West and East Germany). These interests influence the legitimacy of the institutions and the degree to which transformations in the institutions and organizations occur (Czada and Lehmbruch 1998).[1]

In addition, it can be argued that the cultural and institutional inheritance of industrial organization during the GDR period, the framing of institutional constraints into a problem of western dominance, as well as the criticality of the economic and labour market situation which, respectively, indigenous firms and workers have to confront, can also contribute to explain the lack of interest in, as well as the resistance to, institutional transfer in some fields by East German actors. If transferred institutions differ in the degree of their acceptance and hence in their functioning, there might be some implications for the assumption of institutional complementarity[2] (Hall and Soskice 2001a). For example, if we look at some central aspects of the German model, like inter-firm cooperation, the dual system of industrial relations or vocational training and how they developed in the East, we can indeed notice a differentiation in the level of reception and adaptation of those institutions. Some institutions developed surprisingly well, against all expectations; others, although formally introduced, showed stronger deviations in their implementation and could even contribute to the transformation of these institutions in the west. Some of the deviations in the east have been compared and linked to some recent tendencies (see Chapter 2 of this book by Glassmann) or to some structural exceptions to the German model in West Germany itself. Neglecting the problem of institutional transfer, the specificity of the economic- and labour-market situation in which institutions are transferred as well as the regional and sectoral differentiation could lead us also to neglect some specific East German sources of success and change for the German system as a whole.

Hungary too has seen important debates both over the role of external investors in creating possible 'cathedrals in the desert' and over the type of capitalism that might prevail—'Rhenish' or 'Anglo-Saxon' (Albert 1991). Those favouring the Rhenish model point to many characteristics of the former regime (heavily institutionalized system, overall importance of the state, widespread universal welfare services, dense network of catch-all institutions), the impact of the neighbouring Austria and Germany, European discourse on the European social model, as well as the related components of the *acquis communautaire*. The population as a whole seems to prefer a continental European-style welfare model, its stability, security, and relative income equality, and an important role for the state to ensure the provisions of such a welfare state. Many large state-owned business organizations and domestic entrepreneurs who are well connected to local political elites with somewhat paternalistic attitudes also prefer a model of this kind.

Other factors are pushing rather towards a more market-oriented capitalist model. One is that the weak administrative capacity of the state, weak unions, and weak employers' associations mean that the actors required to build up and enforce the institutions of a Rhenish model are not readily available. Also, the lack of strong domestic companies in the all-important export-oriented manufacturing sectors means that the economy is dependent on strategic foreign investors and on FDI in general for investment and economic modernization. Intense competition for investment forces government to adopt policies akin to the so-called Anglo-Saxon model. Part of this regime competition is the race for ever lower taxes, which put important constraints on public expenditure. The liberal model is also pushed by powerful international financial institutions, as well as by the EU through its Stability and Growth Pact, competition policy, and other market-oriented policies.

As a result, at present Hungary cannot be classified as either one of these alternative varieties of capitalism. Institutional innovations have not been conforming to one model or the other. In addition, profound institutional change continues to be on the agenda and no clear equilibrium has been achieved. There have however been a number of quite undisputed elements in the Hungarian 'model search'. First, ultimate priority was given to EU accession (Andor 2000). Second, and a point of key importance to this discussion, is that for all post-1989 governments, regardless of their political colour, attraction of FDI has been the main tool to restructure the Hungarian economy. On the one hand, this stems from the country's high foreign debt inherited from state-socialist times and the respective need for foreign currency. On the other, FDI has been considered the major instrument of economic modernization because it can provide new employment, access to western markets, modern technologies, as well as up-to-date know-how and work practices. As a result, many facilities have been offered to FDI companies, including extensive tax holidays. Such facilities were offered not only by the state but also by local governments interested to attract FDI to their towns and cities (Keune and Nemes Nagy 2001). As a result, throughout the 1990s Hungary was the major FDI destination in CEE, surpassed only after 2000 by the Czech Republic and Poland. The Audi plant that forms the centre of analysis in this chapter has been the major post-1989 FDI project in Hungary.

Third, post-1989 developments in Hungary have been very uneven in geographical terms (Fazekas and Ozsvald 1998; Keune and Nemes Nagy 2001). This disparate performance can be explained by a number of factors, some more and others less directly related to FDI. They include the sectoral structure inherited from the state-socialist era; the embeddedness of enterprises in the local economy; geographical location; infrastructure; historically developed industrial culture, education, and skills; historically developed contacts with the west and western producers; and the character of local development strategies followed by local actors, including their attempts to attract FDI (Fazekas and Ozsvald 1998; Keune and Nemes Nagy 2001; Keune et al. 2004). These factors result in differing regional material and institutional contexts for economic activity. They have influenced both the destruction of state-owned enterprises and employment inherited from state socialism and the creation of new enterprises and employment after 1989, including the inflow and growth of FDI projects. Fourth, as will be discussed in more detail below, is the emergence of a weak and decentralized system of industrial relations. Finally, the informal sector is a major characteristic of the Hungarian version of post-socialist capitalism. Although there are enormous difficulties of its definition and measurement, comparative studies agree that the informal sector in Hungary is among the largest in CEE. Schneider (2002) estimates its size to be 24.4 per cent in 2000–1, and claims that of the population aged 16–65, 20.9 per cent were active in it. This means that an important part of the Hungarian economy is not, or not totally, governed by the constellation of formal institutions.

Zwickau and Győr

Zwickau

Car production in Zwickau dates back to 1909, when it was the initial site of the Audi enterprise. After the Second World War the communist authorities maintained the industry, nationalizing both Audi and its suppliers. In 1979, all car production was organized in a *Kombinat* directly dependent on the Ministry for Machines, Agricultural Machines and Vehicle Construction (IFA). Until the 1960s growth levels as well as the innovation capacity of the automobile industry could be compared to those of West German producers, but both productivity and innovation sank dramatically in the 1970s because of the chronic lack of raw materials and investment flows. This situation led to a wider gap between demand and supply, so that in the last years of the GDR one had to wait on average 13 years to get a car. On the other hand, the plant and the region of Zwickau could count on skilled workers and a high level of occupational qualifications. In 1984, two-thirds of all workers had completed a vocational training and 12.5 per cent had a university degree. The role of unskilled workers decreased strongly in the 1980s.

In 1984 the Ministry for International Trade reached an agreement with Volkswagen AG for the installation of a VW engine in the Trabant, the mass car of the East German market. The idea was to reduce waiting time without investing in a radical restructuring through marginal changes in the production process. Associated with this deal was some advanced training for Zwickau workers by VW. Further, some firms from other *Kombinaten* were suddenly attached to IFA. As a result some innovation, flexibilization, and spread of skills took place in the region, as well as the link with VW, which proved to be important after unification. Already in December 1989, VW and the IFA-Kombinat PKW of the GDR had founded a 'project company' with shared ownership. Later, as unification and economic and monetary union became more concrete, VW took over the plants where the Trabant was produced as well as motor construction in Chemnitz. A new plant was planned in 1994. From initial production of the Polo, VW-Mosel is now producing the Golf 5, the Passat Limousine, and the car body of Bentley and Phaeton, which is projected and assembled in Dresden. Some body parts are also produced in Zwickau and then 'exported' to other VW plants for further assembling.

Győr

Situated in the north-western corner of Hungary, the region of Győr where Audi Motor Hungaria (AMH) is located is one of the most dynamic and successful regions of Hungary (Keune and Nemes Nagy 2001). Like the region around Zwickau, it has long been a highly industrialized region, with a key role for the engineering industry, and already during the 1970s and 1980s a number of state-owned enterprises in the region had close contacts with western firms. Building on its favourable historical, institutional, and geographical characteristics, it managed rapidly to overcome the crisis of the early 1990s and to establish a new regional industry based largely on the concentrated inflow of FDI (Keune et al. 2004). This inflow was strongly promoted by a coalition of the main power blocks in the region: managers of (former) state enterprises, local public institutions, and the Socialist Party (ibid.). As a result, the region enjoys full employment and is among those with the highest wages and GDP per capita in the country.

It forms part of an extensive FDI car-production belt stretching from Prague, through Wroclaw, Katowice, and Cracow (Poland), Martin-Zilina (Slovakia) to western Hungary, eastern Austria, and parts of the former Yugoslavia. Audi was attracted to Győr as the firm tried to cope with the industry's recession of the 1990s. Originally it planned to locate the manufacture of its newly developed engines in Hungary in three stages with a total investment of DM800 million, while the profile of the factory was to be broadened, including the manufacture of the crankcases, engine cases, the connector, and the main shaft (Havas 1997). This would take up just over half of the enormous, 100,000 m^2 site that the firm had acquired, enabling suppliers and service providers to occupy the remainder (ibid.). However, during its initial two years of operation AMH's productivity, quality, and reliability were so satisfactory that Audi decided in May 1996 to re-locate all its engine production from its headquarters at Ingolstadt to Győr and consequently to concentrate all Audi engine manufacture at AMH. In addition, AMH's profile was broadened dramatically since it was chosen as the site for the assembly of the Audi TT coupé sports car and the Roadster models. All this required a further investment of DM200–250 million (ibid.).

The decisive factor in the decision to concentrate engine production and the assembly of the TT models in Győr, besides the positive performance it offered, was that Audi had recovered from the crisis of the early 1990s and had been able to increase both its product range and the total number of cars produced. Increasing sales demanded a substantial increase in capacity at the German factories in Ingolstadt and Neckarsulm, which allowed company management to restructure the company and to introduce an improved production system without resorting to a painful and conflict-ridden process of job reduction. It meant that despite the concentration of engine production in Győr, surplus labour at Ingolstadt could still be employed in car assembly, which was to be concentrated in the two German factories. The company management and the General Works Council agreed that the company would not lay off any staff for economic reasons, and would maintain the number of apprentices at a steady level. Indeed, following the closure of the Ingolstadt engine plant, not a single worker was laid off. What is more, while in 1994 employment at Audi Ingolstadt was at 22,391, in 2003, two years after engine production was terminated, employment stood at 31,013, almost 40 per cent higher. Indeed, Audi's overall performance had improved markedly by then, among other things because of the fact that Audi Győr turned out to be extremely profitable. It had become a key member of the VW-Audi Group.

As a result of further expansion the Győr factory became Audi's central engine plant, producing almost all its engines as well as engines for other parts of the VW-group, that is, VW itself, Skoda, and Seat. In 2003–4 a research and development centre was set up. Some 80–100 engineers are now employed at this department, which is mainly concerned with innovations in the production process and quality control. By 2006 total employment in AMH amounted to 5,200, while another 5,000 jobs in the region were estimated to depend directly or indirectly on Audi.

Since the Zwickau and Győr plants remain branches of VW-Audi, there will be no discussion here of issues of corporate finance and governance. Our attention concentrates on the other components of model comparison.

Production Structure and Inter-Firm Cooperation

Zwickau

The splitting up of the East German *Kombinaten* and the sale of their strategic parts (the so-called *Stammbetriebe*) to West German investors led to anxieties that previous intra-firm and inter-firm relationships might be disrupted, and that western investors would have no interest in using East German suppliers because they could use their networks of suppliers in West Germany. Our evidence throws light on three aspects of this issue: the kind of investment made by VW in Zwickau; the role of local institutional actors; and the introduction of state-financed projects aimed at linking local inter-firm cooperation and innovation.

In fact, there has been a process of revitalization of the local tradition in the sector, due not only to the VW plant itself but also to the influence of Japanese production concepts in the early 1990s. These focused on quality (zero errors), the attribution of further tasks and responsibilities to workers, and above all the reduction of internal hierarchy, elimination of stocks, and introduction of a system of suppliers based on 'just in time'. In the 1980s the western motor industry had experienced a reduction of internal integration in favour of outsourcing, hence of cooperation processes with external suppliers. Coordination of the inter-firm division of labour through just in time increased these tendencies because of the important role of coordination, strengthening reciprocal dependencies between, in the case of VW, the core firm and the 'module-suppliers' or 'first-tier suppliers'. Following the Japanese model, not only have hierarchy levels been significantly cut in the new plant in Mosel (about 30% less than in West German plants), but the main western module suppliers also had to set up new plants near that of VW. In the whole *Land* of Saxony, more than 37,500 jobs were created in production activities linked to VW since the beginning of the 1990s. About 15,000 of these are in service activities, a further 15,000 being in about 450 manufacturing firms. About 60% of these firms are concentrated in the small region of southern west Saxony.[3]

Relations between VW and immediate suppliers are described as very tight, characterized by strong communication processes and coordination. VW dependency on its suppliers is generated by the importance of quality and the maintenance of quality standards (VW also takes decisions about the sub-suppliers) as well as by the important role played by coordination and logistics. For the suppliers, renewal of their mandate for the following production cycle depends upon the quality of relationship in the previous years, and also on their willingness to introduce changes and to further invest to fit their organization with that of VW. Contracts are for one production cycle of about eight years. During this period, the supplier has enough time to develop solid relationships with VW. On the one hand, loyalty has always to be understood in the context of competition among suppliers, not only among external firms themselves but also between them and VW-associated companies specializing in the same activities. These have been created not only for increasing competition but also to avoid the loss of competences in the field that could lead to a strong dependence of VW on the suppliers (Herrigel and Wittke 2005).

The VW plant in Zwickau has not only attracted the immediate module suppliers but also further investments of external firms willing to expand in the sector and therefore with a relatively high degree of autonomy from the parent firm in the west or in the mother country. Furthermore, the tradition of an automobile and machine industry favoured the development of local companies. These enterprises, mainly directed by local entrepreneurs, or in partnership with external investors, soon tried to orient their production towards the motor industry.

The latter type of firm is not specialized in the construction of parts for cars. They rather project and construct machines for the production process in the plants itself, for example, sheet metal bending and profiling machines. They work directly for VW and for its suppliers as well as for other automobile companies situated in other regions. For their activities, they can count on a stable regional network of sub-suppliers. In this case, contracts between VW and first-tiers on the one side and firms producing machine tools on the other are limited to the production of machines at the beginning of a new cycle. However, the suppliers are also responsible for maintenance, which implies more continuous relationships.

According to the 'colonization' argument, the existence of assemblers and first-tier suppliers that do not carry out their R&D in the region implies an absence of innovation. On the contrary, it has emerged from our research that actually the subsequent levels of stratification of production are the driving forces of regional innovation, which is carried out by producing highly specialized machines, and through cooperation with other entrepreneurs as well as with the local university, specialized in *Fahrzeugtechnik*. Local entrepreneurs cooperate mainly with regional firms. As they often underline, personal contact and proximity represent a crucial value added for their activity. In some cases, there is also cooperation with potential competitors. Sometimes this takes the form of sub-supplier relationships in case a firm has not enough capacity to produce what is required. Cooperation can also take place in research if firms are not directly competing in that field.

In this respect, the role of actors in local institutions like the Industrie- und Handelskammer (IHK, Chamber of Commerce) is very important. Some initiatives have been carried out to bring entrepreneurs together. Some of them are not financially supported, like the so-called *Unternehmen Stammtische*. Entrepreneurs meet periodically and listen to presentations on matters of interest. These meetings enable information to circulate and, indirectly, business ideas to develop. Local institutions have also developed a 'rhetoric' or a 'discourse' of cooperation, which has helped to move from initial scepticism to the construction of stable cooperative networks (Piotti 2005). Furthermore, the IHK in Zwickau was also the initiator of a network of firms, which are all producing for the automobile industry called AMZ (Automobilzulieferer Sachsen). Now this programme includes firms from all over Saxony. It is centrally managed in Dresden and strongly supported by the *Land*. This network has the same functions as the *Stammtische* described above. Further, it enables cooperation in concrete research projects oriented towards innovation. Another aim of this programme is to establish connections between local and external firms based on previous circulation among potential local suppliers of information about the demand of the assembler and the first tiers.

Innovation through networks of firms and institutions is also the main goal of a programme financed by the federal government and targeted towards the East German regions, called 'InnoRegio'. Within this programme, Zwickau developed a network constituted by local firms in the automobile sector called IAW 2010. Important institutions involved in these programmes include the local university, which has a long tradition of research in the field, and the Fraunhofer Institut—a West German institution oriented to the diffusion of technology and innovation especially for SMEs. Against expectations and the hostile context, the development of cooperation can be considered to be the result of a successful institutional transfer from west to east both of inter-firm cooperation itself (as a way of conceiving, organizing, and carrying out business relationships) and of its institutional preconditions (IHK, Fraunhofer Instituten). But the process of institutional transfer has been neither automatic nor undifferentiated. VW has certainly played an important role in quasi 'imposing' its way of producing in an organizational form like that of 'lean production' and 'just-in-time'. On the other hand, cooperation is much more developed in the auto industry than in other sectors in the same region in the presence of the same institutional actors. Strong decentralization of production and the important role of R&D activities push entrepreneurs towards cooperation.

The transfer of the institution of the IHK has not occurred in a vacuum. *Handels- und Gewerbekammern* were present throughout Germany since the mid-nineteenth century and were not completely abolished during the GDR. They were strongly dependent on the political sphere, being required to control the activities of the still existing private firms in order to guarantee their conformity to the goals of the socialist state. This meant to support more or less formally the entrepreneurs in the solution of production problems typical of the *Mangelwirtschaft* (shortage economy—a term used to characterize the former GDR) to meet the requirements of socialist plans. The Chambers were also expected to cooperate with local administrations in planning and managing the provision of services like transport and communication.

Immediately after the fall of the Berlin wall, GDR politicians who had been opposed to the regime began to plan for more autonomy for craft firms, small manufacturers and retailers, and for a politically independent IHK, which should support the interests of entrepreneurs instead of those of the state. Hence, the chambers introduced by the transfer of West German institutions were not a completely new institution operating with completely new actors.

In the case of Zwickau, numerous factors contributed to the functioning of the Chamber and strong legitimation by entrepreneurs. Among these were (a) the strong orientation of the Chamber towards the activities of the West German Chambers, especially in similar territories specialized in the automobile industry; (b) the strong interest of local entrepreneurs in having institutional support at the beginning of their entrepreneurial activity and in the attraction of external investments like that of VW and suppliers; and (c) the strong commitment of local actors to regional development. However, this legitimation cannot be considered as automatic but regionally differentiated and dependent upon the concrete policies of the local (Chamber) actors. For instance, it might be weaker in districts where chambers were concerned to attract new external investments with no role for local entrepreneurs. In this case, the interests of local entrepreneurs might even be hurt.[4]

Győr

Hungarian developments need to be seen in the context of more general recent trends shaping supplier relations in the motor industry. When auto assemblers set up production operations abroad in the past, they created new supplier networks in the host countries, be it in Brazil or in Spain (Humphrey and Memedovic 2003). They would identify local firms as suppliers, nurturing them by transferring skills and technologies to them, investing in them, and buying from them (Sturgeon and Lester 2003). This strategy created dense connections between final assemblers and local supply firms, and facilitated the upgrading of domestic enterprises. The 1980s and 1990s saw the beginning of a new phase, characterized by the granting of designing and co-development responsibilities to major suppliers, the creation of global supply chains, and tiered supply networks led increasingly by first-tier mega-suppliers. These changes have reshaped the relationship between assembly plants and potential local suppliers. First, the headquarters of car companies are playing a pivotal role in selecting supply partners through a global purchasing process. This also means that supplier selection is transferred away from the local plant to the central purchasing department. Second, first-tier suppliers play a much more important role than in the past in organizing local supply. They participate in the design of the part or system in conjunction with the headquarters of the auto-manufacturing firm. In many cases, but not always, the design belongs to the component manufacturer, who is responsible for organizing supply or transferring its design to a partner (subsidiary, affiliate, or licensee) in far away locations (Humphrey and Memedovic 2003). American and European lead firms have recently become more dependent on a relatively closed set of global suppliers based in core countries (Sturgeon and Lester 2003). Local assembly plants now have only limited responsibilities in the selection of suppliers and the organization of the supply chain. Also, major suppliers are often following the locational policy of their assembler partners and deploy subsidiaries close to newly established assembly plants. Consequently, relatively small local firms face considerable difficulties in establishing direct relationships with nearby assembly plants (Humphrey and Memedovic 2003).

Another challenge for firms intending to enter into global supply chains is that they have to meet much more elevated quality and cost expectations of car manufacturers, including the various ISO and QS certifications. Also, entering into a global supply chain may require the supply of parts and components for the whole global supply chain, not only for the relatively small local assembly plant. This means a different scale of investment and capacity requirements, which many smaller domestic firms without a stable financial background would have difficulties to meet with. As a consequence, the limited financial and managerial resources of many smaller and medium-sized local firms greatly reduce their possibility to enter into global sourcing networks, while their direct access to local plants is limited. Finally, reducing trade and investment barriers have allowed many established supplier firms in core countries to establish subsidiaries in low-cost locations and to compete successfully with local firms based on their better managerial systems and easier access to financing, while enjoying the same cost advantages as domestic firms. As a result of these changes, when CEE countries entered global capitalism it was hardly possible any more simply to build up local suppliers for incoming car manufacturers, except as lower-tier manufacturers (Humphrey and Memedovic 2003).

When Audi decided to invest in Győr, it was not only welcomed because of its direct effect on local employment, but high expectations also prevailed concerning the trickle down effect this investment project could have through the development of local supplier relations. However, the local content of AMH is only 10 per cent. Here we will first discuss why this is the case, and then turn to relations with the present local suppliers.

A local content of some 10 per cent looks low compared to that of the other major automotive company in Hungary, the Suzuki plant located in Esztergom where it is 40 to 50 per cent. These differences originate in the diverse institutional conditions the two companies face, the distance from headquarters, differences in products, as well as different global strategies followed by the mother companies. Suzuki Esztergom, as a non-European company, had to meet a 60 per cent local value-added content requirement in order to be able to export its product to the EU, in the period before the accession of Hungary. Audi, as a European firm, had no such requirement to fulfil. Second, Suzuki's operational base as well as much of its traditional suppliers were far away in Japan and the company had to develop a strategy to deal with this absence of an important part of its supplier base, while Audi's Győr plant is only 600 km from the Ingolstadt headquarters. Third, the Suzuki plant is a car-assembly plant, which requires a wide number of parts and components, including many low-technology glass, plastic, and metal parts. AMH's engine production rather requires a far lower number of supplied components, and most of them of a higher technology level. Finally, Audi Győr has to conform to the VW Group's global sourcing policy directed from the VW headquarters in Wolfsburg. Global sourcing means that, for each serial purchasing, the company has an Internet-based tender procedure through which suppliers around the world can present offers to produce the respective part. While this tendering process is an open process where the production of parts and components is concerned, there is a more closed tendering process for development projects related to new products to be supplied in the future. This second process, called forward sourcing, is open only to companies that are already global sourcing partners of the VW-group.[5]

Still, Audi urged some of its major suppliers to set up local subsidiaries and supply the new plant directly from nearby, not the least to allow for just-in-time production processes. Also, supplier companies came to the region hoping that this would allow them to enter into AMH's. This was for example the case of Hydro, which established an aluminium foundry in the Győr industrial park, hoping to be able to supply the Audi and GM engine plants in the vicinity. It did so with significant success.

The reconfiguration of the plant from being a relatively small engine plant to be one of the major engine plants of Audi and the VW-group in 1996–7 made the issue of local sourcing more pertinent. The substantial increase of volume and manufacturing depth both required more strategic handling of supply for the plant. Audi sought to increase the value of its Hungarian sourced components from €30 million to €100 million (Havas 1997). Audi Győr organized two supplier conferences, where interested local companies were informed about possibilities. As a result, the local supply content reached 2 per cent of value added in engine production—still a very low figure. Some observers have blamed Audi, saying that it had no real intention to seek local suppliers and to develop their capacities. Others, however, point out that the quality and the technology level of local suppliers are not yet sufficient to become direct suppliers of the engine plant. Also, the global sourcing programme of the VW-group makes it difficult for small local companies to have direct supply to car plants.

At the end of the 1990s VW group headquarters made the Audi Győr plant one of the 18 global purchasing teams of the group. This involved mapping, benchmarking, qualifying, auditing, and maintaining relations with possible supplier firms in its geographical area in order to prepare their involvement into the global supply chain. Here the local purchasing department hence performs a global task. At the same time, the purchasing department also began to try to increase the scope of local supply for the Győr plant. This strategic decision coincided with the preparation to set up the first automobile cluster in Hungary, the Pannon Automotive Cluster (PANAC), mostly with public funding. The aim of PANAC was to help organizational learning of local, especially domestic automotive firms in western Hungary in order to be able to meet the high exigencies of companies like Audi, and to facilitate face-to-face contacts between local firms in the automotive industry to promote the establishment of supplier relations between SMEs and major end assemblers in the region. A further aim was to facilitate innovation and to provide training and cooperation programmes. It would also serve as a meeting point for companies and as an agent of marketing of local industries to potential buyers.

PANAC was set up in 2000, pooling 67 automotive firms primarily from the West Danubian region. Audi itself was one of the founding members. Reportedly, the purchasing department of Audi Győr hoped to use PANAC as an instrument in mapping, evaluating, and organizing potential suppliers. Nonetheless, the management of PANAC opted for running an open learning network. PANAC turned into a horizontal network, offering general services to firms to facilitate their upgrading, and did not engage in any type of evaluation of the members. Hence, the AMH purchasing department made its own search for possible supplier partners for the VW-group. It mapped all potential supplier companies in Hungary, evaluated a shortlist of 180 candidates, and included them into the database for potential global supplier companies. In this process, it also enlarged the pool of companies directly serving the Győr plant. As a result of these efforts, local content has increased to the present 10 per cent. Altogether, according to one estimation, Audi, through its orders of materials and services to local suppliers, generated a further 4,000–5,000 jobs in the region (Somai 2002). Also, the value of Hungarian sourced components to the VW-group increased substantially. It is important to note that Hungarian sourced parts and components to the VW-group have a value at least five times higher than those directly supplied to the Audi Győr plant.

The local content supplied directly to the plant can be divided into four categories. One is the wide range of materials, products, and services necessary for the functioning of the enterprise, but not used directly in the production process, from catering to office supplants to cleaning to security. Most of these relations are market based. Second is the employment of a wide range of business services and production-related services in long-term, cooperation-based relations. A number of local companies are performing such essential services as running the internal supply organization within the plant, providing maintenance of machinery and assembly lines for the plant, participating in development and design of machine tools, participation in various smaller R&D projects related to process development and product development. Third is the direct supply of the plant with parts and components. This is a relatively small value in the total value added; and it should be noted that all directly supplying firms, save one, are local subsidiaries of foreign-owned firms. On the other hand, a number of directly supplying firms are acting as first-tier suppliers, and have their own supply firms. Finally, in 2000, based on cooperation with one established supplier, Audi began experimentation with modular production in a relatively small area. This particular company, which is the local subsidiary of a German supply chain organizing firm, has built a manufacturing hall to produce some of the components in a modular system for the assembly line of the TT model. There are plans to increase the share of module-based JIT system for the new generation of the TT model assembled since 2006 in the Győr plant. Clearly, the relationship with this company includes important elements of longer-term cooperation.

It is clear that AMH's supplier relations run to an important extent through the VW-group headquarters' global sourcing programme. Here relations are in the first instance largely market based, institutionalized in Internet-based tenders for supplier contracts. Tendering is restricted to a smaller group of bidders when new products are concerned, and there is also a stronger element of cooperation within the development of new products between VW and the suppliers. This has little effect on AMH, however, which mainly gets its suppliers 'imposed' through the hierarchy of the VW-group. The situation is different for the suppliers with which AMH itself sets up relations. Here, depending on the product or service supplier, relations with some suppliers (non-core services, parts) are largely market based, while with the suppliers of core services long-term, cooperative, and trust-based relations have developed.

Industrial Relations

Zwickau

The institutions of *Tarifverträge* (collective wage settlements) and of *Mitbestimmung* (codetermination) were transferred from West to East Germany on unification, as were trade unions and employers' associations, most of the officials in these organizations coming from West Germany. The organizations wanted to extend to the East both the so-called *Tarifautonomie* (autonomy of trade unions and business associations to conclude wage settlements) and a strategy of high wages. On the one hand, this supported the interests of West German entrepreneurs and unions who feared price competition from the East; on the other hand, it would have reinforced the organizations by enlarging their membership basis. In the first years after reunification, union membership was very high, but this was rather the effect of an almost automatic transfer of members from the East German unions to the West German ones.

The processes of privatization of the ex-*Kombinaten* led to an increasing heterogeneity of East German firms (those already privatized, those still under the *Treuhand*, SMEs, and large firms, different sectors) and to difficulties in terms of representation (Artus 2001; Czada and Lehmbruch 1998). In addition, the growth of unemployment and the decrease of firm size led to a loss of potential members for the unions (Artus 2001; W. Schroeder 2000). The membership basis of business associations has never been wide because of the low industrial density in the *neue Länder*. The west-driven politics of high wages, carried out by the *Tarifpartner* (trade unions and business associations) in a situation of substantial lack of representation and uncertainty about the economic situation of East Germany, proved inadequate. Especially for East German SMEs, high wages, set independently of productivity increases, could mean exit from the market. On the other hand, workers were ready to accept lower wages in exchange for job maintenance. Therefore, entrepreneurs increasingly refused to attend collective bargaining meetings or more often avoided any form of associational commitment. This went beyond the so-called *Öffnungsklauseln* (originally conceived in West Germany as 'codetermined' deviations from *Tarifverträge* in firm-specific difficult economic situations, not formally violating the collective agreement itself). The unilateral definition of wage by the smaller entrepreneurs became the norm in East Germany. Firm-level agreements (*Hausverträge*) spread, and the strategies for both high wages and a strong role for associations sank dramatically.

The second pillar of the West German system—codetermination at the firm level—is also becoming less institutionalized and much more voluntary. Most local firms, regardless of their size, have no *Betriebsrat* (works council). After the critical phase of privatization, in which management strongly cooperated with representatives of the works councils for the common goal of survival, today they exist only where local circumstances or personal relationships support them (R. Schmidt 1998).

Some of the characteristics of the industrial relations described above are also characteristic for some recent tendencies in West Germany. Many authors underline how collective agreements are much more convenient for large firms than for small ones and how the latter have increasingly withdrawn from the employers' associations at least since the beginning of the eighties (Glassmann, this volume; Silvia 1997; Streeck and Rehder 2003). Others also stress the present processes of decentralization in matters like wage definition. However, if these phenomena take apparently the same forms in east and west, there are differences in the nature and the intensity of the deviations. In the ex-GDR, unions were almost a political organ with no function in terms of representation and work defence. But differently from the institution of the IHK described above, the failure of unions to become embedded after reunification was exacerbated by the transfer of West German functionaries, by difficulties in recruiting local ones, and above all by the lack of an interest among entrepreneurs in accepting constraints to their activities. Some studies of codetermination show differences in implementation in east and west (Bosch et al. 1999), particularly in terms of power asymmetry between employers and employees and in terms of support for the works council by the workforce (R. Schmidt 1998).[6]

The analysis of VW Zwickau in this context is particularly interesting. First, it enables us to demonstrate differences in terms of conceptions of industrial relations among different economic actors—especially VW and its immediate suppliers on the one hand and the smaller external and local firms on the other. Second, these differences are even more evident as the automobile industry in Zwickau was the arena of a strike in 2003 that ended with defeat of the unions. In addition, the employers association involved in the *Tarifvertrag* has carried out a particularly aggressive campaign against collective agreements in order to gain legitimation from small firms. As will become clear, this cocktail of actors and strategies has had consequences in terms of institutional laceration that cannot be found in industrial relations in West Germany.

For VW itself, collective agreements are still the main way of fixing wages. By starting in East Germany with a wage regulation according to the Saxony *Tarifvertrag* instead of creating a company agreement (*Haustarifvertrag*) as it had done in Wolfsburg, labour costs have been cut, but it must be stressed that VW did not want to opt out of the framework of the *Tarifvertrag* as such. When the Saxony metal industry employers' association campaigned against central agreements on wages to favour decentralized contracts at firm level, VW left the association and joined that in Brandenburg, to be followed by many of its local first-tier suppliers. One consequence of this, however, was a further weakening of the Saxony *Tarifvertrag*. As in West Germany, a cooperative approach to industrial relations is accompanied by an increasing exposure to competitors and by an enormous pressure on prices. Therefore, these suppliers have given clear signs of dissatisfaction with the rigidity of collective agreements. On the other hand, as one of the functions of the German system is to keep conflicts outside the firm, it is more convenient not to opt out of the collective agreements. In fact, in a highly coordinated production system, the strike of one firm would have strong consequences for the whole system. One manager of an important module supplier working just-in-time said in referring to the strike of 2003 that the firm was lucky that VW was on strike too, because his firm could not afford to take a strike alone. Some other external firms have decentralized agreements on wages, although they are substantially oriented to the level of existing agreements. In any case, this differentiation generates an unequal competition between the firms paying according to the central agreements and those which do not.

If signs of disaffection are evident among suppliers from the west, local entrepreneurs do not accept *Tarifvertrag* at all. It is perceived as making survival of the firm difficult, and possibly as producing injustice, as a source of inequality between VW on the one hand (where people think employees work less and are paid more) and the other firms of the region on the other hand. Ultimately, the industrial relations system is considered as a decision taken in the west and imposed on the east. Firms use their rejection of *Tarifvertrag* for a number of purposes. For some it is a source of flexibility: if the firm is going well, workers may get wages even above the level established by the

Tarifvertrag. Others use their freedom merely as a way to push down labour costs. Differences can be identified not only between external and local firms but also among workers at different skill levels.

Quantitatively, Saxony has seen a decline in acceptance of collective agreements in the metal industry as a whole. Slipping from 19.2 per cent of firms (covering 29.1% of employees) in 1999 to 8.3 per cent of firms (20.8% of employees) in 2003. The proportion of company-level agreements involving unions actually increased (from 5.9% of firms in 1999 to 6.5% in 2002, involving, respectively, 65% and 72.5% of total employees), but that of firms with no agreements at either local or company level has been growing (from about 75% of firms (65% of employees)) in 1999 to 87.6 per cent of companies (72.5% of employees) in 2003 (Verband der Sächsischen Metall- und Elektroindustrie 2004).

Differences in the acceptance of works councils follow a similar pattern. The external firms generally have a *Betriebsrat* whether they take part in collective agreements or not. It is largely accepted because of its role in facilitating communication with the workforce, or as an instrument for motivation of workers and for improving the organization of production. But with the exception of VW itself, in which codetermination is now carried out as in the western plants,[7] entrepreneurs and managers of other firms consider the *Betriebsrat* as positive only if it acts accordingly to the interests of the firm. Some admit that the works council has to push them for the observation of the Works Council Constitution. The majority of local firms have no works council at all. This is not perceived as necessary, mainly because work organization and wages are informally regulated between entrepreneurs and workers. In some cases, the absence of the works council is rather the result of a more hierarchical style of conducting the firm, and hence of a strong power asymmetry between employers and employees. Nonetheless, it has not necessarily to be interpreted as a sign of lack of social engagement in general.

In conclusion, in the field of industrial relations the automobile region of Zwickau shows a dualistic structure. The external investment of VW as such was not sufficient to guarantee and/or reinforce the institutions of collective agreements and codetermination that are coherently implemented within the firm. One could even argue that tensions and conflicts are even deeper in Zwickau than elsewhere because of the comparatively high industrial concentration, the stronger role of local entrepreneurs, and the strategic role of the motor industry for unions.

Győr

The Hungarian industrial relations system is decentralized and trade unions and employers' associations are fragmented. There are six national trade union confederations, divided along political cleavages. In the metal sector, two major federations belonging to different confederations are competing with each other. According to the law, it is up to employees working at a non-unionized company whether they set up a union to represent their interests. Such a union has the right to join any sectoral, regional, or national trade union associations, or to maintain its independence as a company union. Legal regulations compel management to inform, consult, or negotiate with company unions. Employees also have the right to elect works councils. Statutory works councils function primarily as bodies for information and consultation; they do not have codetermination rights.

Within this context, at the start of production in 1993, AMH management organized work in teams and regarded these as the main instruments for communication between the company and the employees. As a greenfield operation, at the outset there was no union presence and management had no interest in seeing unions emerge. In addition, in the decentralized Hungarian system, there are hardly any sectoral collective agreements setting minimum standards for incoming investors, the metal sector being no exception to this. Hence, initially, the individual employment relationship was the basis for setting wages and working conditions. AMH management did not intend to create an industrial relations system similar to that in Germany and initially enjoyed the absence of trade union influence. It was one of the best-paying employers in the region and offered interesting opportunities for personal development and careers. It considered this a sufficient basis for a good relationship with its employees.

Since the opening of the factory, workers have wanted to create a body for interest representation. The Metalworkers' Union (Vasas Szövetség) played the key role, in 1994 its regional secretary persuading a group of leading AMH employees that a union was the most appropriate form for the representation of their interests. Vasas Szövetség is a member organization of the MSZOSZ confederations in Hungary, the successor to the former communist union confederation. In March 1994 the AMH Metalworkers' Union organization (or 'Vasas') was founded. Membership increased rapidly and by the turn of 1995 it had a membership of between 150 and 200. Members had clear expectations. In particular they expected the union to fight to increase both the basic wage and the various shift supplements. The management accepted that the union had been founded, and guaranteed the conditions laid down in the Labour Code for its operation. At the same time, it did not automatically accept the union as a negotiating partner. It was open to contact with union activists, so that they could discuss employment problems, complaints, and exchange information, but no formal system was created for general consultation, problem solving, or collective bargaining.

In the works council elections of spring 1995, Vasas received some 90 per cent of the votes cast, and all but one of the members of the new council were union candidates. Immediately afterwards, Vasas contacted company management to begin negotiations on a collective agreement but the company was not interested. As a result, discontent with the union grew considerably among the employees, who expected wage increases. This created space for an alternative, more militant union, the workers seeking this receiving help from the independent union of the neighbouring Rába plant, which belonged to the Metalworkers' Federation of Liga, a competing confederation to MSZOSZ. The new independent union was formed in May, not long after the works council elections. Its membership fee was set at a much lower level than that of Vasas, it drew up a much more militant programme, and started an active campaign to recruit members. Membership rapidly surpassed 500, while that of Vasas fell to 50 or 60. In a spring 1997 by-election for two new members of the works council both successful candidates came from the new union. Despite its speedy increase in membership, the independent union grew in hostile soil within the company. First, the company management did not recognize it as a representative union. A legal battle ensued between company management and the union, which the union finally won. However, this did not solve the problem of communication between it and the company management.

However, since its formation, the works council itself has played an active role in the company. By late 1997 it had its own office in the plant. Also, because of the problematic relations between the independent union and management, the works council's activities went beyond those defined by the Labour Code, and it began to play an active role in negotiating employee grievances.

In 1997, AMH suggested it would be ready to negotiate a collective agreement with Vasas. This was given a major impetus by the visit of the President of the Audi AG Central Works Council and the chief steward of IG Metall. Following this IG Metall and its Audi AG branch organized a training course for the leadership of the Audi Vasas. More important was the backing of the powerful German union for the Hungarian unionists. At the end of 1997, there were also changes in the leadership of the independent trade union. The resulting change of style and strategy led to an agreement between the independent union and Vasas to negotiate the prospective collective agreement together and to press for common demands. The new leadership also sought to make a new start with company management. Nonetheless, it was only in 2001 that a collective agreement was concluded; management until then dragged its feet. Three factors facilitated the eventual conclusion of the agreement. First, the July 2001 amendment of the Labour Code allowed collective agreements to set more flexible working time schedules than the standard regulations. Through this amendment, AMH management became interested in concluding a collective agreement to widen its options for work organization and the use of employees' time. Second, both the expansion of Audi and the rapid inflow of FDI into the region had resulted in a very tight local labour market. In addition, the wage advantage of Audi compared to other local businesses had eroded. The result was an increase in labour turnover. Audi appointed a new HRM manager to address this and to strengthen the commitment of the workforce. Wages were increased and a more cooperative relationship developed with the unions. Third, despite the fact that the Vasas union was the minor one, IG Metall, the German union active in Audi AG, recognized only it and did not maintain any relationship with the independent union. Once the two company unions had set up the Érdekvédelmi Szövetség (Interest Representation Alliance), the independent union was also recognized and supported by IG Metall.

The main issue of the 2001 negotiations was how to balance increasing working time flexibility and the related elimination of overtime benefits. Unions successfully persuaded management to introduce a 'cafeteria' system of welfare benefits, which allows each employee to choose a package which best fits his or her individual needs, ranging from support in buying a computer to a company pension system. The unions also negotiated a support scheme for buying cars. Based on the 2001 agreement, there now are annual wage negotiations.

By 2005 the Vasas union has a membership of 3–4 per cent of employees, while the independent union has about 35 per cent, and the company was providing good facilities for the works council and both unions. There are weekly meetings between the HRM manager and trade union representatives. Beyond that, both sides are open to ad hoc meetings, depending on actual needs. In the interviews conducted, both sides expressed their willingness to engage flexibly in the solving of problems. The unions expressed their commitment to a flexible adaptation to the requirements of production as long as the basic interests of employees as well as the regulations of the Labour Code are respected. This includes their acceptance of the fact that management to a large extent determines working conditions, including the setting of flexible working time schedules.

When Audi first invested in Hungary, it had no intention to replicate the German industrial relations model. It did not obstruct the formation of trade unions, but at the same time it did not foster it nor did it seek close cooperation once unions were established. A transplant of the German model to a Hungarian subsidiary would also have faced the problem that the Hungarian system of industrial relations is completely different than the German system. Union membership is low, unions are strongly divided among themselves, industrial relations are decentralized, and there are practically no sectoral collective agreements. Nonetheless, after 2000, a kind of shallow micro-level cooperation developed between local workers representative bodies, including both unions and the works council, and management. Local, national, and international factors played a role in this change. Cooperation is made possible by the compromise-seeking attitude of trade unionists and the openness of local management to worker representatives. It was however also motivated by clear interests. AMH wanted to reduce labour turnover and secure labour supply in an increasingly tight local labour market. Also, it wanted to fully exploit the possibilities the Labour Code offers for working time flexibility, and this can only be done through a collective agreement. Unions accepted that flexibility is a major source of competitiveness, which in turn results in new jobs and continuous investment. At the same time, the unions wanted to increase workers' benefits in exchange for this flexibility, and they succeeded in this. Finally, the support of IG Metall and the Audi AG Central Works Council helped to convince management to adopt a more positive attitude towards workers' representatives.

The cooperative relationship between top management and union leadership had its effect on the everyday policy of line managers and supervisors. If they order an unusual working time scheme or practice, they usually consult the union and seek its approval. Union leaders normally approve such moves, provided they are compensated financially, such a decision being reinforced by a quick meeting between union representatives and the employees affected by the possible changes. This cooperation and continuous exchange of goodwill is continuously reinforcing trust between management and unions. It also strengthens the relationship between union leaders and their members and has an impact on unionization: employees feel that unions matter and that their voice is heard. Still, the cooperation between management and workers' representatives remains limited to direct work organization issues and does not include more strategic issues.

Vocational Training

Zwickau

If we consider another milestone of the German model—vocational training—the literature generally underlines strong differences in the implementation in East Germany as compared to the West. On the one side, the so-called *duale System* (the dual system of apprenticeship in companies and schools) was transferred top-down like other institutions. On the other hand, the ex-GDR also had a strong tradition in apprenticeship at school and in firms, although not in a market context. The problems of implementation, which can be observed in East Germany, are therefore essentially due to economic uncertainty and a substantial lack of firms, which cause a mismatch between demands of apprenticeship of young people on the one hand and the supply by firms on the other (Brussig 2003). Even those young people who have the possibility to be trained within the framework of the traditional dual system have no guarantee that they will be offered a job at the end of their training. On the other hand, training is costly for the firm and it is even more costly if there is no perspective to integrate the apprentices (*Auszubildende*) afterwards or if inter-regional 'free-riding' occurs. The scarce supply of trainee places as well as the lower wages in East Germany have, however, the opposite effects: strong migration processes of young people into the old *Länder* and a stronger engagement of local institutional actors in the creation of apprenticeship opportunities within the dual system—often with a stronger role played by schools instead of firms.

Culpepper (2001) underlines the role of involvement of employers' associations in the definition of vocational training policies as the explaining variable between success and failure of those policies. While on the one hand 'employers' associations from the west succeeded in facilitating the establishment of strong organizational capacity among East German associations' (ibid. 278), the failure of the policies are considered as a consequence of political decisions not to involve associations in decision-making. This has consequences in terms of lack of information transfer about content and firms' training needs.

The automobile industry and its supplier chain in Zwickau represent a sort of exception in the East German context. Although the firms interviewed do not train as many young people as they should according to the norm, they have at least all programmes of vocational training in the firm. In 2004, VW was training 233 people, about 81 each year, the majority in the plant of Mosel (61), the rest in the engine production plant in Chemnitz (20). The company has its own vocational training centre (VBI—Volkswagen Bildungsinstitut) which is also used by other firms, especially by module suppliers. Local entrepreneurs use mainly regional training centres, which are sometimes continuations of older GDR training schools. As already mentioned, the region has a strong tradition in the automobile industry, and during the first five years after reunification there was a general process of training and retraining for other sectors. As firms linked to the automobile industry experienced a growth in the following years, they faced a lack of qualified and highly specialized workforce. For the smaller firms, vocational training is also a way to gain the commitment of young and qualified people. As in West Germany, some firms even pay for further qualification of their workers at the *Berufsakademie* (a combination between a university of applied sciences and training on the job) or at the university, while they continue to work for the firm. Both external and local companies have contacts to the local university that supplies highly qualified and specialized engineers. This form of interaction between firms and university is quite widespread, though entrepreneurs fear that, since well-qualified workers and young people with a higher education degree are paid less than in other German regions, they will be likely to move away once local firms have paid for their training.

Overall, firms have developed an interest in apprenticeship combined with a sense of social commitment to young people in the region. The IHK is also strongly supportive. This is sectorally specific, as other industries are much more reluctant to invest in qualification, but it can be concluded that vocational training in Zwickau functions relatively well, considering East German standards and the general economic situation. However, at the same time it functions independently of the support of the traditional institutions of industrial relations that are considered as complementary by the literature on the varieties of capitalism. Employers' associations and unions are too weak to be able to play the traditional role of insiders, collecting information, and fighting free-riding through 'pressuring major firms to take on apprentices and monitoring their participation in such schemes' (Hall and Soskice 2001*a*: 25). It seems that direct, non-mediated engagement by firms in different committees and regional forums, and some forms of wage adaptation oriented to the market without associational commitment are acting as functional equivalents.

Győr

Before the Second World War, vocational education and training in Hungary shared many characteristics with the Austrian and German dual system, combining school-based and enterprise-based learning. In the state-socialist period, both the school and vocational training system and the economy were nationalized. Following this, the link between state enterprises and vocational training schools became even closer. Although most vocational schools were formally independent from the state enterprises, they often catered to specific groups of companies. Also, often, after two years of school-based training, a year of enterprise-based training followed, and trainees would often be employed in the same enterprise afterwards. In smaller towns, where one state enterprise provided most employment, the local vocational school was basically run by this same enterprise. Consequently, the vocational training system was based on strong institutionalized links between schools and enterprises, including channels for enterprise-based training facilitating the school-to-work transition. However, even though institutional links between enterprises and schools were strong, the central state defined most of the curriculum of the school, leaving little room for flexibility and local adaptation in this respect.

Since the early 1990s the school system has undergone profound changes. The two most important have been the ending of the state-socialist enterprise-based model and the reform of vocational training to provide more up-to-date and flexible training. The former practically ended close linkages between vocational training schools and enterprises. Training facilities in companies were closed, the school–company relationship was disrupted, and the school-to-work transition became more problematic: at present only some 30 per cent of vocational students participate in an enterprise apprentice shop or a practical workplace experience, compared to some 70 per cent in 1989. Vocational training hence has become more school based. The end of the dual training system is especially accentuated in manufacturing, and today the majority of apprenticeship arrangements can be found in services.

At the same time, reforms of the vocational training system aimed at adapting both the training organizations and their curricula to the new exigencies of the market economy. Political and economic actors shared the view that a general reform of the vocational training system was necessary. The skills provided by the 'old' system were deemed obsolete and not corresponding to a 'modern' market economy. Also, the way curricula were defined was judged too inflexible for the adaptation to sectoral and technological change and to the short-term requirements of changing and new enterprises. In addition, curricula were seen to be too narrowly focused on production skills and lacking more general skills important for continuous skill acquisition, 'lifelong learning', and flexibility on the side of employees. The need for reform was further underlined by the downsizing or bankruptcy of many traditional state enterprises, the growing importance of multinationals as well as SMEs and new human resource strategies.

Today, local governments largely own the Hungarian vocational training system, which comprises two main types of schools. Vocational training schools are rather narrowly focused on the acquisition of specific skills for specific occupations, providing a three-year curriculum; vocational secondary schools, with a four-year curriculum, provide a broader education that also serves as an entry to higher education. Vocational training schools have seen a decline of student numbers by almost 40 per cent since the early 1990s, while vocational secondary schools have rapidly increased participation.

The central state no longer imposes detailed curricula. Rather, the Ministry of Education defines a frame curriculum, providing for the local definition of actual curricula. It also maintains the National Vocational Qualifications Register, a framework of state-recognized qualifications that provides the basis for the development of common training profiles for both initial and continuing vocational education. The Development and Training Fund, financed by a specific enterprise contribution (called the Vocational Training Contribution at the rate of 1.5% of wage costs), is a sub-fund of the Labour Market Fund and is used to finance both the vocational training school system and the training of the employed. Nonetheless, enterprises have the right directly to finance particular vocational schools instead of paying the levy to the central fund.

In the late 1990s Audi started to feel the tightening of the regional labour market as far as skilled workers and engineers were concerned. Also, because of the increasing volume and complexity of production, it required many skilled workers with specific types of training. As a result, it started to build a network with local vocational training schools (*szakmunkásképző iskola*) and vocational secondary schools (*szakközépiskola*) to harmonize training programmes, to provide school-based practical training with the technology used by the Audi plant, and to organize practical training within the plant. It made ample use of the option that companies can decide to fund their own vocational training organizations instead of paying into the central fund.

Given the size of Audi, 1.5 per cent of wage costs is a large sum and gives important leverage to the firm to induce cooperation with local institutions. Moreover, its good contact with the local government ensured support for strengthening the relationship with local training institutions. The firm now has a well-developed cooperation network with a number of schools in the field of engineering, including many elements of the concept of dual training. Audi granted state-of-the-art machinery and technology to the training shops of these schools to provide the option to learn about and use the technology in use at the firm. They have jointly developed training materials and special curricula adapted to the skill requirements of Audi, and prepare students for the transition from school-to-work (provided they select Audi as their employer). Audi has also set up a training hall within the factory and students can come to do their practical training there, working on real production tasks supervised by the firm's engineers and skilled workers.

An example of such cooperation is the Lukács Sándor Szakképző Iskola (vocational training school), which annually sends some 75 students to Audi for practical training. In exchange, since 2000, Audi has already given more than 100 million HUF support to the school to develop facilities. In June 2004 a new laboratory with CNC machines was set up in the school with a value of 60 million HUF, out of which 32 million were provided by Audi. Altogether, since 2000, 213 students have taken part in this exchange, and most of them now work at Audi. Following the start of car-assembly at the Audi plant in 1998, a car-manufacturing vocational skill training course was set up at this school with support from Audi, a unique course in Hungary.

Practically all students finishing a course and a practical training experience within the Audi training programme can expect a job offer from the company. In many cases, especially in the case of vocational secondary schools, however, students are opting to go for higher education, especially engineering at the local university, instead of seeking employment as skilled workers. Still, many of them seek employment at Audi after having finished their engineering studies.

Hence, Audi, in cooperation with these local vocational schools, developed something resembling a micro version of a dual system, based on close cooperation between the company and the schools. In this micro-system, the public schools are responsible for general education, according to the requirements of the national education system. The teaching of more specific knowledge as well as practical training are however largely catered towards the needs of Audi, and the company plays a major role providing both this knowledge, in providing materials for school-based practical training and in offering practical training places within its plant. As a result, students can easily make the school-to-work transition, as long as they are willing to work for Audi.

To some extent this is a 'return' to the kind of relationship that prevailed between state-owned companies and vocational schools under state socialism, as well as a partial and micro adoption to the German system. These 'double roots' of the Audi system certainly helped to forge a successful partnership between the schools and the company. Both partners, that is, the German expatriate managers and the Hungarian school directors, could build on practices familiar to them and could adapt these to the new economic and political circumstances as well as to the peculiarities of the Hungarian educational system. It should be noted that the current reform plans of the Hungarian government for vocational training are consistent with this model. It is seeking to launch a programme offering financial incentives for firms that provide practical training possibilities for vocational students and thus facilitate the school-to-work transition (*Népszava* 2005.06.18).

Conclusions

A major source of interest of this study for examining local and branch-level variations in capitalism has been the 'natural laboratory' of comparing the operation of a West German multinational corporation in two central European locations with state-socialist histories, but in one of which West German institutions have been formally established since 1989. Such differences as we have found between the two locations have been consistent with what institutional theory would teach us to expect: for example, structures like IHK have been playing a role in Zwickau that nothing approaches in Győr. However, as many institutionalists would warn us to expect, the formal eastward extension of western institutions did not necessarily mean that they were immediately effective. This is perhaps particularly the case, as with industrial relations, where power relations are concerned.

More generally, we have also seen how similar existing traditions can facilitate institutional transfer, especially if a common interest and thus consensus is built around them. Further, some resources or blockages for institutional functioning are to be identified in the strategies and in the role-interpretation by the institutional actors. Introducing the local dimension is therefore important to explore variety and enlighten different institutional constellations that support or discourage development and that could remain unexplored if exclusively the national dimension is considered.

In Zwickau in general, inter-firm cooperation developed surprisingly well, considering the economic situation in East Germany and the premises of the 'colonization idea'. This was possible, partly because of the role of some local institutional actors, but also because of sectoral peculiarities, the role of hierarchy, and its influence on the interests of the local economic actors. The dual system of vocational training was also working relatively well in the automobile sector and in the local economy of Zwickau, as compared to other sectors and to the rest of East Germany. On the other hand, industrial relations experienced problems in terms of both implementation and legitimation. This should not surprise us, as industrial relations are not concerned solely with technical issues but with power relations between employers and employees, and labour markets have been weak throughout CEE. (Indeed, in both Zwickau and Győr it was a tightening of the labour market that led to a strengthening of industrial relations institutions in VW-Audi itself.) Here developments might represent precedents that may influence institutions in the west as well.

The study of Győr showed Audi's position in the region developing from being an isolated high-tech island to being an institutional entrepreneur and network organizer. Initially, it developed an arms-length, market-based relationship to its local environment, much resembling a 'cathedral in the desert'. In particular, the local content of production was absolutely minimal, and AMH acquired the required workforce through strict market processes. For the rest it relied on its Ingolstadt headquarters, which provided management and technical expertise, designed the product and production process, and organized the supply of parts and components. The local government and the central government were Audi's main partners in this initial period, providing financial and other incentives, infrastructural investments, as well as the necessary transport infrastructure. However, this approach quickly turned out to have its limits. Because of its own rapid expansion as well as the quite successful development of the region as such, the company ran into problems to find sufficient and sufficiently qualified employees on the labour market and it started to experience increased labour turnover as its wages and working conditions stopped being competitive. In addition, AMH started to need certain types of business services that did not fit the initial approach. Hence, it was in need of different public and private goods as well as of different employee relations. To ensure the provision of these goods and a change in employee relations the company had to change its relations with the relevant actors in the region, increasingly complementing its market approach with elements of cooperation. Indeed, it had to become more embedded into its local environment.

Its development of closer relations with local actors should be seen in this light. The institutionalization of patterns of cooperation remains relatively weak in the sense that cooperation takes place at a micro-level and is not embedded in broader formal structures in which similar types of cooperation take place and reinforce each other. Also, although some of the forms of cooperation seem to have become more solid and institutionalized in recent years, whether they will be consolidated or would disappear in the future is hard to predict. In this sense, institutional change and innovation are in full swing and no stability has as yet been reached. In addition, cooperation remains to some extent arms-length in the sense that the partners do not commit totally to each other, often try not to become totally dependent on each other. Rather, cooperation is contract based and may be terminated once new conditions or opportunities so require. This 'arms-length cooperation' allows flexibility for both partners in finding additional 'suppliers' and 'customers', respectively, and additional support for their own development trajectory. AMH is clearly the dominant partner in this relationship, which provides it with extensive flexibility. However, there are also certain advantages for suppliers and educational organizations. In this era of highly mobile industries, a plurality of customers might be a better long-term survival strategy than depending completely on one company.

But the two cases both demonstrate more than anything else the capacity of a major MNC itself to mould institutions. While we have established the overall project of which this study is a part primarily as a confrontation between national versus local and sectoral institutions, it is this other actor that emerges as *victor ludorum*. Where an existing West German institution proved useful, as with vocational training, VW-Audi managed to implement major features of it in Hungary almost as much as in East Germany, where the system had been formally introduced at a general level. In both locations the strong associational base of employers' organizations and unions, normally considered essential to the West German training system, was missing—even though again in Zwickau they had been formally established after unification. But VW-Audi itself seemed to provide a functional equivalent of the associations. Similarly, in both Zwickau and Győr industrial relations institutions that to some extent resemble a weak version of West German ones can be seen in plants of VW-Audi itself, and perhaps of its West German first-tier suppliers; but not among local firms. And the institutions were strengthened when they served the firms' recruitment and retention needs. Here there seemed little difference between a *neues Land* and Hungary, neither the formal transfer of West German institutions in the former nor their absence in the latter making more than a small difference. There are limits to the implications of this conclusion: VW-Audi is a particularly powerful firm; the institutional structures of the countries of CEE are rather weak. Nevertheless, we do see here the capacity of major firms to act as institution-makers, and not just as institution-takers as in the normal expectations of neo-institutionalist theory, whether it is concerned with the national, the local, or other levels.

Notes

1. Czada and Lehmbruch (1998) underline, for instance, how the integration of electricity system and of public transport (S-Bahn) in East Germany occurred relatively easily. In the sectors exposed to more exogenous transformation, the influence of market and actors is more evident. In public sectors like the health system or television (Rundfunk) interests with 'public status' (e.g. health insurances) pushed the institutions of the West German system to avoid possible changes in their own field. They could also partly count on convergent interests of other decisive actors (like the young East German doctors who could profit much more from the West German system of the Krankenkasse in comparison to the central health system

of the ex-GDR, or like the East German politicians at *Land* level, who could count on a higher influence on the media). On the other hand, sectors like local press and agriculture, in which economic performance is a primary condition for competition, self-dynamics were more clearly identifiable. However, an important role was also played by strong local interests in the former case and more fragmented West German associations in the latter. Maintenance of the organization of production based on large farms instead of adaptation to the (collapsing) European and German model of small farmers proved to be economically successful.

2. The problem of institutional complementarity has recently been at the centre of the debate in the literature on varieties of capitalism. See Crouch 2003, 2005; Crouch et al. 2005; Deeg 2005; *Socio-Economic Review* 2005.

3. The data on South West Saxony refer to the district of the local Industrie- und Handelskammer (IHK, Chamber of Commerce). This district includes the areas of Zwickau, Chemnitz, and Plauen.

4. This was for example true for the region of Bautzen in East Saxony, not far from Zwickau. In this case, cooperation among entrepreneurs and local institutions was much more the result of the commitment of the local political actors and administration (see Piotti 2002).

5. This is not necessarily the case for the relation between the suppliers in this pool and the VW-group as a whole. Indeed, VW does regular audits and evaluations of its suppliers, which include elements of cooperation as well.

6. R. Schmidt (1998) argues that a certain degree of 'easternization' of the Western industrial relations could occur exactly through the pressure of those western firms producing also in East Germany in far less constraining institutional conditions.

7. At the beginning of the 1990s, the management in Zwickau was less motivated to act in conformity to the Works Council Constitution Act; and in some cases the controversy was even presented to the judgement of the Labour Court. The claims laid by the work council prevailed. In the following years, there was also a process of stronger integration of the Work Council in Zwickau within the VW-Central Work Council. Because of the different juridical status (VW-Saxony is an extra-limited liability company) the representative of the *Betriebsrat* in Zwickau was initially only present as 'guest' at the meetings of the Central Work Council.

6

The Development of Munich and Cambridge Therapeutic Biotech Firms: A Case Study of Institutional Adaptation

SIMCHA JONG*

Recent comparative studies of the German economy suggest that many of the country's national political and social institutions such as rigid labour markets, a system of firm financing dominated by regional banks, and a shareholder-unfriendly corporate governance system seriously impede the formation and development of entrepreneurial firms in technologically volatile and risky markets, which require firms to adopt 'radically innovative' product strategies (Crouch and Streeck 1997; Hall and Soskice 2001*b*; Hollingsworth and Boyer 1997; Kitschelt and Streeck 2004). Rather than a small entrepreneurial firm in a technologically disruptive market, the typical German firm is generally considered to be found in a more stable, established industry in which it is able to benefit from the support of Germany's settled institutional environment for firms by following more incrementally innovative, long-term strategies.

Since the late 1990s, however, German entrepreneurs in the biotechnology sector seem to have managed to defy institutional stereotypes by building up a growing biotech industry. In fact, according to Ernst and Young (2003) the German biotech industry is currently Europe's largest, measured by the number of firms. The aim of this chapter is to understand better how, despite their supposed comparative institutional disadvantages, German biotech entrepreneurs have been able to build up their firms' key capabilities and tackle organizational challenges. This contributes to the present book by showing that national varieties of capitalism may allow for local and sectoral diversity. The development of a vibrant biotech industry in Germany over the last decade also constitutes an interesting case study of institutional mechanisms, which lead to change in *national* capitalist systems too—both in general and in the German capitalist system in particular.

In order better to understand the development of the therapeutic biotech firms in the Munich region, Germany's largest and most successful biotech

* Fuller details of both cases will be found in Jong (2006).

cluster, this study contrasts the development of Munich firms with that in the Cambridge region, in the United Kingdom. The UK is considered to be the prototype of the European liberal market economy and is regarded to offer all the institutional settings which are required to support the development of entrepreneurial radically innovative high-tech firms, which the German economy lacks (Casper and Glimsted 2001; Hall and Soskice 2001*a*).

Moreover, this study focuses on therapeutic biotech firms in the Cambridge and Munich regions that focus on the discovery and development of new pharmaceutical drugs, which is a very risky, long, and costly process. These firms have been identified in the comparative institutional literature as being especially reliant on the type of institutions such as venture capital and 'hire and fire' labour markets that are present in the liberal market economies of the UK and the USA but are absent in Germany (Casper 2000; Casper et al. 1999). Therefore, focusing on therapeutic biotech firms is particularly appropriate in the context of this study, which attempts to examine the extent to which entrepreneurs are able to defy institutional settings that constrain the pursuit of certain innovative strategies and find alternative institutional paths to sustain the development of their firms, thus constituting productive incoherences to their national institutional environment.

The United Kingdom houses Europe's oldest and most vibrant biotechnology industry. The findings of this chapter confirm that biotech entrepreneurs in the United Kingdom were able to benefit from the institutional support infrastructure for firms in high-tech industries that is associated with liberal market economies. During the 1980s entrepreneurs founded the first biotechnology firms, with scientists leaving their positions at major pharmaceutical firms playing a particularly important role in the formation of new firms. Moreover, the findings of this chapter highlight that these entrepreneurs were able to rely on well-developed equity markets in the United Kingdom to fund these firms.

Moreover, this study finds that biotech entrepreneurs within Germany's coordinated market economy have been remarkably creative in finding alternative institutional paths, bypassing potential institutional obstacles that could have prevented them from achieving their goals. Although this study confirms that 'rigid' German labour markets and the system of firm financing which heavily relies on local banks have indeed posed formidable challenges for Munich's biotech entrepreneurs in building up their firms, these obstacles did not prevent them from developing capabilities to effectively deal with these challenges.

In the absence of open, flexible German industry labour markets, biotech entrepreneurs have relied on the German academic community to recruit scientists and on international labour markets to recruit their most senior managers. In the absence of a German domestic venture capital industry and German equity markets accessible to young high-tech firms, German entrepreneurs have relied on international venture capital firms that have proven to be all too eager to profit from investment opportunities in Munich-based biotech firms, which were not taken up by private German financial institutions. Interestingly, the isolation of Munich-based biotech firms from labour markets for professionals entrenched in established industry practices and their close ties to academic communities, seems to have pushed Munich biotech entrepreneurs towards the pursuit of product strategies that are more rather than less technologically disruptive and 'radically innovative' than the product strategies of their Cambridge-based counterparts.

This chapter proceeds as follows. First, it discusses how the comparative case study, which follows, will increase our understanding of the mechanisms through which entrepreneurs in a new industry are able to overcome pre-existing institutional barriers to their firms' development. Second, the main organizational challenges with which biotech entrepreneurs in Cambridge and Munich have been confronted in building up a biotech firm are outlined. Third, it is analysed how Munich's and Cambridge's therapeutic biotech firms have relied on their institutional environments differently to develop their firms' capabilities to deal with these organizational challenges. Fourth, it is discussed how the different institutional paths which Cambridge's and Munich's biotech entrepreneurs have followed to deal with key organizational challenges have affected the development of these firms. Finally, the main findings are summarized and some implications of this study for broader debates in the comparative institutional literature are suggested.

A wide range of recent studies of the German economy have reached a consensus that German institutions, while providing significant support for established firms in technologically stable markets that follow more incrementally innovative product strategies, at the same time significantly inhibit the development of small, entrepreneurial high-tech firms in new technologically volatile markets. The inability of the German economy (as opposed to the more liberally organized market economies of the USA and the UK) to foster the development of Silicon Valley-type high-tech firms has widely been attributed to a number of well-defined institutional factors (cf. Casper et al. 1999; Hall and Soskice 2001*b*; Katzenstein 1987; Kitschelt and Streeck 2004; Streeck 1997).

First, German rigid labour markets, while providing incentives for firms in technologically stable markets to make long-term investments in firm-specific skills of employees, significantly impede the development of German firms in technologically volatile markets that rely on their ability to rapidly hire and fire employees for their organizational and strategic flexibility.

Second, even though allowing established firms to take a more long-term look at their product development strategies, Germany's financial system, with its strong local banks and underdeveloped equity markets, significantly impedes the formation of high-tech firms that rely on equity investments to finance their growth.

Within recent debates in the political economy literature on the state of the German capitalist 'model', disagreement exists on the extent to which efforts to make it more liberally oriented would improve the current dismal state of the German economy (see Kitschelt and Streeck 2004 as opposed to Hall and Soskice 2001*a*). However, a consensus does exist within these debates regarding the immobile and self-reinforcing nature of the current German capitalist model. However, this consensus has not been shared by policymakers eager to position Germany at the frontier of the so-called knowledge-based economy and high-tech entrepreneurs determined to build up profitable enterprises in new and rapidly growing markets. Concerned by the comparatively weak performance and relative absence of German firms in new high-tech industries in which innovation is driven by small entrepreneurial 'radically innovative' firms, German policymakers since the early 1990s have tried to design policies aimed at challenging entrepreneurs to defy the outlined institutional barriers and find creative ways to build up successful new high-tech firms. In particular, the biotech industry was identified by the federal government as a high-tech industry of great strategic importance for the future competitiveness of the German economy and significant policy resources have been dedicated to creating an internationally leading German biotech industry.

A first set of initiatives focused on streamlining the process of transferring potentially valuable scientific 'founding ideas' from scientific institutions to entrepreneurial spin-off firms. One important step has been to reform Germany's intellectual property legislation governing university research and to model this legislation on American legislation, primarily on the Bayh-Dole Act of 1981. The Bayh-Dole Act attributes intellectual property over publicly funded research to the universities in which this research is conducted (rather than to the individual scientists alone), and thereby gives these institutions an incentive to invest in the commercialization of their research. Another important step to support the transfer of research from scientific institutions to entrepreneurial biotechnology start-ups has been the 'BioRegio' programme through which coalitions of local governments, business associations, and university administrators were provided generous funding to develop support services and start-up subsidy programmes for German scientist entrepreneurs.

A second set of initiatives focused on increasing the financing opportunities open to biotechnology entrepreneurs in Germany. In particular, German policymakers have attempted to help German biotech entrepreneurs overcome the lack of financing available for starting up a firm in Germany through a broad range of subsidy schemes. Various publicly funded agencies such as the Kreditanstalt für Wiederaufbau (KfW), the Technologiebeteiligungsgesellschaft (tbg), the regional BioRegio offices, and various state-owned investment agencies have made available significant funding since the mid-1990s to help German biotech entrepreneurs through the first growth phases of their firms. Moreover, in order to stimulate the development of financial products and services, such as venture capital, geared towards the financing needs of small risky high-tech start-ups during the early stages of their development, the 'Neuer Markt' was created in 1997. Modelled after the American NASDAQ exchange, the Neuer Markt was meant to provide an incentive for investors to provide financing for small high-tech firms by creating an easy exit option for these investors. With the creation of the Neuer Markt as a specialized separate equity market for risky high-tech firms, German investors would be able to sell their investments to the public, something which was not previously possible since young high-tech firms generally could not meet the stringent listing requirements of the main German Frankfurter Stock Exchange on which Germany's large established firms are traded. However, due to the disappointing performance of the companies listed on the Neuer Markt, the exchange was closed in 2003.

Although indeed taking away important sector-specific barriers to the formation of a German biotech industry (Adelberger 1999; Lehrer 2000), German biotech policies have not changed the defining features of the overall German socio-economic system such as its rigid labour markets and its bank-based financing system, which have been considered to impede the formation and development of entrepreneurial German high-tech firms. Nevertheless, German biotech policies have resulted in a rapid increase in firm formations in the industry. From being practically non-existent during the early 1990s, the number of biotech firms in Germany grew to 380 in 2002 (Ernst and Young, 2003). So it seems that Germany was able to create a second institutional system, which worked according to a different logic than the old one and thereby provided the functional equivalent of an Anglo-American business environment.

In order to understand better the opportunities and constraints within which German biotech entrepreneurs had to operate within their institutional environment, this chapter contrasts the development of biotech firms in the Munich region in Germany with biotech firms in the Cambridge region in the United Kingdom. The biotech industry, which is concentrated in the Cambridge region, constitutes Europe's largest biotech cluster. The first pioneering biotechnology firms in the Cambridge region, among which Cambridge Antibody Technology is the most notable firm, were formed during the late 1980s and like the biotechnology industry in Munich the biotechnology industry in Cambridge experienced an accelerated growth during the late 1990s. However, compared to the role of German public policymakers at the state and federal level in the Munich case, the role of UK policymakers in the development of a biotechnology industry in Cambridge during the 1990s was more limited. Instead, biotechnology firms in the Cambridge region were mostly able to rely on existing networks of investors within the UK's equity-based financing system.

The formation and rapid growth of a number of clusters of entrepreneurial biotech firms of which the Munich cluster has become the most successful seem to pose a serious challenge to the consensus in the political economy literature that Germany's capitalist model does not support the formation and development of competitive firms in new technologically disruptive high-tech industries.

One hypothesis, which has been proposed to account for the formation of a biotech industry in Germany that would be compatible with the ortho-doxy on the German economy, is that German biotech entrepreneurs have adopted sub-sector specializations in the biotech industry that avoid partic-ularly science-intensive areas where technological risks are high, such as the market for therapeutic products. Instead, German biotech firms are expected to specialize in more technologically stable sub-sectors such as those for platform biotechnologies and 'service and support' activities (Casper 2000). However, empirical data on the activities of German biotech firms dismiss this hypothesis.

An examination of the product strategies of Munich-based biotech firms founded after 1993 indicates that therapeutic biotech firms which have been identified in the neo-institutional literature as firms in the most technologi-cally disruptive sub-sector of the biotech industry, focused on the develop-ment of new therapeutic drugs, are very well represented; the Munich region houses 15 therapeutic biotech firms which is only slightly less than the 19 therapeutic biotech firms founded after 1993 which are located in Cambridge.

Moreover, although performance data are difficult to obtain on young firms in an industry in which product development trajectories span up to 10 years, there seems to be no clear indication that Munich-based therapeutic biotech firms founded after 1993 are less sustainable than their Cambridge-based counterparts as the existing neo-institutional literature on the German economy would suggest. Among the 10 Cambridge firms and 11 Munich firms which made available to the public financial performance data for the year 2003, revenues were almost the same, namely, €4.4 million for the average Cambridge firm and €4.5 million for the average Munich firm. In addition, in terms of the numbers of employees the average Munich firm, which employs 65 employees, even appears to be larger than the average Cambridge firm, which employs 46 employees.

This study aims to understand the paths German entrepreneurs have fol-lowed to support the development of their firms while surrounded by German national labour market and financial institutions, which are considered to impede the formation of such firms. Rather than attempting to reconcile the behaviour of German biotech entrepreneurs with the national institutional settings which define the 'German model' of capitalism, this chapter takes a broader look at the interplay between the development of Germany's biotech firms and their institutional environment and examines in-depth how biotech entrepreneurs, relying on their institutional environment have been able to develop the capabilities required to deal with each of the key organizational challenges that are related to building up a sustainable biotech firm.

The group of 19 Cambridge- and 15 Munich-based biotech firms studied was identified with the help of the comprehensive PharmaProjects database, which tracks the progress of therapeutic product development projects in the pharmaceutical industry and identified these firms as having at least one therapeutic product in a preclinical or clinical testing phase by the beginning of 2004. As has already been indicated, at first sight, the populations of Cambridge- and Munich-based therapeutic biotech firms in this study are well suited for a comparative study, since these firms are on average more or less of the same size and generate similar revenues. Moreover, the examined Cambridge- and Munich-based therapeutic biotech firms are on average of the same age; the average firm in both Cambridge and Munich was founded in 1998.

Three Organizational Challenges

Three key organizational challenges are identified with which Cambridge's and Munich's biotech entrepreneurs have had to deal in order to turn a good idea into a sustainable business. Moreover, it is outlined in what way this chapter analyses how Cambridge's and Munich's firms have dealt with these challenges.

Corporate Financing

A first key challenge for biotech entrepreneurs is to attract investments to finance the different growth stages of their firm. Usually biotech start-ups have few tangible assets or income that could be used as collateral for loans and therefore their ability to rely on banks for financing their growth is very limited. Instead, during the initial growth stages of their development, biotech start-ups rely on equity investments of venture capitalists who are experienced in assessing the high risks associated with early stage biotech ventures and monitoring the development of these firms. During later growth stages, after having proven the viability of their products and after having generated their first income, successful biotech firms generally rely on public equity markets to finance their further development.

We need to discover how Cambridge- and Munich-based therapeutic biotech firms have been able to rely on their institutional environment to attract the financing necessary for implementing their business plans. Using information obtained from Thomson Financial's SDC Platinum database, which provides information on which investors participated in the different investment rounds of all but 2 of the 39 examined Munich and Cambridge biotech firms, we shall analyse which financial institutions played a role in funding the growth of Munich and Cambridge based biotech firms. As a result, it is possible to determine the extent to which the absence of the type of liberal market institutions such as venture capitalists and easily accessible equity markets for high-tech firms in Germany has formed an obstacle to the growth of Munich-based firms.

Finding a Professional Management Team

A second key challenge for biotech entrepreneurs attempting to build up a therapeutic biotech firm is to attract a senior management team with the skills and expertise that are required to turn the firm's founding ideas into a set of marketable products. Developing therapeutic innovations often involves bringing together insights from the frontier of science in complex therapeutic product development projects and moving these projects through highly complicated clinical testing processes, in which these innovations are tested on their effectiveness and safety in treating targeted human diseases. Moreover, biotech firms need to embed themselves in a web of research, marketing, and licensing alliances with other biotech—and pharmaceutical—firms as a way of generating early revenues and accessing critical knowledge input required in the product development projects of the firm. Dealing with these challenges requires the presence of senior managers in a biotech firm with extensive pharmaceutical industry experience.

This chapter examines how Cambridge- and Munich-based therapeutic biotech firms have attracted most of their senior managers. Analysing the career histories of key managers, obtained from company websites, this chapter is able to determine on which recruitment networks Cambridge- and Munich-based firms relied to attract their senior managers. Both Germany and the United Kingdom house significant national pharmaceutical industries on which biotech firms can potentially rely for their recruitment efforts. However, studies on the career trajectories of professionals in German labour markets indicate that these career trajectories are largely organized inside firms, and that professionals who have achieved a certain level of seniority within an established German firm are rarely willing to move to another firm (Hall and Soskice 2001a; Mayer and Hillmert 2004; Sorge 1988). If German labour markets for professionals are as closed as they have been portrayed to be in comparative institutional studies, Munich's biotech firms likely have encountered significant problems in attracting managers with industry experience. In contrast, in the United Kingdom, professional labour markets are often seen as more open, suggesting that Cambridge-based biotech firms are in a more advantageous position than their Munich-based counterparts to recruit professionals with pharmaceutical product development expertise. By analysing from which institutions Munich-and Cambridge-based therapeutic biotech firms recruit their management, this chapter is able to determine to what extent the organization of German national labour markets for professionals put Munich's biotech firms in a comparatively disadvantageous position in their ability to attract skilled managers.

Inter-Company Relations

A final challenge for biotech entrepreneurs is to embed their firms in therapeutic research and development networks which will enable these firms to attract the right skills and knowledge input in their drug discovery and development programmes. Drug discovery and development programmes often require input from the frontier of science and demand a wide range of skills which biotech firms are not able to develop internally. As a result, a key challenge for biotech entrepreneurs is to embed their firms in a web of relationships (i.e. consultancies relationships, corporate alliances, academic collaborations, licensing agreements) to academic laboratories, pharmaceutical firms, and biotech firms to access these skills (Liebeskind et al. 1996; Powell 1998; Powell, Koput, and Smith-Doerr 1996; Zucker, Darby, and Brewer 1998).

Analysing the collaborators that are listed on the scientific publications published by scientists affiliated with the studied Cambridge- and Munich-based firms, this chapter considers the extent to which entrepreneurs have been able to rely on their institutional environment to access the skills and knowledge required in their drug discovery and development programmes. In particular, we are interested in learning how the earlier observed limited ability of German entrepreneurial firms to entice research scientists from established German pharmaceutical firms to join risky start-ups (Casper et al. 2004) has affected the ability of these entrepreneurs to access the drug development expertise networks in the pharmaceutical industry.

Building Up a Biotech Firm in Cambridge and Munich

This section discusses how Cambridge and Munich entrepreneurs, relying on their institutional environment, have dealt with the key challenges that have been associated with building up a therapeutic biotech firm.

Corporate Financing

Confirming expectations formulated in comparative studies on firm financing in Germany, Munich-based firms seem to have been positioned in a comparatively disadvantageous position in attracting equity financing. Both in Cambridge and in Munich, local banks, which have been considered to be the main source of financing for German small- and medium-sized firms, have not played a significant role in financing biotech enterprises. For the rest, an analysis of information on investors in Munich- and

Cambridge-based biotech firms shows stark differences in the types of investors on which Munich- and Cambridge-based firms have relied.

Whereas public funding has played practically no role in the formation and early development of Cambridge-based therapeutic biotech firms, Munich-based firms which have been set up without the support of multiple public funding agencies are an exception. The average Munich-based biotech firm has attracted investments or soft loans from 2.7 publicly funded investment agencies. The most active public investor in Munich-based biotech firms has been the federal Technologie Beteiligungs Gesellschaft (tbg). This has made investments in at least eight Munich-based biotech firms. Among the other public funding agencies, which have several investments in Munich-based firms are the BioRegio Munich, and Bayern Kapital, an investment firm, in which the state of Bavaria has a significant stake.

Not only for seed funding and early stage financing but also for later stage financing, Munich-based firms have not been able to rely on a German domestic venture capital industry as their Cambridge-based counterparts have been able to rely on British venture capitalists. While investments and soft loans provided through various (semi) public federal and state agencies have satisfied most early stage financing needs of Munich biotech firms, foreign venture capital firms have played an important role in satisfying the financing needs of Munich-based biotech firms during the later stages of their development; 63 per cent of the private investors in the average Munich biotech firm are foreign (predominantly British or American) as opposed to 36 per cent of investors in the average Cambridge-based firm. In fact, the most active private investor in the Munich region with investments in 6 privately held firms is the British venture capital firm '3i' with a stake in 6 of the 13 privately held therapeutic biotech firms in the Munich region.

Moreover, the proximity of well-developed and accessible equity markets for young high-tech firms in the City of London seems to have put Cambridge-based biotech entrepreneurs in an advantageous position in terms of accessing these equity markets as an important source of financing for expansion beyond the initial privately funded growth phases. Having reached similar growth stages, Munich-based firms are much less likely to have accessed public equity markets for financing than their Cambridge-based counterparts; of six Cambridge-based firms with revenues of over €1 million, five are publicly traded firms; only two out of seven Munich-based therapeutic biotech firms with revenues above €1 million are publicly traded.[1] In contrast to their Cambridge counterparts, successful Munich-based biotech firms seem to have largely relied on their predominantly international group of private investors to finance their expansion after their initial growth phases instead of attempting to acquire a listing on a stock exchange. Only three of the privately held Cambridge-based therapeutic firms have relied on private investors for their financing beyond a second round of financing and none beyond a third financing round; In contrast, 10 Munich-based biotech firms

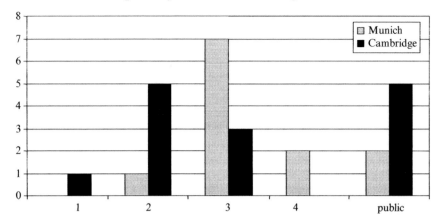

FIGURE 6.1. Latest financing round Munich and Cambridge firms
Source: Thompson Financial's SDC Platinum database.

have relied on private investors to finance either a third or a fourth investment round. Figure 6.1 shows the contrasting financial development of Cambridge-based and Munich-based therapeutic biotech firms.

Thus, despite efforts by policymakers to stimulate the formation of a German venture capital industry, problems for young high-tech firms, in attracting private equity financing in the context of the German socio-economic system, have persisted. Munich-based biotech firms, however, seem to have found a creative way to sidestep these financing constraints by relying to a large extent on foreign private institutions for their equity financing needs.

Finding a Professional Management Team

Confirming expectations formulated in comparative institutional studies on career trajectories of professionals in the German economy, Munich-based firms seem to have been comparatively disadvantageously positioned in their ability to recruit an experienced management team from German industry labour markets. In analysing the career histories of the CEOs of Cambridge- and Munich-based firms, the relative absence of managers heading Munich firms, who were recruited from the German pharmaceutical industry, is indeed striking. Munich's biotech firms seem to have experienced significant difficulties in finding managers at German pharmaceutical companies who were willing to leave the internal labour markets in these companies and join a risky biotech firm. Whereas all but one of the CEOs of Cambridge-based firms worked in the British pharmaceutical industry before accepting their current post, only 3 of the 14 CEOs of Munich firms worked in the German pharmaceutical industry prior to their current position.[2] Rather than relying on German labour markets to recruit their CEOs, Munich-based therapeutic biotech firms overwhelmingly went abroad to attract most of their senior managers.

Thus, the form of the German labour market with its closed nature for professionals, extending to the pharmaceutical industry, seems to have isolated Munich's therapeutic biotech firms from German markets for management expertise in the pharmaceutical industry. However, they have largely managed to deal with their inability to attract experienced managers from pharmaceutical firms by tapping into international labour markets.

Linking the Firm to Research and Development Networks

Citation data obtained on the institutional affiliations of the research collaborators of scientists of Cambridge- and Munich-based therapeutic biotech firms uncover the very distinctive knowledge networks in which the research organizations of both groups have embedded themselves (see Fig. 6.2 for a breakdown of the collaborative ties underlying the scientific production of Cambridge and Munich firms).

Reinforcing previous findings by Casper et al. (2004), who found that German biotech firms have been cut off from labour markets for pharmaceutical industry scientists and have instead relied on academic labour markets—in particular on ties of firms to the founding laboratories in academia from which these firms were spun-off—to recruit their scientific personnel, this study finds that Cambridge-based firms seem to have been more closely linked to industry knowledge networks than their Munich counterparts.

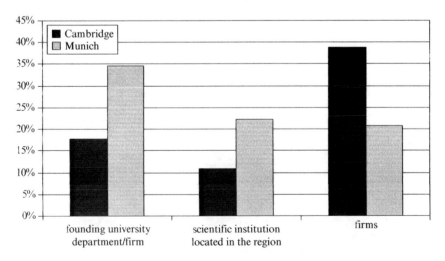

FIGURE 6.2. Institutional breakdown of collaborators listed on firm publications
Source: ISI Web of Science.

Collaborations with firms formed the basis for 39 per cent of the scientific publications of Cambridge firms, whereas only 21 per cent of the publications of Munich firms were the result of scientific collaborations with firms.

On the other hand, by the same token, Cambridge-based firms seem to have been largely cut off from academic knowledge networks as compared to their Munich-based counterparts. The findings of this study seem to confirm findings in the existing literature on the isolation of British universities from industry research networks and illustrate well the problems the British economy is still experiencing in reaping economic benefits from publicly funded basic research that is conducted inside universities. Especially, the limited extent to which Cambridge biotech firms have developed ties to world renowned scientific institutions which are located in the Cambridge region— such as the various academic departments of Cambridge University, the Sanger Centre, and the MRC Laboratory for Molecular Biology, all world leading in the field of molecular biology research—is striking. Of publications by scientists at Cambridge-based biotech firms, only 11 per cent was the result of scientific collaborations with academic laboratories located in the region other than founding laboratories. In contrast, in Munich 22 per cent of publications of biotech firms was the result of collaborations with laboratories of regional scientific institutions other than the founding laboratories.

Thus, confirming insights from the comparative institutional literature, the closed nature of labour markets in the German pharmaceutical industry seems to have isolated Munich's therapeutic biotech firms from important drug development expertise that is embedded in pharmaceutical industry networks. However, in their reliance on the academic community as its main recruitment ground, Munich's biotech firms have managed to develop relatively strong ties to various knowledge communities in academic fields of relevance to their drug discovery programmes.

This section has examined the extent to which the German institutional system has constrained the development of therapeutic biotech firms in the Munich region. It has been argued that although many of the constraints that have been identified in the comparative institutional literature on the German economy exist, entrepreneurs have found alternative 'institutional paths' that enable entrepreneurs to deal with these constraints. The next section addresses how the alternative 'institutional paths', Munich-based therapeutic biotech firms have followed, have affected the development of these firms.

The Divergent Development of Biotech Firms in Cambridge and Munich

As has been discussed above, the lack of open labour markets for scientists, with experience in established pharmaceutical firms in Germany, led Munich's biotech firms to recruit predominantly academic scientists to staff their laboratories. These academic scientists are coming from a very different background from scientists from pharmaceutical firms, and have brought their distinctive professional networks and research practices into Munich's firms, embedding the research organizations of Munich's therapeutic biotech firms in knowledge networks that are distinctive from the knowledge networks in which the research organizations of their Cambridge counterparts have been embedded. As a result, this section discusses how Munich's firms, being more closely embedded in academic knowledge networks, have developed stronger scientific capabilities, giving them an edge in dealing with more fundamental therapeutic drug discovery research problems; while Cambridge's firms, being more closely embedded in industry knowledge networks, have been proven better at dealing with more conventional organizational challenges in the field of drug development.

Data on the quantity and quality of the research output in terms of publications in academic journals indicate that the research organizations of Munich's biotech firms have been more 'in tune' with the latest advances in academia in different therapeutic research fields as opposed to those of their Cambridge-based counterparts, which to a much lesser extent rely on collaborative ties to academic research communities in their research activities. Scientists affiliated with Munich's 15 therapeutic firms published together a total of 211 articles in scientific journals, compared to 129 articles published by scientists affiliated with Cambridge's 19 therapeutic biotech firms.

Not only did Munich-based therapeutic biotech firms publish on average more than twice as many articles in scientific journals, but the quality of the scientific output of Munich-based therapeutic biotech firms was also significantly higher as measured by the average number of citations to these articles by other articles in academic journals. On average publications by Munich firms were cited 12.5 times and publications by Cambridge firms 7.6 times.

While Munich firms have tried to capitalize on their close ties to the academic community by building up superior research capabilities, which focus on developing new disruptive therapeutic innovations, Cambridge firms have tried to capitalize on their experienced teams of pharmaceutical industry managers and scientists by focusing on the rapid identification of potentially valuable therapeutic compounds and pushing these through clinical trials more cost-effectively than established pharmaceutical firms. This contrast between the product strategies of Cambridge and Munich therapeutic biotech firms becomes very clear if the corporate profiles published on company websites in which firms elaborate on their product strategies are systematically compared.

Whereas Munich-based firms tend to emphasize the ability of their research organizations to take a radical new approach to solve certain fundamental therapeutic research problems, Cambridge-based firms tend to emphasize the long track record of their management team in bringing therapeutic innovations to the market. For example, the main product strategy of 6 out of the examined 19 Cambridge firms is to find new medical uses for already known therapeutic compounds; none of the Munich-based firms follows such a strategy. Instead, all but one of Munich's biotech firms have a product strategy that focuses on the discovery of new therapeutic compounds using a newly developed scientific approach.[3] The following two excerpts from corporate profiles published on company websites highlight what Cambridge-based therapeutic firms consider to be their comparative advantage in the marketplace. In its corporate profile, Alizyme (2004), Cambridge's most successful biotech firm both in terms of its market capitalization of £200 million and in terms of its number of therapeutic products in clinical trials, states:

Alizyme has developed its business with a high emphasis on outsourcing, controlled by its core management team and specialist advisors. Rather than establish its own laboratories and development facilities, it has worked with collaborators and service providers such as contract research organisations. This has the benefit of allowing Alizyme to focus its investment onto its development programs in a cost effective way.

In its corporate profile Arachnova (2004), a more recently founded Cambridge-based therapeutic biotech firm, states:

With venture capital backing, Arachnova uses a virtual R&D pharmaceutical strategy to incubate novel projects for partnering. Named after the web-building activity of the spider, Arachnova is expert in outsourcing, making use of a huge international network of contractors and specialists to take its projects through to proof of principle in the clinic. A pioneer of therapeutic switching (finding new therapeutic uses for existing drugs) the company has two important projects in early-stage clinical trials.

The more short-term product focus on downstream product development projects of Cambridge-based therapeutic firms relative to their Munich counterparts also seems to be reinforced by the distinctive financial system in which Cambridge-based firms operate. Entrepreneurs and investors who have built up biotech firms in the Cambridge region are able to cash in on their firms' successes much earlier than their Munich-based counterparts through an initial public offering on London's public equity markets. This has given them an incentive to adopt product strategies that are more focused on tangible short-term payoffs.

Comparative data on the number of drug candidates in clinical trials confirm that the comparative strength and focus of Cambridge-based therapeutic biotech firms on the later stages of the therapeutic product development process has put Munich-based biotech firms in a significant disadvantage relative to their Cambridge-based counterparts in terms of the number of therapeutic compounds in the various clinical testing phases, which is an

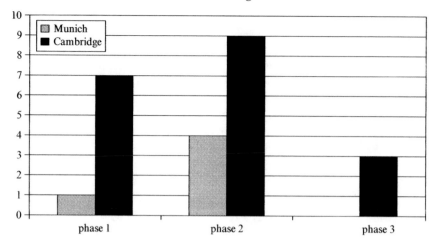

FIGURE 6.3. Product pipelines Cambridge-and Munich-based biotech firms
Source: PharmaProjects database, November 2003.

important indicator of how close firms are to actually being able to sell
therapeutic innovations on pharmaceutical markets (see Fig. 6.3).

By November 2003, the 19 Cambridge-based therapeutic biotech firms had
7 drug candidates in Phase 1 clinical trials, 9 drug candidates in Phase 2
clinical trials, and 3 candidates in Phase 3 clinical trials. In contrast, Munich
firms by November 2003 had only one drug candidate in Phase 1 clinical
trials, four drug candidates in Phase 2 clinical trials, and no candidates in
Phase 3 clinical trials.

Although it has been argued that the reliance of Munich biotech firms
on academic recruitment networks has likely provided these firms with a
comparative advantage in creating significant early-stage product opportunities based on disruptive technologies, the problem of Germany's closed pharmaceutical labour markets for scientists and managers with essential skills
and expertise to capitalize on these opportunities has remained an important
challenge for them. Their management teams seem to have recognized this.
While maintaining their headquarters and research facilities with close ties to
the academic community in the Munich region, firms have overwhelmingly
started to open up facilities abroad where more open labour markets allow
Munich-based firms to attract industry scientists and managers entrenched
in established pharmaceutical industry practices to deal with downstream
product development problems. More than half of Munich's biotech firms
had by October 2004 followed this approach to overcome their comparative
disadvantage in developing downstream product development capabilities
and have opened facilities abroad, predominantly in the major biotechnology clusters in the USA. In contrast, only two Cambridge-based firms have
opened facilities abroad.

Conclusions

The development of a vibrant cluster of biotechnology firms in the Munich region over the past decade illustrates how entrepreneurs are able to develop local support infrastructures required to support innovation in new industries. Whereas during the mid-1990s the competencies required to develop commercial product innovations in the field of biotechnology were practically absent. By the middle of the first decade of the twenty-first century, policymakers and local entrepreneurs had succeeded in building up a local infrastructure within which entrepreneurial therapeutic biotechnology firms have been able to thrive.

Although the findings of this chapter are based on the development of one relatively small industry in one particular country, some insights developed in this chapter seem to be valuable in the context of broader debates on how social actors construct local institutional support infrastructures in specific industrial sectors. In particular, the findings of this chapter suggest that socio-economic systems are often more dynamic than anticipated by academic scholars and highlight several mechanisms through which entrepreneurs are able to sidestep constraints of national socio-economic systems in building such support infrastructures.

Existing studies in the neo-institutional literature often make strong claims about which political and social institutions within national institutional frameworks matter in determining the behaviour of economic actors and how these institutions matter.

This chapter has attempted to contribute to the development of a more dynamic understanding of the interplay between institutions and economic actors. By analysing how German biotech entrepreneurs have been able to deal with key organizational challenges, this study has highlighted the importance of a more actor-centred view, which does not fail to account for 'Schumpeterian' entrepreneurs, trying to circumvent national institutions. The findings of this study outline two important mechanisms through which entrepreneurs are able to develop the competencies required to sustain innovation within local industrial agglomerations in the absence of existing institutions at the national level that are able to support the product strategies undertaken by entrepreneurs in a new industry.

First of all, this study has demonstrated that although comparative institutional frameworks are often correct in highlighting the absence of institutions within a national institutional system which in other national institutional systems play an important role in supporting a given innovative strategy, these frameworks often are wrong not to recognize that firms could rely on other institutions within their national system that play a similar role. As this chapter has argued, multiple institutions can perform a similar institutional support function. It has been demonstrated how in the absence of German flexible labour market institutions in the pharmaceutical industry,

Munich-based entrepreneurs have been able to rely on alternative institutions, namely, the German academic system (within the German institutional system) to recruit employees with valuable skills and expertise.

In addition, although national economic and political institutions are an important source of support for the development of firms, these institutions are not the only ones on which firms are able to rely for support. The findings of this study have once again indicated that in today's increasingly intertwined global economy entrepreneurs are able to rely on foreign institutions as well for support to develop competencies required to pursue certain innovative strategies if such support is absent inside a given national institutional system. This chapter has analysed how the absence of a German venture capital industry and equity markets for high-tech firms did not impede the ability of Munich-based biotech firms to attract financing for their growth from foreign institutions, mainly British and American venture capitalists and private equity firms. These venture capitalists and private equity firms proved more than eager to fill a 'gap' in the German socio-economic system and transfer their expertise to local subsidiaries these firms have been setting up in the Munich region.

Finally, this chapter has highlighted how the absence of German labour markets for senior pharmaceutical industry managers did not impede Munich-based biotech firms to rely on international labour markets to attract managers to develop the key managerial competencies that are required to successfully develop product innovations for therapeutic product markets.

Notes

1. Statement based on revenue data on the 2003 fiscal year which was available for 11 Munich firms and 10 Cambridge firms and was obtained from the Amadeus financial database.

2. Of all 19 analysed Cambridge therapeutic biotech firms, 12 had a CEO recruited from large pharmaceutical firms in Britain, 6 had a CEO recruited from biotechnology firms in Britain, and 1 had a CEO recruited from an America-based biotechnology firm. Of all 15 analysed Munich therapeutic biotech firms, 1 did not have a CEO, 7 had a CEO recruited from foreign pharmaceutical firms, 3 had a CEO recruited from a large pharmaceutical or a biotech firm in Germany, 2 had a CEO coming from academia, 1 had a CEO recruited from a chemical company in Germany, and 1 had a CEO recruited from the German office of an international management consultancy firm.

3. The one firm which does not have a main product focus on the discovery of new therapeutic compounds using new scientific insights is Nascacell, a firm which focuses on conducting contract research.

7

Creative Local Development in Cologne and London Film and TV Production

SABINE ELBING, ULRICH GLASSMANN, AND
COLIN CROUCH*

In both Germany and the UK, during the 1980s public broadcasting organizations reduced the proportion of programmes that they produced by themselves and started to buy products from private producers. In the former case this was a practical response to the growing quantity of programme content being made possible by new technology; in the UK it was a political command from central government. In both cases this led to a growth of small firms, some being very small, project-based firms, devoted to making films for television. In both again, this new industry is strongly concentrated geographically, in central Cologne and in the Soho district of London. This kind of new, informally structured sector is an example of the kind of activity for which German capitalism is usually considered to be ill equipped. On the other hand, while British capitalism seems likely to be more adept at the flexibility embodied in the sector, it too faced a certain challenge. The British public broadcaster, the British Broadcasting Corporation (BBC), organized an extensive and highly rated training programme for television skills. Given the relative weakness of vocational education in the British private sector, how would the new firms acquire the skilled labour force they would require? Both German and British forms of capitalism faced challenges in the changes to public broadcasting of the past quarter century.

The Two Local Economies

Cologne

Cologne has the highest concentration of employment in radio and television of any city in Germany, with 15.62 per cent of national employment

* Elbing worked on the British research, Glassmann on the German; Crouch integrated the studies. Further details of the British case will be found in Elbing (2006) and of the German case in Glassmann (2006).

(Schönert 2004:8). Employment in broadcasting has a higher importance for the local labour market than anywhere else. Moreover, the degree of sectoral specialization of radio, television, and film (Standard Industrial Classification (SIC) categories 92.2 and 92.1, respectively) shows the highest coefficients for sectoral specialization (Schönert 2004; the localization coefficient showed 9.30 for radio and television in Cologne and 5.74 for film production).

The Cologne media cluster evolved in the 1980s and 1990s. The only large media enterprise present in Cologne at the beginning of that period was the Westdeutscher Rundfunk (WDR), one of Germany's public broadcasting companies. Due to the federal structure of the political system each *Land* runs an equivalent institution to WDR, and each is able to broadcast nationwide, thus all of these public broadcasting stations are larger enterprises and play a significant role for the national media industry. WDR is the largest among these. It is in charge of the media content for North-Rhine Westphalia and contributes to ARD, the first national television programme, but its main facilities are almost entirely located in Cologne.

Even before the public broadcasting monopoly broke up in 1984, the *Land* government had plans to expand the role of the media industry in Cologne to compensate for declining employment in the city's previously dominant manufacturing industries. Due to the legislative autonomy of the *Länder* with respect to cultural policy, each *Land* was able to license frequencies to private broadcasting firms when the dual system was set up and private broadcasting firms entered the television market. Although this responsibility was initially provided in order to secure cultural standards and create a binding but decentralized regulatory framework for media content, it soon transformed itself into an economic policy means. The social democratic *Land* set out to bring private media firms to Cologne, succeeding in attracting RTL, which became one of Germany's biggest such firms, in 1984.

In 1986 the city council of Cologne, which shared the *Land's* policy, decided to build a whole new quarter in the north-western part of the city centre: The Mediapark. It was completed in 2004 and today hosts some 250 firms (mainly SMEs), with 5,000 employees, some of which are engaged directly in the production of media content, while others primarily service collective competition goods, especially in the field of vocational education and further training. In 1993 VOX and the music channel Viva also began operating in Cologne. Viva expanded with another channel in 1995 (Viva Zwei), relaunched in 2002 as Viva Plus. RTL set up Super RTL in 1995. In 1999 the channel Onyx moved to Cologne. After a while, some other regional TV-channels started to run their programmes, like WDRpunkt Köln in 2000 and TV.NRW in 2002. In 2004 the French AB Groupe launched its 24 hours documentary channel Terra Nova and n-tv, the German news broadcasting equivalent to CNN, moved to Cologne in the same year (Stadt Köln 2004). However, very recently Cologne also had to accept a movement of firms out of town.

In 2003 the Deutsche Welle, Germany's famous overseas news broadcasting station, moved into a new and modern building in Bonn, which fulfilled the requirements of the company much more than the asbestos contaminated building from the 1970s in Cologne. Certain firm sections of Viva have been relocated to Berlin and rumours about RTL leaving Cologne for better local conditions elsewhere produced an outcry among the public and local officials responsible for the media industry.

While RTL was persuaded to remain, this development has clearly demonstrated that local conditions are most important in order to make the private flagship enterprises stay. Second, it demonstrated that the Cologne media cluster is extremely dependent on these larger firms as customers of smaller producer companies. After decades of success and employment growth in the audiovisual media industry, Cologne is today experiencing signs of a crisis in the sector.

The presence of WDR in Cologne promoted the creation of a large pool of freelancing personnel engaged in media. While in early days WDR relied heavily on in-house production, it later started to outsource activities to smaller supplier firms in the area. The reason for this new strategy may be seen in two important forces for change. First, WDR expanded its media content and therefore needed additional support from other production companies. Second, the digitalization of radio and television production demanded a new technological environment, which WDR could not implement as quickly as small production firms. As it became extremely difficult to know which system for digital production of radio and television content might be superior in the developmental phase, an early decision on certain hardware and software products could have had disastrous financial consequences. Supplier firms in this new technological field were not yet established companies. Their failing on the market would have paralysed WDR's technological infrastructure as well. As digital technology needed time to mature, large media firms hesitated to incorporate this technology as whole systems into their own production facilities. The inflexibility of large firms soon became the comparative advantage of small firms which used this technology from early on and even specialized in certain technologies as well as in particular work stages within the value chain.

While digitalization is a recent process that influenced the media market, outsourcing began at an earlier stage and coincided with the arrival of private media firms. But even RTL did not immediately stimulate the agglomeration process of smaller enterprises, because in the beginning it either bought in cheap media content, like older American TV-series, or it accessed firms in other media clusters in Germany, especially Munich. But Cologne politicians successfully lobbied RTL and WDR to commission more local production (Baumann and Voelzkow 2004: 270 f.). Public and semi-public institutions then initiated further collective competition goods to support the industry.

Soho, London

No more than in Germany has the reform of the TV production industry in the UK implied an all-encompassing privatization of public structures. The growth dynamic of the numerous small companies in the film and TV production industry is rather the result of a re-regulation of the industry that provided potential space for them.

There are two key dates of governmental regulation: 1980 and 1990. The 1980 Broadcasting Act (UK Government 1980) gave permission to add a fourth television channel to the existing three channels, BBC1, BBC2, and ITV: Channel 4. Channel 4 set out to provide an alternative to the three existing channels. Without any in-house production, Channel 4 was committed to using independent production companies causing more decentralized production structures. The growth of the independent production sector since the launch of Channel 4 is reflected in the growth of independent production hours: in 1982 there were no such hours at all; in 1983 there were 268; and in 1990 there were 2,585 (Pratt 1999). Like the BBC, Channel 4 has a public service remit and is operated by a non-profit corporation. Unlike the BBC, it is not funded by a licence fee but by advertising and is therefore a hybrid of public and commercial broadcasting. This hybrid broadcaster not only provided for decentralized production structures in the film and TV production industry, but it also provided for a concentration of independent production businesses in Soho and the immediately adjacent areas, as a result of its own initial location in Fitzrovia, on the fringes of Soho. At that time property in Soho and the immediately adjacent areas was cheaper than the London average, Soho being then well known as London's red-light district. There were no specially developed media-industry sites; the gentrification of Soho and the creation of a cultural quarter have been neither encouraged nor discouraged in any significant way by tax breaks or by subsidized infrastructure. It has developed without direct state intervention, but the effects of changing state regulation have shaped its structure dramatically during the past 25 years.

Not only in terms of production structures but also the content shown on and produced for Channel 4 was different from that of the other broadcasters. More innovative formats were shown, and since its launch, it has been known as successful creator of innovative show formats. The channel's attitude and broadcasting content are regarded as non-conformist, provocative, and thought provoking, culturally diverse and distinctive. Remarkably, it is legally required to be innovative and to provide content for different interests. This, and a 'safety-net approach' for Channel 4, are the reasons for a very particular approach of governing the channel and the independent production industry. Commercials were to be sold on it, but competition for advertising with Independent Television (ITV)[1] was avoided. The budget was fixed by the Independent Broadcasting Authority (IBA) on the basis of funds levied from ITV companies. This safety net was created since it was considered that

Channel 4 would not otherwise be able to fulfil its obligation to be innovative and creative. This was no free-market approach, the channel's innovative potential and task were seperated from advertising industry's pressures.[2]

In 1990 a new Broadcasting Act (UK Government 1990) proposed another independent channel, Channel 5, a new structure for the allocation of franchises for ITV regional companies, and, most important, required the terrestrial channels (which had an audience share of 77.4% in 2003) to buy 25 per cent of their programming from independent producers.[3] Since the implementation of the Act, the BBC, ITV, Channel 4, S4C, and later Channel 5, are required to allocate in each year at least 25 per cent of 'qualifying programmes' measured in hours, to the broadcasting of a range and diversity of independent productions. ('Qualifying programmes' comprise basically everything except acquired programmes, repeats, news, and items shorter than two minutes.) The aim of the statutory independent quota is not only to tackle vertical integration but also to multiply sources of supply—particularly of SMEs—and to stimulate creativity as well as foster new talent. The independent production quota originated from the report of the Peacock Committee in 1986. This had recognized that the way to innovation and creativity was through a greater range and diversity of production supply; also: 'We are concerned about the level of costs and efficiency in broadcasting generally ... [T]here is suggestive evidence that BBC costs are higher at least in some cases than those of small independent producers' (UK Government 1986).

After the implementation of this Act the number of independent production hours doubled within six years, and there was a further growth of new firms, again particularly concentrated in Central London. A considerable number of former employees of the main broadcasters set up their own companies, predominantly in the Soho area. Most of them used to work and live in Central London and had the contacts there necessary for the establishment of new companies and for the organization of production projects. As a reaction to these regulations and the following structural changes within the industry, the BBC reorganized its production and created the possibility of 'producer choice' in 1993. Here, the producers have control over their own budgets to purchase resources and labour either from other departments of the BBC or outside the BBC. Another result of the new regulations was that BBC training budgets were cut.

Radical though these changes were, and personally hostile though the prime minister of the day, Margaret Thatcher, was to the BBC, the primacy of public broadcasting remained, and the UK has not followed the US route of a commercially dominated system.

Today the media production industry in London is the second largest in the world after New York (Krätke 2002: 209) and by far the densest and most significant concentration of the industry in the UK. There are several media clusters in the city; in this chapter we concentrate on the film and TV production cluster in Central London, concentrated at Soho and the adjacent areas.

The number of enterprises involved in 'Motion Picture and Video Activities' and in 'Motion Picture and Video Production' (MPVP) has considerably risen in recent years: The UK SIC, covering all businesses registered for VAT and PAYE, registered 1,927 enterprises concerned with 'Motion Picture and Video Activities' (SIC 92.1) in 1995 and 6,146 in 2001, the bulk of which belonging to MPVP (SIC 92.11) with 1,392 registered enterprises in 1995 and 5,391 in 2001. In the category of 'Radio and Television Activities' (SIC 92.2) 919 enterprises were registered for 1995 and 3,885 for 2001. More than 95 per cent of enterprises in each category are SMEs, with the highest concentration in the 'micro-size' section consisting of one to nine employees: 85 per cent of 'Motion Picture and Video Activities' related enterprises and about 80 per cent categorized in 'Radio and Television Activities' are micro-sized businesses. Although the particular organization of production does not allow us directly to relate annual turnover to size of businesses, very small firms also seem to be dominant in terms of turnover with half of VAT-registered businesses having had an annual turnover of less than £100,000 and only 3 per cent with more than £5 million in 2000 (DTI 2000).

The production of exact data is a problem for many reasons. First, there are no statistics identifying numbers of individual firms and only different physical units are identified. Second, the sectoral production specificities, working within 'project ecologies' (Grabher 2002a,b) as common practice in parts of the industry, do not facilitate the study of small media production companies. And third, differentiation between the segments of TV and film production as well as related segments is very difficult since companies are working within different segments at the same time or might change between them, thus leading to overlaps in figures (Marrs and Boes 2002).

Growth in the number of MPVP businesses (UK SIC 92.11) has been particularly concentrated in the smallest turnover size band as opposed to the UK all-industries trend: the proportion of MPVP companies in the £1,000 to £99,000 turnover range increased from 40.7 per cent in 1996 to 55.7 per cent in 2003. The same size band for the UK all industries shows a reduction from 52.8 per cent in 1996 to 45.5 per cent in 2003. Significant reduction in MPVP (92.11) is found in the £100,000 to £999,000 turnover size band: 45.3 per cent of businesses were registered for 1996 and 31.5 per cent for 2003. The following size band with a turnover of £1 mn to £5 mn also shows a reduction, from 11.5 to 8.7 per cent. Growth is again to be found in the category of £5 mn+ turnover: Here, 2.6 per cent of businesses were registered for 1996 and 4.0 per cent for 2003 (UK Film Council 2003).

More recent figures produced by the UK Film Council show that the majority of companies produces only one film a year, and might 'lie dormant' for the rest of the year depending on the length of production. Furthermore these figures might also indicate that a company produces one film only and is dissolved thereafter. Nonetheless, two trends might be deducted from these figures: an increase in very small companies and an increase in very large independent production companies as found in TV production, both at the expense of a decline in middle-size firms.[4]

The audio-visual sector is prospering: according to the Sector Skills Council for the Audio Visual Industries (Skillset), the audio and visual industries comprising broadcast, film, video, interactive media, and photo imaging generate £23 bn for the UK economy annually, around 2.5 per cent of GDP. Their growth in 2000 was higher than in UK-service-industries as a whole: the Gross Value Added (GVA) per job in 2000 was £195,000 in film and video distribution, £67,000 in television and radio and £55,000 in film and video production compared with an average of £27,000 for UK service industries as a whole. Skillset states that all these sectors are predominantly London-based.[5]

Furthermore, all sectors are represented in Central London, but the concentration of television companies (terrestrial, cable, and satellite) is particularly high and the three sectors of independent production, commercials, and post-production are almost entirely based in Central London[6] and concentrated in Soho, with the concentration of post-production leading to Soho's description as the 'post-production cluster'. Eighty per cent of UK film industry employment and 50 per cent of jobs in radio and television are concentrated in London (London–New York Study 2000).[7] About 70 per cent of companies engaged in activities associated with film and TV production are in and around Soho (Cheshire and Gornostaeva 2003: 153; Nachum and Keeble 2000).[8] Film production, post-production, editing, film distribution and sales agents, photography, music, design, and advertising—the entire chain of production is available in this area, which is commonly defined by Oxford Street to the north, Regent Street to the west, Charing Cross Road to the east, and Leicester Square and the streets immediately adjacent to it to the south, a one square mile area within the W1 postal code area[9] of Central London. Not only are approximately 70 per cent of UK enterprises engaged in activities associated with film and TV production located in this area, but specialist services are rarely purchased outside Soho (Nachum and Keeble 2000). Approximately 75 per cent of the major service providers to film and TV production enterprises, including post-production services and photographers, are based there (Nachum and Keeble 2000).

Figures on workforce concentration in London and Central London vary. These differences are connected to sectoral particularities as stated before, including overlaps in figures of the fragmented industry and variety of sectors: According to the London–New York Study of 2000, 235,000 people worked within the media production industries in London in 1997. Among them, 40,000 worked in advertising, 52,000 in publishing, 46,000 in telecommunications, 28,000 in radio and television, and 25,000 in film. While, with the latest figures, the Office of National Statistics estimated an employment of around 33,000 people working in 'Motion Picture and Video Production' for the UK (Skillset 2002*b*) of which about 70 per cent are located in London. And the London Development Agency produced a figure of 100,000 'employed' in the 'film and media sector' in London in 2004 (see http://www.lda.gov.uk/workofthelda/industry/creative/). About 70 per cent of the workforce engaged in film and TV production in the UK are employed by enterprises located in Soho (Nachum and Keeble 2000) and reside in Greater London (Skillset 1994).

Financing the Sector

Cologne

In Cologne we conducted a survey via e-mail questionnaire with 21 film and television production firms. An interesting outcome in itself was the fact that of 154 firms that had been contacted on the basis of the latest edition of the Media Firm Guide Cologne (Stadt Köln 2002), 44.8 per cent no longer existed. It is a sectoral specialty of the media industry that companies act on the financial basis of short-term projects, making it difficult for them to survive when a project is terminated (Grabher 2002). The questionnaire dealt with all matters of collective goods provision from financing to vocational training.

In 1991 the *Land* government founded the Filmstiftung NRW, a regional foundation in charge of financing television and film production. This foundation very soon became the most powerful 'support agency' for the media industry in Germany and certainly embodies the most impressive act by the *Land* government to induce structural change in the region. Today, the annual budget of the Filmstiftung for its promotional activities amounts to €36 mn. Initially the foundation was co-funded by WDR, while Second German Television (ZDF) as well as RTL later joined as responsible bodies, giving a perfect example of how flagship enterprises and political actors cooperated in order to produce collective competition goods for the regional media industry. During this phase, when public and semi-public institutions started to produce collective competition goods, the media firms in Cologne entered their boom years. However, this effect was to a large extent due to public funding. Employment in the audiovisual media industry in Germany is heavily subsidized. Kurp (2004) estimates that every worker in the German film industry is subsidized with €5,000 annually by public institutions, if all national and European institutions are taken into account. The federal government additionally promotes the film industry with the 'Filmförderungsanstalt' (FFA— Institute for the Promotion of Films) that was founded in 1968. Its budget in the year 2003 amounted to €76.5 million. The 'Bundesbeauftragter für Kultur' (federal responsible for culture) again disposed of €23.1 mn in 2003.

The *Hausbankprinzip* is still an important instrument of enterprise financing in many German industries, and some major German banks do promote local media enterprises, for instance the Deutsche Bank, which offers special consultancy for media enterprises by their branch offices in Cologne as well as the Dresdner Bank, which also offers support to media firms by specialized experts in their Cologne offices. However, the Cologne Savings Bank (Stadtsparkasse Köln, SK) turns out to be the most important actor. This is a public institution, controlled by the city of Cologne. Fifty per cent of all surveyed firms (*n* = 20) cooperated in some ways with the local savings bank in order to finance their entrepreneurial projects. One may argue that this local bank simply copied the *Hausbankenprinzip*, especially as SK holds shares of some larger media firms, like the Magic Media Company, which recently built one of the largest studio production sites in Europe (Coloneum) in Cologne, but in this case banks should have attained some influence over enterprise decisions. However, the great majority of firms we interviewed said that this was not the case.

From the very beginning SK, the largest communal savings bank in Germany, played a major role in the local media industry. In 1991, the same year in which the Filmstiftung NRW was founded, it opened its Entertainment Finance Department, creating one of the largest banking teams directly occupied with the financing of media firms (Media Guide NRW 2005). It has developed concepts for project finance, not only acting as a credit institution but sometimes being directly involved as a financing body for feature films. Its entertainment finance experts provide advice beyond mere financial issues. It forms part of an international network for the promotion of media enterprises and is thus capable to mediate contacts to other producer firms, lawyers, etc. SK clearly acts as a local policymaker, capable of doing so since it maintains its status as a public institution. On the one hand, its activities resemble those of a local development agency, because SK promotes many public events, which create a marketing effect for the local production system. On the other hand it imitates strategies of venture capital firms by fostering communication between companies and service providers and by supporting the production of collective competition goods through co-financing. For instance, it holds shares in the Multimedia Support Centre, which was founded in the late 1990s in order to promote start-ups in the media industry by providing venture capital, counselling firms on possible strategic alliances and cooperation with public institutions, such as universities and so forth.

Why has SK distinguished its activities from the *Hausbankenprinzip* and acted more like a venture capitalist development agency? House banks consider long-term profits, and these are difficult to realize in the media industry since the market is shaped by individual projects in a fast-moving market. The constraining property rights-regime in Germany creates an even higher risk for producer firms and investors because, according to the regulations in this policy area, the producer company cannot claim author rights after selling the accomplished work to broadcasters (Baumann and Voelzkow 2004). Consequently, producers and investors cannot share the profit if a movie sells well. In turn, broadcasting companies very often leave all the investment risk to producer companies, which are compelled to pursue an all-or-none strategy. In this situation start-ups of small producer firms only succeed with some kind of institutional backing beyond a more or less generous money lending policy. For this, banks must be able to calculate risks through pooled project financing and venture capital instruments. However, this has been a rather underdeveloped mode of entrepreneurial support in German capitalism. It was therefore important for the local industry that SK fill this gap. It could only successfully promote the local media industry if it accepted its role as a local development agency, also pursuing collective aims of the local production system.

London

Similar problems faced the London firms, equally involved in a project ecology. They have to raise money on a film-by-film basis, and are in a weak position when negotiating the acquisition of rights. Two mechanisms are here important which are rather unusual and surprising for a British industry. First, and particularly surprising given the Cologne experience, some elements of a *Hausbankprinzip* are to be found in London: some local banks have developed specialized departments to serve the needs of the industry. These banks are parts of the local 'project ecology'. Second have been public subsidies based on money from the National Lottery and tax incentives (via 'sale and leaseback'), the latter providing for an incentive system for investments in film production, have been established by the government.

There is no one manner of financing in the film and TV production sector in London. Venture capitalists do not like investing in production projects; they prefer to invest in businesses.[11] Production costs can be enormous and the success of a film is not, or only rarely, predictable. The way of raising capital differs depending on the kind of business, its specialization, and its age: an established TV production company, probably founded and led by a former employee of one of the major broadcasters and therefore having important business contacts, might have no funding problems; whereas an inexperienced and not established production company lacks contacts and negotiating practice. Large distributors can be of help in terms of funding, but small production companies are in a rather weak position when negotiating distribution and IP rights with the distributor.

The question of venture capital versus loans in London-based film and TV production was answered by a representative of one of the leading London-based banks, who stated that: 'Loans are preferred. They are cheaper. In general, 3–7 years running loans are granted.'[12] To apply for venture capital financing, enterprises have to have a turnover of £5–10 million. For these reasons, only 2 per cent of film production companies and less than 5 per cent of TV production companies are generally regarded as being in the position to qualify for venture capital financing. Banks do not only have an impact in financing of post-production projects with bank loans rating at 20 per cent, but they also play an important role in other segments of film and TV production: Leading banks located in Central London have established specialized departments focusing on services for the media production sector. These comprise funding for TV production, film production, and post-production, as well as intellectual property finance. Funding for film production is offered via borrowing up to the full budget of a film production, comprising all costs and legal fees, but only if pre-sales contracts, equity, lottery funds, or grants can be provided as coverage.

Barclays Media Banking Centre (with headquarters in Soho Square, in the very centre of Soho) claims that 25 per cent of all UK film productions since 1996 have used its banking services. This centre works in three segments: a small business team for companies with an annual turnover of up to £1 mn with about 700 clients; a medium business team for companies with a turnover of £1–10 mn with 500–600 clients; and a large business team for those with a turnover of £10–15+ mn with about 200 clients. Their average customer in TV production has an annual turnover of £3–5 mn. Approximately 80 per cent of their clients are London-based.

The same percentage of London-based clients has been stated by Coutts Media Banking Centre. They focus on the independent production sector and have no 'major clients' like Barclays Media Banking Centre. Media Banking at Coutts is concentrated at their premises at The Strand, Central London. They work in three sections with the following numbers of nation-wide clients: 'TV, Film and Entertainment'; 'Music'; both sections with about 250 clients each; 'General Media', which includes advertising, with about 800 companies. The existence of 'Special Purpose Vehicles' (SPVs), as possibly being included in these figures, has been emphasized. SPVs are companies that do not 'work seriously', or lie dormant for a while, or are helpful as tax shelter entities.

Specialization in banking services is particularly important for various reasons: First, film and TV production demands specialists with an under-standing of the industry's needs, who might have worked in media production before establishing their career within a media banking department, as well as with the capability to speak 'the right language'. Second, funding structures are various, IP rights and intellectual property finance are crucial and difficult subjects to deal with; finally, sale and leaseback deals as part of the film production tax incentive system, which will be referred to in the following, can only be handled by specialists.

Place-based networks play an important role in the TV and film production sector. These centrally located media banking centres, which are part of the local network, have more control over 'their' production companies through concentration and proximity, and share in up-to-date knowledge about the reputation and performance of the companies as well as the ability of staff and owners.

Apart from banks, broadcasters, and distributors, an important means of financing film-making in the UK is funds from the National Lottery via the UK Film Council. The government's Department of Culture, Media and Sports (DCMS) sponsors the film industry as well as broadcasting, while the Department of Trade and Industry (DTI) is responsible for New Media and E-Cinema. The Film Council is the richest public funding body with about €40 mn from the lottery and an equal annual grant from DCMS.

When sources of funding for first time film-makers have dried up, projects tend to build around joint financing from the Film Council, broadcasters, and regional funds, often providing the only way for newcomers to fund their projects. Regional funding is available only since very recently via The London Capital Fund and Film London. The London Capital Fund was launched in 2002 with a budget of £50 mn. It aims at helping SMEs to make first investments of up to £250,000 with the potential to make follow-on investments of the same amount. Further regional funding has been available since 2004 through Film London. This strategic agency for film and media in the capital was set up under the auspices of the UK Film Council, Skillset and the Mayor's Office. It is co-funded by the Film Council (about 60%) and the London Development Agency (about 40%).

National government also affects governance structures in the film and TV production sector through funding schemes particularly designed for SMEs, and through tax incentives. In 1994 the government launched the Enterprise Investment Scheme (EIS) designed for small production companies (Alberstat 2004). It allows for an income tax relief accounting for 20 per cent of the amount subscribed for shares up to £150,000 a year in an unquoted company. It has been particularly designed for smaller companies. It is difficult to appraise its success. UK independent financial advisers have judged it as having been not very successful (see, for example: http://www.moneyextra.com/glossary/g100154.htm), but the findings of our questionnaire and interviews with production companies in London suggest that the EIS is often used by small production companies (UK Film Council: http://www.britfilmusa.com/dincentives/othertax.php).

The question of success can be answered without any doubt when investigating the influence of sale and leaseback tax incentive schemes. Initially used to finance both film production and TV production, it was later restricted to 'theatrical release' only. These schemes provide tax incentives benefiting the makers of British films and stimulate larger amounts of outside investment in them. They have existed since the 1970s. Under their most recent form (Section 48 Finance Act 1997) they amount to 100 per cent of the production costs for films costing up to £15 mn during the year of expenditure.[13] Although no incentives have been designed for TV production, the definition of a 'British film' for the purposes of tax relief has been rather liberally interpreted to include TV programmes.

Albeit some uncertainties resulting from 'misuse' of sale and leaseback-based tax advantages, with the sale- and leaseback incentive system, the British government here designed a funding possibility not only used by larger companies but also by SMEs, thereby tackling the traditional difficulties of small firms in the UK in attracting external investment. DCMS (2003) considers that the tax relief system has worked well. The British film industry has experienced a boom in recent years, to an important part due to the unparalleled tax breaks offered for film production.

The British innovation regime normally demands and favours venture capital financing, and UK firms are considered to prefer seeking investment capital in the private capital market. However, in the film and TV production sector in London, various and varying means of funding have been created and been established for and by SMEs: pre-sale contracts, bank loans, funding by distributors, funding via sale, and leaseback deals (with the Treasury being one of the biggest investors in film production), grants based on lottery money, local development grants (since recently), and venture capital. Schemes for the use of the latter have been provided for by the government, which has created venture capital investment schemes on a smaller scale.

Vocational Education and Training

Cologne

The German vocational training system assumes clearly defined skills. In the media industry, especially when digital technology opened up a new product market, new training institutions were demanded, though skills could not be standardized quickly. As a result, a multitude of training courses and on-the-job training opportunities emerged, offered by public and private institutions. These activities were quite useful in specialized niches, but they condemned workers to stick to individual technologies and work-stages, irrespective of market opportunities and technological development. This experimental phase of vocational training clearly lacked a broader knowledge base on the side of the workforce, a more active involvement on the entrepreneurial side and transparency on both sides. It was neither possible for workers to know whether their courses taught up-to-date disciplines and subjects nor for entrepreneurs to estimate whether their workforce was adequately trained.

In order to create more transparency, an initiative emerged from local firms, which was taken up by a regional association, the Association for Television, Film and Video Production Industry in North-Rhine Westphalia (VFFV). It demanded a new agency for the coordination of vocational training in the sector. Again the *Land* acted in a traditional manner. In 1995 the

KoordinationsCentrum Ausbildung in Medienberufen (AIM) was founded to supervise the vocational training market in Cologne and the larger region. It receives funding from the *Land* government, the EU and its own fund raising activities. Its board is constituted by the usual suspects of corporatist support agencies: the union, the city of Cologne, the chamber of industry and commerce, various associations, the Filmstiftung NRW, the local Agentur für Arbeit and the flagship enterprises, WDR and RTL Television.

The agency defines five different categories, for which it provides coordination activities: the development of human resources in media enterprises; counsel for freelancers to develop career strategies; pooling information on vocational training schemes and on opportunities to find access to relevant vocational training courses; contacts for institutions of higher education; and definition of job specifications and examination of deficiencies in the vocational training market of the industry. It also offers job databases and an information archive on all training schemes in the media industry and opportunities for training and posts offers for apprenticeships (AIM 2005).

AIM had been contacted by only two of our surveyed firms, but its competition goods are more tailored to serve individuals in their need to develop skills. In order to assess the work of such institutions, firms were asked whether they think that conditions for vocational training have improved, stayed the same, or worsened due to the activities of the city and the *Land* in the recent years. Of 19 firms that responded to this question, 9 said the conditions have improved, though 8 said it had stayed the same and 2 firms even claimed that conditions had become worse.

To assess the numerous activities on the supply side of the vocational training market, one needs to know how the demand side reacts towards them. It is important to understand how qualified employees are on average, how employees are recruited and furthermore, whether or not firms train employees in-house. If vocational training is supposed to work according to the orthodox rules of the dual system, a high proportion of certified employees should be able to offer their skills successfully to an external labour market, where recruitment takes place through specialized placement organizations, etc. Only 13 per cent of employees of SMEs in the Cologne media industry have not obtained any kind formal qualification, while almost one-third has accomplished an apprenticeship, 28 per cent have a university degree and 13 per cent have visited a technical college, but the proportion with no formal qualification at all increases to 31 per cent of employees among the smallest firms. Informal institutions appear to be much more important than usual in German capitalism: only 8 of our 19 firms seek new employees through conventional and anonymous institutions like employment offices, the newspaper, or the Internet. Instead, 11 of the 19 ask friends, other employees, or colleagues about someone who can be recommended for the job.

The reason why formal placement strategies do not work in the sector is that creativity, a quality sought from many employees, cannot be certified.

Nevertheless, Cologne and the *Land* government have created numerous formal institutions: university institutes such as the Institut für Rundfunkökonomie (Institute on the Economics of Broadcasting) and the Academy of Media Arts, both founded in 1990. The *Land* government financed the Internationale Filmschule, organizing professional courses for script writing, and local schools for journalism were set up. Most importantly, local institutions in Cologne supported the introduction of new apprenticeship schemes, tying vocational training again to orthodox German institutions. The local IHK could not offer a complete training scheme that would fit firms' needs. When approached by the VFFV to address this problem, it turned initially to outdated schemes such as the laboratory assistant for film and video processing, adding new formation modules to create provisional training opportunities (Baumann and Voelzkow 2004). This initiative generated what came to be known as the 'Kölner Modell' of apprenticeship training. It has been modified for various requirements and then adopted by the national institute for the regulation of training schemes (BIBB). As a result the dual system now provides regular vocational training for media. While our survey suggested that SMEs rate the new system highly, 16 of the 19 confessed that they did not train according to these profiles, while only 4 trained apprentices. Informal mechanisms still dominate.

London

In London also, new forms of training provisions have been needed in the TV and film production sector, for three reasons. First, a consequence of deregulation was the discontinuation of training formerly provided for by the BBC's in-house training programmes. Second, deregulation and the subsequent fragmentation of the production sector has led to an increasing freelance workforce, which is in need of training provision on flexible terms and affordable costs. Third, standardized training has been problematic in the sector. As stated by the UK Film Council, it has been ad hoc and relatively disorganized since the end of the traditional studio system, when film became essentially a freelance production activity.

To tackle these problems, the Sector Skills Council for the Audio Visual Industries (Skillset), covering Broadcast, Film, Video, Interactive Media and Photo Imaging, was founded in 1994, with the status of a National Training Organization. This gives it the legal status of a charity and public funding as well as backing by key employers. Its board of directors is made up of people working in the industry, occupying a lead position and representing all concerned interests: SMEs, trade associations, unions, large and small employers, the nations of the UK. Skillset does not provide training but encourages and raises investment to subsidize it for individuals and organizations. It also certifies the skills and expertise of people working in the industry, undertakes research, and provides career advice. Skillset has a significant influence in shaping new vocational qualifications, which will be referred to below.

Working in partnership with the Qualifications and Curriculum Authority (QCA), Skillset develops a Sector Qualifications Strategy (SQS). An Audio Visual Qualifications Forum was founded in 2004, chaired by the Head of Partnership Management, BBC Training and Development, and attended by representatives from the awarding bodies which offer qualifications in the sector. It is one of the first four 'pathfinder' Sector Skills Councils which are to pilot the new Sector Skills Agreement, endorsed by the Government's Skills White Paper of March 2005. The development and implementation of sector-specific qualification strategies across all sectors is driven by the Qualifications and Curriculum Authority (QCA) supported by Learning and Skills Councils (LSCs)[14] and the Department for Education and Skills (DfES).

With Skillset, in cooperation with the UK Film Council, training needs in the TV and film production industry are for the first time strategically addressed. National Vocational Qualifications (NVQ) are not regarded as having been particularly successful in this industry because of their inflexibility—reasons similar to those affecting formal training in the Cologne case.[15] Further, training according to NVQ standards is said to focus too much on 'hard skills' while neglecting 'soft skills'.[16] In March 2005 the industry's NCQs were formally abolished. About 700 employers nation-wide have been invited to take part in the development of new training standards. These are likely to be based on accredited Skillset Courses.

Alternative training provisions have been provided for the industry before. When the percentage of freelance workforce increased and problems in the provision of both initial and further training emerged, several alternative training provisions came into life through corporatist structures, dating back to 1985. The industry's associations, PACT and the NPA, provided training, predominantly at central locations in London, through the Film and Television Freelance Training (FT2) scheme. This was reinforced through collective agreements.

An important role in funding of training within and for the sector has a cooperative funding system consisting of two larger funding sources: The Freelance Training Fund (FTF) is the largest 'cross-industry fund' consisting of a combination of contributions from the major television employers, independent producers and public money. It is sourced 50:50 from the industry and the state. The fund has been created to give freelancers the opportunity for affordable training and to provide for structured new entrant training. Part of the Freelance Training Fund scheme is the Independent Production Training Fund (IPTF). IPTF was created as a Charity in 1993 by PACT. It is controlled by a board of independent TV producers. The IPTF levy is a voluntary levy on independent television productions. The levy is calculated as 0.25 per cent of the total production price up to a maximum of £8,750. The BBC, regional ITV companies, C4 and Five have agreed to deduct the IPTF levy from programmes that they commission and to forward it to the IPTF. For the period between January 2001 and March 2002, contributions to the FTF were as follows: BBC £136,485; Channel 4 £487,500; ITV £547,250; Independent production companies through the IPTF £454,500 (Skillset 2002).

The FTF funds the Independent Companies Researchers Training Scheme, the Film and TV Freelance Training Scheme and subsidizes freelance places on industry training courses in London and nation-wide. The Freelance Training Fund also contributes to the National Film and Television School (NFTS). Thus freelancers pay a subsidized training fee when taking part in short courses at the NFTS. Finally, the fund contributes to business skills and company development by funding PACT's short course programmes, company development schemes, and a pilot project of IPTF contributors' in-company training.

The second funding scheme is the Skills Investment Fund (SIF), launched in October 1999. It is managed by Skillset on behalf of the industry supported by the Department for Culture, Media, and Sport (DCMS), PACT, and the Motion Picture Association (MPA). The SIF is based on contributions from UK-based productions due for theatrical release. The fund is voluntary, with UK productions asked to contribute 0.5 per cent of their total production budget up to a maximum of £39,500. These contributions from film productions are joined by contributions from the DCMS based on lottery money. The money is invested in new entrants training, health, and safety training, and production accountant training. The fund also contributes to the Skills Investment Fund Trainee Network. (With the system of 'Public Match Funding', Skillset achieved between January 2001 and March 2002 £3,973,262 invested in the funding of training.) Between January 2001 and March 2002 grants comprising £735,088 were agreed, which supported a total of 397 training places during this period (Skillset 2002).

Industrial Relations

Cologne

Industrial relations in the German media industry in general, or indeed other private services sectors, are not highly backed by corporatist arrangements of the kind familiar from manufacturing. The Cologne TV and film sector follows this pattern.

According to our survey, only 10 per cent of the workforce is organized in a trade union. Interestingly, smaller firms (<10 employees) show a higher degree of labour organization than larger firms (>10 employees). This could mean that unions have realized their potential to offer collective goods to smaller firms.

In general in the sector, trade associations like the VFFV play a much more vital role than employer organizations and unions. As mentioned before, in crucial domains of associational collective goods provision the VFFV has acted on behalf of the local industry and put up some important initiatives. However, such associations cannot substitute union agreements. Firms were therefore asked whether they voluntarily adopt wage standards of collective agreements and how they bargain over these issues. Only 3 firms out of 21 were simply oriented towards collective agreements and followed standardized procedures of wage negotiation. Instead, 16 firms relied on individual negotiation. But this does not mean that they pressure the workforce and rely on a low-pay job market. It is well known that firms in the media market tend to ask for extreme flexibility from workers. However, only one firm stated that individual negotiations were used in order to implement low-pay strategies. Eleven firms confirmed that they regularly paid more than was demanded by collective agreements.

The reason for this becomes clear if one examines the fast-moving project-based media market. Firms are in need of high flexibility, which the German industrial relations system fails to provide. As we have noted, they rely on personal contacts to recruit employees. All matters of wage conflict therefore have to be internalized and solved by the firm itself. Informality is thus a means to secure compliance with workers who are forced to agree on special market conditions, like flexible working-hours, a very short-term contract, etc., but may negotiate individually over their salary. Depending on the position taken, some employees gain very high wages for a short period of time. The labour market in Cologne has survived and has been able to create employment because both capital and labour actors withdrew from traditional organizations of industrial relations.

London

Surprisingly, collective agreements between employers' associations and unions seem to be more important in London than in Cologne. Their reach extends even to the freelance workers who constitute a high proportion of the workforce. In its Employment Census of 2002, Skillset found that about half of the workforce is working in independent production (47%), the great majority working in the production of commercials (70%), and virtually the entire workforce in film production are freelancers (Skillset 2002*b*). Fifty per cent of freelancers experienced unemployment within the 12 months before the census day, and pay levels are lower than those of employed staff. These problems have been tackled by the Producers Alliance for Cinema and Television (PACT) and the Broadcasting Entertainment Cinematograph and Theatre Union (BECTU) via the Freelance Production Agreement, setting out (minimum) standards for the domestic film and television production industry. The Freelance Production Agreement was effective from January 2001.

Revised in November 2003, the agreement comprises the method of payment, holiday entitlement and pay, working hours, payment of unsocial hours, provisions in cases of sickness and injury, health and safety provisions, regulations for ending or suspending engagements, and disputes procedures. Findings from our questionnaire show that, not only production companies that are members of PACT but also non-member firms, use the Freelance Production Agreement as a basis for negotiations with their freelance staff. Additionally, PACT and BECTU state in the agreement to maintain and develop the Freelance and Television Training (FT2) schemes.

More generally, outsourcing production activities produced a fragmentation of the industry, to which it responded by constructing new forms of coordination. New associations like the Production Alliance for Cinema and Television (PACT) and the New Producers Alliance (NPA) emerged in 1991 and 1992. The Broadcasting Entertainment Cinematograph and Theatre Union (BECTU) was founded in 1991 after a series of mergers between separate unions during the 1980s. BECTU, with its more than 25,000 members of which 6,550 (only) were London-based members in 2004, is structured in branches and grouped into six divisions. It is financed entirely by subscriptions from members and offers an impressive range of services: various insurance schemes, free legal assistance, a 24-hour legal helpline, a 'free' MasterCard, a stakeholder pension scheme, and particular help for freelance workers including the Freelance Production Agreement negotiated between PACT and BECTU. Furthermore, the 'skillsformedia' career development service for the media industries is jointly owned by BECTU and Skillset.

PACT is governed by a council elected by and from its members, predominantly consisting of independent production companies. Council members are representatives and owners of independent production companies, the vast majority of which are based in London. It describes its domain as being the 'UK trade association that represents and promotes the commercial interests of independent feature film, television, animation and interactive media companies'. PACT is mainly funded by membership fees, which are set in relation to the annual turnover of a production company, and of a minority funding based on the levy on TV productions collected for the contribution to the Freelance Training Fund (FTF). Part of this fund is based on independent productions via the Independent Production Training Fund (IPTF) administered by PACT. The PACT UK Directory of Independent Producers of 2004 indicates a membership of over 900 members nation-wide. (Membership has decreased during the past 7 years: In 1997 PACT had a membership of 1,300 nation-wide compared to 900 in 2004.)

Since no official figures are available to provide information about the density of associated London-based production companies, density can only be deducted from industry directories like the Kemps Film and Television Production Services Handbook Online (http:www.kftv.com): 622 London-based production companies are indicated for 2003 and 2004.

Of these 622 companies, 184 are members of PACT and 108 are a member of other associations, either of the Advertising Film and Videotape Producers Association (AFVPA) or of the International Communications Associations (IVCA), or are members of more than one association, summing up to 292 production companies or 47 per cent of the production companies indicated in the directory are associated. Approximately 30 per cent of all production companies as indicated are a member of PACT.

PACT provides services including training, business advice, and subsidized legal services for its members. It has an important role in corporatist training funding as a partner in the Skills Investment Fund, which will be referred to in the following, and as administrator of the Independent Production Training Fund levy for television producers. PACT negotiates collective agreements with guilds and unions, is involved in EU regulatory issues, and negotiates terms of trade with all public service broadcasters in the UK as well as supports its members in business dealings with satellite and cable channels.

The New Producers Alliance has about 800 members in the UK, two-thirds of which are located in London. It aims at providing help for the development stages 'from short films into feature films' and particularly concentrates on small and very small businesses. The NPA has a minority sponsorship of 30 per cent of the UK Film Council, 70 per cent are contributed by membership fees and sponsorship. The NPA provides a network and training as well as 'direct information from the industry' by means of 'networking events' living up to the motto 'by filmmakers for filmmakers'. Tackling the problems of very small companies, they aim at providing contacts with larger producers and post-production companies. The manner of cooperation of 'their' production companies is described as being 'collaborative', while TV production has been experienced as being more competitive than film production.

PACT and the NPA offer a range of training courses. NPA courses take place in Central London; the majority of courses offered by PACT take place at their premises in Central London. Courses offered by PACT are subsidized by the Independent Production Training Fund. They comprise Business Development, Legal Issues, Production Skills, Personal Skills, and Finance Skills. The NPA emphasizes the importance of training of management skills for small production companies, since 'creative people' are regarded as concentrating more on the creative side of their business. They tackle this problem with the '9 Point Producer Training' delivering seminars and lectures at low cost basis, followed by open discussions with invited speakers and panel members from within the film industry.

Inter-Firm Relations

Inter-firm relations may be roughly framed in two different ways: they may be primarily cooperative, where inter-firm relations are close and where firms look for synergies both on the vertical as well as on the horizontal level of inter-firm relations; or they may be primarily competitive, at arm's length, where firms try to control the market by furthering in-house competitiveness, simply buying up beaten competitors.

In the Cologne survey, media firms were asked whether they were organized in cooperative networks or not. Seven out of 20 firms were organized in such networks, while 13 firms responded they were not. Interestingly, not a single case was reported in which public institutions formed part of these networks. Size of networks varies from 3 to 20 firms cooperating. Very different reasons for cooperation were given: 'in order to be able to execute large orders', 'in order to get together for informal exchange of information', 'in order to exert common influence on the media policy of the *Land* government', 'for reasons concerning the protection of formats' or 'to increase accessibility for customer firms'. In short, all sorts of collective action problems were approached by these networks, including those in which associations typically try to act on behalf of their clientele. Again, the classic institutions supporting the cooperative culture in German capitalism were rather absent.

Asked in general on whether media firms in Cologne were rather cooperative or not, three-quarters of all surveyed firms ($n = 20$) answered that cooperative engagement existed but that these inter-firm ties were of a rather weak nature. This result may be taken as the 'weakness of strong ties', since the term 'weak' may simply point to the fact that inter-firm relations, where they tend to emerge as cooperative relations, are rather informal and short term. They do exist, but unorthodox cooperation is not heavily backed by formal institutions.

Firms were asked whether they would consider helping other media firms in the local economy in times of need. This was supposed to test whether friendship and trust backs the local firm cluster in addition or as a substitute of formal institutions. Nine firms out of 20 asserted that they would help and 9 were undecided, which means that under specific circumstances they would help. This shows a large openness of entrepreneurs and it demonstrates that firms also relate to other firms on the basis of friendship. Informal collective action is thus possible because people communicate without just the aim of coming to terms with each other. This may well be a sectoral requirement and not a characteristic of the town, however obviously the city of Cologne offers the opportunity to accommodate supply and demand in this respect.

The city's so-called Belgian quarter, where media SMEs are concentrated, is a hot spot of informal exchange, supporting the impression that Cologne has solved some collective action problems just by being an urban agglomeration with the right mix of breweries and museums. This may not be adequate, because it means that formal institutions leave many collective action problems unresolved, relying on informal cooperation of entrepreneurs instead. Thus, it comes as no surprise from the survey that the entrepreneur who mentioned 'friendship and personal relations' as an important condition for his willingness to support another media firm is the same one who said that 'city officials should turn to smaller producer companies in order to learn about their needs and demand, therefore they should make contacts and communicate with smaller firms'. Summed up, informal cooperation serves as a functional equivalent for public support. Actors in the public institutions willingly accept this.

Local Collective Competition Goods: Why Cologne? Why Soho?

When asked in the survey why production companies had chosen Cologne as a location for production, 16 out of 21 companies said that a short distance to customer firms was decisive, while only 7 mentioned suppliers, 6 firms subcontractors and only 2 answered that it is important to have competitors in easy reach (multiple mentions possible). The short distance to customer firms appears to be the most important issue. This was demonstrated by locating television, film, and video production companies according to the postal code of their addresses on the basis of the Cologne Media Guide. It is important to remember that many of the firms no longer exist. Nevertheless, the survey outcome was confirmed: the area of maximum concentration of producer firms is not far from the largest office and production studios of WDR. This interpretation of the cluster process is completely in accord both with orthodox theories of economic geography (Greenhut and Norman 1995), which claim that transaction costs are reduced by choices concerning enterprise location, and with orthodox assumptions about the typical governance structures of local production systems in Germany, where collective competition goods are predominantly accessed through vertical inter-firm relations. However, another perspective on this in-town concentration is also possible.

The quarter where the maximum concentration is measured is called Belgisches Viertel (Belgian quarter). It may be characterized as an 'in-quarter' in town, where many of the music clubs and bars can be found. In an interview with a managing officer of WDR, he explained, that the agglomeration of companies in the Belgisches Viertel results from the fact that:

... this is a more intellectual quarter, where many of those who work for smaller production companies and the WDR live. There exists a good bar infrastructure and you simply meet there ... This is not a matter of entrepreneurial infrastructure, because many firms concentrate there, but [agglomeration] results from the idea: we go out tonight and have a drink together and then we might agree on a common ... project. I have a creative artist ..., what do you think about recording him in your studio ...

And earlier on the same issue:

We live on interlocutors, we live on contacts, we do not run a push button factory, but we manufacture something that is not tangible, something very ephemeral. This means that organizing connections, talks, and contacts is our prior concern...(Interview WDR)

Another interpretation of the maximum concentration within the Belgisches Viertel, which is not set up as a rival hypothesis but rather complements the argument on the relevance of large customer firms, can be given if informal relations between market actors are analysed. It may be a sectoral speci-ficity that the audiovisual media industry is very much dependent on such informal contacts. However the question arises how actors, whose initiatives are largely steered by strong formal institutions of the German kind, may create a market environment in which such informal sectoral needs can be accommodated.

First, the *Land* government has created a powerful institutional environ-ment for the production of collective competition goods supporting the local media industry in cooperation with the city of Cologne. Some formal institu-tions have been quite successful in shaping this rather untraditional and fast moving market. On the institutional level of the *Land* there is no evidence for any innovative departure from the German model. However, some local institutions in Cologne clearly deviate from this pattern of exclusively formal and orthodox support. One may speculate whether the strong Catholic sub-culture of Cologne has influenced the functioning of formal institutions in a manner that resembles some of the features of production systems in Italy, where informality forms an important part of the political economy (Regini 1997).

In any case, what may at first glance give the impression of a disadvantage in a competitive market environment paradoxically turns out to be advan-tageous as soon as sectoral peculiarities demand rather informal market relations. The relaxed formal institutional order in Cologne creates a much more experimental market environment, where self-employment in a media firm is equally dependent on informal contacts as many other career options in local public or private institutions. This in turn promotes an extraordinary urban atmosphere in which creative artists and journalists as well as other employees in the media industry enjoy living and cooperating.

There has thus been an interesting mix of formal institutions on the one hand—including large flagship enterprises and an active *Land* government, typical of German capitalism—and informal institutions on the other. Of course, it is not claimed that everything that appears to be deviant in this case is caused by informality, but it is claimed that deviance in the case of the Cologne media industry is primarily produced by local organizations, not federal or *Land* organizations.

One might argue that the city of Cologne has followed quite orthodox concepts of structural policy by creating such challenging and trend-stetting projects as the Mediapark. This project has indeed been important to host suppliers of competition goods that service the media industry, it surely created growth and employment, but it did not attract as many media firms in the SIC 92.1 and 92.2 sectors as expected. This is the reason why the Mediapark area is not emerging the locus of maximum concentration. Out of the 415 firms in the audiovisual industry only nine are directly located in the Mediapark. Many of the 250 firms that have moved into one of the representative modern buildings of the Mediapark produce in different sectors (insurance companies, lawyers, management consultancies, etc.). It has finally been a success, because it constitutes a collective good in itself: it helps to market the city as an important place for media production, and it does this well for instance due to its architecture: the semicircular arrangement of the many modern buildings surround a large 'piazza'. This architectural concept is intended to foster informal communication between employees of the target industry and to encourage clustering. However, the real cluster-concentration of audiovisual media firms can be found elsewhere in the city. That hints at the fact that the physical infrastructure and orthodox concepts of structural policy, although they have been quite successfully carried out by the city council, do not alone explain the competitive advantage of media firms. Consequently, it comes as no surprise that the survey points to other important factors.

Ten firms out of 21 said that the social environment was an important reason choosing Cologne as a location, this ranking second only to 'closeness to customer firm'. In comparison, not a single firm considered the local economic support policy to be important. Only one firm had ever contacted the Amt für Wirtschaftsförderung (office of business development) and only four had contacted the specialized Stabsstelle Medienwirtschaft (staff office media industry) of the city of Cologne. This result is in line with our hypothesis that the city's immediate influence through formal institutions does not sufficiently explain the high concentration of media firms. Nevertheless, the physical infrastructure as such was regarded as being important by exactly one-third of all surveyed firms. However, enterprises did not mention collective goods produced by the *Land* or the city of Cologne in particular, but rather they highlighted the importance of the WDR-studios and the general studio infrastructure. This does not mean that private firms and studios create the competitive advantage of the media industry in Cologne almost entirely by themselves. If one examines the classic fields of collective goods provision, state organizations emerge as important actors, although apparently taken for granted by private entrepreneurs.

Similarly in London, the exceptional growth of the film and TV production industry and the structural changes of the industry producing the emergence of small independent production companies are connected to the government policy; but this does not answer the question of the exceptional high extent of geographic concentration of these companies in Soho and the adjacent areas. An explanation of the geographic concentration is the availability of local collective competition goods, like vocational training and research and development, which are provided for the SMEs and freelancers working in the industry by a superstructure of local or national institutions concentrated in or confined to London.

As in Cologne, location in geographic proximity to other production companies but also to large broadcasters is advantageous and can even be vital, since organization in project ecologies necessitates face-to-face contact. Here in particular the location of Channel 4, the BBC, and, later, Channel 5 have encouraged geographical concentration.

Elite training courses for the industry are also concentrated in London: internationally renowned MA courses are run by The London Film School (adjacent to Soho) and the National Film and Television School (rather further out); MA courses in filmmaking and screenwriting are provided at The London Film School. Their alumni list shows many successful film directors and producers. MA courses in animation, Cinematography, Composing for Film and Television, Documentary, Editing, Producing, Production Design, and Screenwriting are on offer at the National School. While larger colleges are located outside London, the London College of Music and Media with more than 40,000 registered students predominantly studying for BA and BSc degrees has three locations in the Thames Valley; smaller colleges offering training also designed for freelancers are situated in or near Soho, such as the Academy of Radio, Film and Television, and the 01zero-one Creative Learning Lab at the Westminster Kingsway College. Production companies in Central London offer placements to students, in general on the basis of a one day a week placement over one term.

Greater London hosts several specially developed sites for film- and TV-production. The major studios for film are located on the outer suburbs of London, Pinewood and Shepperton Studios being the oldest, existing since the 1930s. The BBC's production studios are located in inner West London (White City). Larger studios with central locations are The London Studios, designed for TV production and located at the South Bank, not far from Soho, and 3 Mills Studios.[17] Several smaller studios are located at Central London and at Soho.

A very important local collective competition good is offered by the famous Sohonet, a broadband Local Area Network (LAN) developed by private initiative. It has broadband links with Hollywood, thus enabling post-production work to be done overnight in London. Sohonet, founded in 1995 by a group of Soho-based post-production companies, also links Shepperton and Pinewood studios to post-production in Central London with direct optical fibre connectivity. It has also provided for a Wireless Area Laser and IR ATM network linking its key clients across the growing Sohonet Metropolitan Area Network.[18]

However, the argument that the film and TV production industry is concentrated in London for reasons of the availability of collective competition goods for SMEs that are confined to Central London is questionable. Here, the reality is a more complex one: Some local collective competition goods have been provided for after the 'first stage' of concentration. It can therefore not be finally concluded, which or how many companies have established their businesses in this area for reasons of availability of these goods. A second reason for the dense geographical concentration in Soho becomes obvious when carrying out empirical research there: just as in Cologne, the project ecologies in which independent production companies and their freelancers work necessitate proximity and face-to-face contact.

Their work is highly disintegrated, with networks of many small trans-actions that are constantly changing. Production is often organized around teams formed for a single project, which are dissolved when it is completed. This leads to a state of constant movement of labour and service providers. Network organizations are constantly created and re-created. Short-term oriented action particularly dominates in film production. Transactions tend to be frequent in occurrence, small in scale, but involve prolonged personal contact. These factors encourage geographic proximity between producers, service providers, and workforce, creating an environment of 'project ecolo-gies' (Grabher 2002a,b). Such proximity facilitates inter-firm relationships and can lead to rather dense inter-firm relationships which are vital in the media production system, since they increase the speed and efficiency of information exchange as well as facilitate transactions between producers and between production companies and service providers: 'Firms in the Soho cluster, many of them small and medium-sized enterprises, are linked by dynamic processes and learning and innovation into a collective entity, dependent on and benefiting from highly localized competitive advantages' (Keeble and Nachum 2000: 13).

While examining foreign and indigenous firms in the media cluster of central London, Nachum and Keeble (2000: 17) found that both '... seem equally to value geographic proximity to the cluster in facilitating informa-tion gathering and accessing specialized and customized expertise needed for particular tasks'.

Further, in general smaller companies have more difficulties in recruit-ing staff than larger ones. Geographic proximity is vital for recruitment, between 90 and 95 per cent of the employees being recruited locally (ibid.). Only certain types of labour are recruited outside London, for example, film directors, who are recruited globally. Proximity and organization in project ecologies also enhance recruitment dominated by reputation rather than by certificates. Whom you know is considered as important as what you know (Pratt 1999), the transportation of professional reputation being crucial in particular for freelancers (see also Baumann 2002a,b; Nachum and Keeble 2000: 24).

Face-to-face contact taking place informally at Soho meeting places is the most common way of communication. Knowledge is easier to get the smaller the distances between potential service providers and production companies are and the more often they meet, on formal and on informal terms. Referring to Pratt (1999), Grabher (2002*a*: 1922) states: 'The essential requirement is that many actors, collaborators, and rivals who perform similar or related tasks are located where they can monitor and observe each other in a formalized and strategic fashion', but that the opportunities for hanging out and for casual conversation are of the same importance as the formal structures. All in all, we find a number of factors creating spatial concentration in Soho: A pool of specialized labour, a rich infrastructure of specialized suppliers, in particular post-production facilities, and knowledge spill-overs further driven by the 'evening economy' and its centrally located meeting places.

Conclusions

These two case studies demonstrate several examples of actors at local and sectoral level taking initiatives to resolve apparent deficiencies for their purposes in the 'normal' national array of institutions. A particular surprise of the finding is that in doing so both German and British film and television makers have occasionally, usually by chance, hit on institutions more typical of the other country. This last point will require some explanation below.

In both cases too informal and often micro-structures, so easily ignored in broad-brush studies of national systems based on official data, are important. The Belgisches Viertel and Soho may be unusual places, but they are far from unique in their role of local ecologies that support particular kinds of economic activity, whatever the dominant national or even regional pattern.

At first sight, UK broadcasting looks like a 'typically neo-liberal' case of deregulation producing a fragmented structure and fierce competition among many small production companies. However, within this competition and strong market-ruled structure, we find a rather densely regulated system that maintains standards through governmental regulation as well as cultural norms and standards, and coordination through associational and corporatist agreements and structures.

Our studies of corporate finance showed a curious example of unconscious institutional borrowing between the two countries, the local savings bank in Cologne acting as a venture capitalist development agency, backed by its status as a public institution, and banks in Soho adopting some of the characteristics of *Hausbanken*. Although there might be a trend in Germany that shows that many banks withdraw from the house bank principle, the local savings bank acted in this unorthodox manner from early on and furthered the production of collective goods through shareholding in semi-public support agencies and the establishment of other financing measures.

Similarly, in vocational training, in Cologne there were several mainly informal training and recruitment procedures by firms themselves—though the

Land and the city both acted as supporting institutions, adapting vocational profiles of the dual system as well as founding new organizations in the field of higher education and training. At the same time, London saw the development of corporatist structures, with unions being involved considerably more than in Cologne, to introduce and monitor new training schemes and solve the chronic free-rider problem of British vocational education.

Again in industrial relations, at times the British seemed '*plus allemands que les allemands*', and vice versa. In Cologne there was individual bargaining over wages by the majority of employees. Consequently, only 10 per cent of the local workforce seems to be organized in labour union organizations. In London, not only is density far higher but even freelancers are being covered by collective agreements.

One is tempted to conclude that the conditions in this emerging new industry of micro-firms is so delicate that extreme versions of any standard economic model are likely to crush it; it will flourish where a particular balance of the features of alternative systems is achieved. This is a 'temptation' because it may lead us into functionalist forms of argument, implying that somehow local economies will find the form of governance they will need. There is no necessity about this; there are after all far more places where no dynamic SME sectors based on project ecologies exist, whether in this sector or in others that might make use of them. Chance plays its part here, but also we return again to the extreme geographical concentration of both these locations. This made possible an unusual degree of interaction from actors in all parts of the industry and its related services, giving them an unusual opportunity to discover and to implement new, innovative institutional solutions, borrowing from wider national structures where convenient, but creating something new where it was not.

Just as culture represented a collective competition good enabling decision-makers in the city of Cologne to realize that creativity, and therefore creative sectors, could not be fully managed, so institutional innovation in the governance of sectors is itself a creative act. Our cases confirm what Florida has shown for the USA—an urban atmosphere of tolerance and diversity may contribute heavily to growth and employment in creative industries (Florida 2002, 2005*a,b*). They also suggest that responsive institutional design requires the same context.

Notes

1. ITV was the first commercial television channel in the UK. The ITV network comprises 15 independent regional television licences in 14 regional areas (there are 2 licences for London).

2. The Broadcasting Act of 1990 introduced a funding formula enabling Channel 4 to sell its own advertising. but still guaranteed funding from Channel 3 (ITV)

companies, in case Channel 4's income from advertising fell below 14% of total national television advertising revenue. The safety net was in fact not needed, since Channel 4 was very successful and 'profit making' with its advertising section. Funds had always flowed from Channel 4 to Channel 3 companies (ITV), approximately £350 million, until the formula was ended in 1998.

3. An 'independent producer' is defined in the legislation (Independent Productions Orders 1991, 1995, and 2003) as a producer who is not an employee of a broadcaster, who does not have a shareholding greater than 25% in a broadcaster, and which is not a body corporate in which any one broadcaster (who directs their services at the UK) has a shareholding greater than 25% or in which any two broadcasters together have an aggregate shareholding greater than 50%.

4. This trend has also been confirmed by Barclays Media Banking Centre, Soho, London (Interview with the Head of Barclays Media Banking Centre, 20 April 2004).

5. See Skillset: Some facts and figures: http://www.skillset.orgnation_regionenglish_regionslondonarticle_1825_1.asp

6. See Skillset: A snapshot of the Audio-visual sector in London: http://www.skillset.orgnation_regionenglish_regionslondonarticle_1824_1.asp

7. Film London: Facts about Film and Television Production in London, Appendix D, 2004: 80% of the UK's film and television industry are concentrated in London.

8. See also Skillset: Some facts and figures: stating that about 125,000 people work in the audio-visual industry in London: http://www.skillset.orgnation_regionenglish_regionslondon article_1825_1.asp

9. Functionally speaking, Soho can be extended to include the immediately adjacent areas of Fitzrovia, Covent Garden, the South Bank and Victoria.

10. We would like to thank Daniel Weber for his valuable support in gathering survey data.

11. This has been confirmed by Coutts Media Banking Centre, Strand, London, Head of Media Banking, and by Barclays Media Banking Centre, Soho Square, London, interviews 20 April 2004.

12. Barclays Media Banking Centre, Soho Square, London, interview 20 April 2004.

13. Section 42 Finance Act 1992 allows for a tax write-off over a three-year period for producers or acquirers of qualifying British films of any size budget.

14. In 2001 Learning and Skills Councils took on the training functions previously performed by the Training and Enterprise Councils (TECs) and the funding responsibilities of the Further Education Funding Council (FEFC). There are 47 Local Learning and Skills Councils in England, 5 of which are in London. While the Learning and Skills Councils are occupied with initial training only, Skillset as the sector skills organization is also concerned with the provision of opportunities of further training and freelance training ('industry training').

15. This has been confirmed by experts of the Learning and Skills Council Central London, Skillset, and the Westminster Kingsway College (Interviews LSC and Westminster Kingsway College 20 January 2005; interview Skillset 18 January 2005). See also as indicated in the report the 'British Film Industry': 'Formal training and development have not historically made a significant contribution to the British film industry. This is changing, but the situation needs attention to make sure that problems are dealt with' (DCMS: British Film Industry 2003: 46).

16. The same problem is mentioned concerning training at college courses: They focus on 'hard skills' (Interview Westminster Kingsway College 20 January 2005).

17. 3 Mills Studios have been acquired by the London Development Agency.

18. The laser rooftop network system offers transmission over distances ranging from 100 to 4,000 m. The narrow transmission angle offers security for data transmission for the Soho clients.

8

Conclusions: Local and Global Sources of Capitalist Diversity

COLIN CROUCH, MARTIN SCHRÖDER, AND HELMUT
VOELZKOW*

The original aim of the research project on which this book is based was to identify 'productive incoherences' in the governance of regional economic clusters. By 'incoherence' we indicated situations where the governance of a cluster deviated from the economic governance of its national context. An incoherence would be deemed 'productive' if it could be shown to be associated with a higher competitiveness of firms in the cluster, and if the tension between local and national enabled local institutional entrepreneurs to innovate, bringing elements of local and national together in new and creative combinations. We were particularly interested to identify clusters where 'deviant' local institutions enabled a sector to succeed against the norm of the national economy concerned. The research project therefore challenged the claim of other institutionalist literature, that insisted on the need for coherence, for homogeneity among different components of economic governance if economic success was to be achieved (Hall and Gingerich 2004). We planned to set our Schumpeterian concept of the relationship among institutions against this functionalist one that has tended to characterize much neo-institutionalist writing.

We were not seeking to replace the claim of 'coherence' theorists that homogenous institutional arrangements would always be more successful than heterogeneous ones with the rival opposite assertion. Rather, in keeping with our Schumpeterian stance, we were seeking what might be *possible*, not what should be routine. The study of entrepreneurial activity necessarily seeks surprising departures from the routine; and it must always be remembered that more entrepreneurial ventures fail than do routine ones. As explained in Chapter 1, this same logic justifies and in fact requires the case-study methodology that we have used.

We have certainly found cases that support our initial search for productive incoherence. Swedish furniture-makers in Tibro, resisting the logic of the

* All colleagues within our project contributed ideas that have been used in this collective conclusion, but we are particularly grateful for stimulating comments on an earlier draft from Maarten Keune, Geny Piotti, and Pernilla S. Rafiqui.

overall Swedish economy towards concentration in large production units; biotechnology firms in Munich, combining the local with the global to over-leap certain German national institutions and access the capital and labour that they need; new TV production micro-firms in both Cologne and London, inventing new institutions as neither the formality of strong institutions of the former location nor the institutionally thin structures of the latter suit their particular survival needs. (For a fuller summary of our findings related to the productive incoherence framework, see Crouch, Schröder, and Voelzkow 2009.)

However, in the event our findings were not limited to the 'productive incoherence' concept; to concentrate on that topic alone would mean ignor-ing much of what we have learned in the course of our case studies. To some extent this is because that concept implies too strong a confronta-tion with the literature on national systems and generalized typologies of forms of capitalism; but this conclusion in itself is, paradoxically, the result of a greater challenge that our findings really make to these generalizing approaches.

Concepts of systems, at whatever level, are scientific constructs, or some-times the constructs of actors and decision-makers themselves, and as such will correspond only approximately with the underlying reality. Of course, both scientific concepts and the projects of social actors will be more suc-cessful (in their different meanings of success) the more closely they do so correspond; but the gap is usually there. For micro-level actors, who oper-ate with pieces of the reality they find around them, these overall concepts may not be so important. Thus, when the London TV-production indus-try allocates to trade unions a role in a training scheme that theorists of British economic governance regard as inconsistent with the national model, they are not necessarily aware of doing anything odd. They are just tack-ling a practical problem with the resources they have at hand. For such apparent 'deviations' from national models to be seen as 'transgressive', we need some evidence of confrontation between local actors and those at a higher level trying to prevent them. Such cases certainly exist: for exam-ple, in many parts of the world it is not possible to give a full account of how economic activity operates without considering the black or shadow economy (Burroni and Crouch 2008). Such an account will normally need to include how the interface between the shadow economy and the forces of law and order is managed—though even here there are many cases of complete complicity, such that the relationship is not one of tension or incoherence.

To argue in this way is not to make an ethnomethodological case for abandoning theory and just seeing the world through the eyes of local actors, for this is to abandon the scientific task. We should however construct our the-ories from the bottom up, modelling institutions as they present themselves to social actors on the ground rather than as they are planned by, or seen from the perspective of, leading policymakers and strategists. This was the central plea made by Hall and Soskice (2001*a*) for the study of 'the varieties of capitalism' in the introduction to their eponymous volume: institutions should be viewed from the perspective of the firm, they argued. Curiously, however, they failed to carry this through in their methodology, which completely takes for granted national systems, with no local or regional variants, which form an iron cage for firms. That those firms might reach out to find resources in other countries that cannot be provided by their own national institutions, in the manner of the Munich biotech firms, is not envisaged.

To fulfil Hall and Soskice's original vision of a firm-centred account it is necessary to depict several different layers of institutions as they confront firms of varying sizes in various geographical locations and sectors: national layers, certainly, but also local, sectoral, world-regional (e.g. EU), global, and others. Firms will have different degrees of access to these. The actions they take and the organizational problems they solve will depend on the particular array of institutional layers with which they are surrounded, and their ability to access them, as well as on their own institutional entrepreneurship. Also relevant will be the connections of the advisors, consultants, and public-policy actors who seek to help them. These all assist in forging new combinations among institutional components when necessary. We should speak of 'incoherence' in this process of making new combinations only when there is clear evidence of a clash between the terms offered by two or more institutions, or by an institution at different levels. For example, local employers in a country where business associations are weak might be able to create an associational basis of their own to provide training—both diverging from the national situation and providing something more directly relevant to their situation than had they been working within an inherited associational system. Without that evidence, we should merely note variation within a system. Similarly, incoherence can only be found if there is indeed a coherent system, against which it is to be established. A mere plurality of institutions is not yet incoherence in the sense that we use the term.

Taking this approach, we see that a 'national system' does not comprise solely those institutions established at the level of the nation state, *but the full complexity of national, local, sectoral, and extra-national institutions to which firms located within that nation state have access.* There will certainly be differences here among nation states, as some have been more concerned than others to impose centralized national systems and extinguish access to diverse local and/or extra-national resources by their citizens. Historically this was of course how nascent European nation states in particular imposed their hegemony over their territories. Local systems were crushed or made subordinate to national structures, while tariff barriers and nationalism were used to weaken cross-national links. However, since the latter half of the twentieth century this assertion of the priority of the national has become considerably attenuated, especially in Western Europe. There is more tolerance of local and sectoral specificity, even in France and the UK, the two main bastions of national centralism; EU institutions are a reality in many spheres; and, particularly following the liberalization of capital movements, the global level is accessible. A further aspect concerns openness to transnational influences through immigration. For example, as hinted at various points of Jong's chapter, the greater openness of US higher education, in comparison with most European systems, to scientists from a diversity of national backgrounds enabled US science to tap into insights and perspectives from a wide variety of different systems of formation. It is not so much the substantive content of US science education itself that has been so successful as its willingness to combine elements from many approaches.

All this requires a changed approach to the study of institutions, leading us to include in 'national' accounts not only that which exists at the national level itself but also all that is accessible from within that nation. To some extent it is possible to envisage the idea of different layers of institutions in terms of a Russian doll, with its successive layers of ever smaller dolls contained inside each other. Thus, the smallest doll might be the immediate local institutions of a cluster, the largest being the global economy. But the analogy cannot take us far. First, it assumes the same basic institutional shape at each level, when in reality different levels will produce very different ensembles of features (e.g. very different kinds of resource are available at the level of a sector and that of the EU). Second, it assumes a clear distinction between levels; bigger dolls do not interfere with the shape of smaller dolls—except to the extent that smaller dolls have to be able to be accommodated within the larger ones, a point where the analogy with institutions is valid. Among institutions, such interference in (or interaction between) levels is normal; in particular, national institutions are likely to intervene in more local ones. Third, the Russian doll analogy also assumes a 'super-embeddedness' of institutions, that is, that lower-level institutions are fully embedded and supported by higher level ones, with no capacity to reach outside them. This would rule out some of the findings of our research. There are strong functionalist implications in the Russian doll image that must be avoided; Talcott Parsons used it to depict the successive levels, from culture to individual psyche, at which his overall theory of the social system was supposed to operate (Parsons 1951).

A better analogy would be a road map, with firms as travellers and with different institutional levels depicted as different cities that are more or less accessible. Access to them and the resources they can provide to the traveller runs through a complex series of roads. The ability of a traveller to reach any particular city is determined by three factors:

1. Simple distance: some institutions may be literally too remote for small firms in particular to access; hence the importance of local clusters for them, and the importance of considering the local and the sectoral as much as the national when analysing their situations;

2. Gatekeepers: access can be gained to some cities only by passing through others, who may not permit use of the road. This represents the important hypothesis of neo-institutionalism, that actors cannot simply wander where they like to access resources, but are channelled and regulated by many gatekeepers. In institutional analysis gatekeepers are only occasionally task-oriented actors—as, say, when banks make it difficult for small firms to have access to credit. More typically institutions operate as passive, unconscious (because institutions, unlike organizations, are not constructed with strategic capacity) elements that steer firms in some directions and away from others. However, as some of our cases have shown, there may sometimes be alternative routes that do not pass through the gatekeeper city, for those who have the resources and ingenuity to seek them out;

3. Capacity to use a road: not all vehicles can use all roads; in particular a multi-national like VW-Audi can get at institutional resources in a manner that is impossible for a small or medium-sized firm—unless of course (to bring our central theme into the analogy) the latter is highly entrepreneurial, just as an excellent driver can do exceptional things with an inadequate vehicle.

But, again, analogies take us only so far: institutions are not such separate, discrete entities as cities; one is typically 'within' more than one of them at any particular time, and they are typically layered upon each other. Bearing in mind these limitations, it is possible to revisit the findings of our case studies in this light, from which will emerge an image of the firm, not just as a user or exploiter of institutions as in the above discussion, but as an institution-shaper in its own right.

Findings of the Case Studies

To start where we ended, the *Cologne and London TV production* cases present in some ways the biggest puzzle. This was where we encountered most institutional innovation, but where in principle the actors, very small, project-based firms, had the weakest capacity to make bold attempts to access the resources needed for such innovation. There were considerable similarities between the cases. Both clusters consisted of large national broadcasting organizations networked to a vast and changing number of smaller companies. In both, freelancers had an important role. Thus, 'project ecologies' (Grabher 2002*a,b*) have been created based on shorter project-based working periods and prolonged personal contacts. Companies cooperate in networks, which evolve around these projects and are supported by a cultural milieu, the 'evening economy', consisting of a lively bar scene, numerous restaurants, cafés, etc. that are in geographic proximity.

Due to the rapid setting up and dissolving of companies based on projects, neither long-term oriented credit-financing by banks *alla tedesca*, nor normal venture capital financing, satisfy financing needs. In both cases state subsidies and tax schemes have been important. Partly therefore the image of weak, marginal little firms conceals the fact that governments see the cultural sector as one of national importance; the sector is not so remote from the high roads of institutional access as one might imagine. But there have also been interesting financial innovations. Contrary to expectations of how German banks behave, local savings banks in Cologne have provided short-term capital that would conventionally be provided by venture capitalists. Banks were able to take up risky projects because they target their investment objects by building up intensive links to companies. With this expert knowledge, banks also assume a role close to that of a development agency, linking successful firms and thus providing services for the cluster as a whole (i.e. they provide a local collective competition good). Also contrary to expectations, some London banks have built up an expert position in the cluster by providing capital to companies and linking their financing needs to services offered. This is interesting, since in the UK we should rather expect financing of small firms that takes place through bank overdrafts, not through local branches of banks who try to become knowledgeable of a specific industry and establish long-term relationships to companies.

Vocational training schemes have similarly defied the expectations of those who believe fully in the power of national models. The rather formal German model of vocational training is described as being inadequate for the qualification needs of the Cologne media industry, since it is not formal knowledge but largely flexibility and creativity that are needed in the media sector. Although the state is trying to establish qualification structures and schemes, the system of vocational qualification in Cologne is not mediated by associations, but by informal collaboration among firms. In London, too, the situation deviates from national expectations, but in a very different direction. Although 'on-the-job training' is a common mode of training in the industry, state-initiated projects as well as the social partners have taken up important roles in the establishment of qualification schemes—more important indeed than in Germany, where one expects to find such institutions. The union and the employers' association have even set up funds to which production companies and broadcasters are supposed to contribute in order to pay for vocational and freelance training.

There was a similarly paradoxical story in the related field of industrial relations. Not being able to rely on a formally trained workforce, in both locations companies and projects relied on freelancers hired on a project basis, whose 'quality' is ensured via inter-personal networks where reputation is more important than certified knowledge. Wages and working conditions were predominantly negotiated individually. The alleged rigidities of the German industrial relations system seem to have done nothing at all to be a gatekeeper impeding this development in Cologne—though their existence might have delayed the search for alternatives. Even more surprising is the way in which industrial relations in this sector in London are subject to collective regulation, with a stronger union role than in Germany and the extension of collective bargaining and social security schemes to freelancers.

Overall, these clusters seem to be converging towards a model that conforms to neither country's stereotypical national type. How has it been possible for a sector comprising such weak firms to make such bold innovations? Answering in terms of the road map analogy, one points first to the strength of informal social ties in these tightly geographically defined and virtually subcultural sectors. Both have easy access to rich collective competition goods at the extreme local level that small firms can form through networks. It was of course not guaranteed that mere ease of access to such rich potential would actually be realized: entrepreneurial actors were needed; and, as our chapter on this sector noted, if it is characterized by anything it is creativity. Second, and contrary to the expectations of national systems theories, national structures did not operate as gatekeepers barring access to innovative institutional approaches. No one seems to have said: 'You can't do that here!', either because the writ of national structures did not run to the sector, or because its success was seen as too important (and perhaps too dimly understood) by formal policymakers for them to want to interfere. Finally, although these small firms cannot easily access the institutional 'high roads' available to large corporations, big national organizations—the BBC, the WDR, and the other large broadcasting corporations—were supportive. Since at least in the UK 'deregulation' partly took the form of requiring the large organizations to make use of SMEs, the former could not adopt the predatory approach towards small firms that one would expect in the market economy. It became therefore in their interests to facilitate improvements in the latter's quality and performance.

The main 'surprise' for national systems theories of the *Munich and Cambridge biotechnology* cases concerns the relative success of the Bavarian cluster. Again, companies in the two cases were roughly comparable concerning size, turnover, and markets. The Munich cluster is linked to the University of Munich as well as to a Max Planck Institute, whereas the Cambridge cluster has established links to its eponymous university. Due to sectoral specificities, both clusters are concentrated geographically but linked to international networks. Both need access to research institutes, venture capital, and a management that is capable of linking research to market use of the products.

It was not surprising that the UK venture capital industry should cater well for the needs of the biotech cluster in Cambridge, nor that the German bank-based mode of financing was not adapted to the needs of Munich-based biotech firms. These shortcomings were however compensated for by two functionally equivalent institutions. Since the under-developed German venture capital market was not used, firms relied on public funding and used foreign venture capital markets. They similarly avoided certain rigidities of the German labour market by using international labour markets to recruit their CEOs—something that the Cambridge firms did not do. Other elements of the German labour market, such as co-determination, were simply not relevant, as these institutions (which are required to be established only if employees request them) tend not to reach either high-tech activities or SMEs in general.

The varieties of capitalism approach would expect a high degree of cooperation with public research infrastructure for the German cluster (Hall and Soskice 2001*a*: 26). This was indeed the case, as the share of scientific publications produced in collaboration with public research institutes was twice as high in Munich as in Cambridge. However, the outcome of this is rather surprising: The academic embeddedness of the Munich cluster leads to better performance in developing radically innovative products; thus these are more pronounced in Munich than in Cambridge. While governance of the biotechnology cluster in Cambridge largely corresponded to the national stereotype of a liberal market economy, this had the paradoxical effect that incremental innovations are more prevalent in the British cluster. This points to certain British specificities, in particular problematic relations between universities and industry, rather than to general characteristics of so-called liberal market economies, as the same would not be true of the USA (Jong 2007).

As with the TV production cases, one is impressed here by the absence of any intervention by gatekeepers of national systems to stop firms finding the institutional resources they need. Again, this is a sector characterized by innovation and creativity in the actual work task, which seems to extend to actors' approaches to institutions. In addition, and unlike the TV cases, people working in this sector are thoroughly international in their approach, as scientific advance is rarely interested in national institutions. It should therefore not be surprising that firms in this sector should take advantage of global deregulation in order to access the resources they need. Even if relatively small, their internationalism gives them access to international high roads. Furthermore, biotechnology has been identified as a key industry for Germany to succeed in future markets. A considerable amount of public finance is available to these companies. As policymakers realize that domestic institutions do not cater to the needs of this industry, they and not only the companies try to act entrepreneurially and find ways for the companies to thrive by circumventing them.

The challenge presented by the comparison of *furniture-making in Ostwestfalen-Lippe and southern Sweden* was whether Swedish firms could stand comparison with German ones in a sector favouring craft production in medium-sized enterprises—a context for which German institutions are often considered particularly well, and Swedish ones particularly poorly, adapted. In fact, as Chapter 2 has warned us to expect, the so-called German model is itself changing. While the majority of firms in our cluster were family-owned, this is increasingly combined with a professional management team, and some companies have been taken over by foreign competitors (including Swedish ones). These expect to see high yields from their investments. At the same time, corporate takeovers have a tendency to replace traditional company networks. Even though bank-based corporate financing is still prevalent, thus ensuring the stakeholder model to a large degree, there were strong trends to shareholder-value in the German companies, with a detrimental effect on the previously typical corporate governance model.

While firms in one of the three Swedish clusters, Virserum, were suffering the fate one would predict for family-based SMEs in Sweden, those in Tibro were surviving and even thriving. It seems to have been the nature of the local production system with its high degree of cooperation, and associated commitment of public and other institutions in the town to enhancing the industry, that made this possible. This was something that companies and institutions in Virserum had been unable to achieve. For example, in Tibro companies managed to share production sites that no single one could afford to acquire itself. Therefore, the capacity of SMEs to act collectively was a functional equivalent to the hierarchical structure of a large enterprise. The third Swedish case concerned one large corporation, IKEA, rather than a local SME-based economy. To some extent this was less deviant from the stereotypical case of Swedish success based on large firms. However, as we saw, IKEA is in many respects not a typical Swedish firm, and has so positioned itself that it has a virtually global choice of institutions available to it.

The changing nature of the German furniture-making model was also evident in industrial relations, collective agreements providing the basis for remuneration, working time, and other issues, with at the same time an increasing flexibility being integrated into agreements, so that they became rather broad frameworks within which further negotiation could be conducted at company level. Increasing price pressure led supplier companies to outsource production to sub-companies that had not joined the collective pay agreements. Meanwhile, in Sweden a relatively cooperative approach towards industrial relations could be cited as one factor of success of the Tibro cluster over that of Virserum. In IKEA there was also an approach to cooperative relations with the workforce, but one rather deviant from the main union-based Swedish model, with a company-level effort to create a team spirit and company identification. In Sweden, if not in many other countries where it operates, IKEA is unionized—but it tries to make all its employees associate with and remain loyal to the firm and its needs rather than with their respective unions.

Similarly in vocational training, the bulk of training in Germany is carried out by the 'dual system', but with erosion at numerous points, including the increasing importance of something closer to a university for applied sciences

(*Fachhochschule*). The now familiar variety held true of the Swedish cases. Whereas firms in Virserum engaged in no more than the absolute minimum training, which was delivered 'in house' and 'on the job', in Tibro training included successful collaborative arrangements among firms. In IKEA training was largely internalized within the company, which maintained its own vocational schools and thus tried somewhat to insulate itself from the Swedish state system. However, it should be noted that company schools have been explicitly provided for in Swedish legislation since the early 1990s. This was therefore behaviour that 'conformed' to the Swedish model, in the sense that, as with the German case, we here have to come to terms with a model that is itself in the process of change.

It appears that in furniture production SMEs can only survive if they are supported by local collective competition goods, an infrastructure that increases their competitiveness and gives them access to possibilities that would usually be barred due to limited individual resources (Le Galès and Voelzkow 2001). For the cluster in Ostwestfalen-Lippe the German institutions of a coordinated market economy, albeit in their changing form, are able to do this, in compliance with the national framework of diversified quality production.

In Virserum we gained our first real instance of national arrangements impeding a particular form of organization of production, as firms there fell foul of the lack of support from Swedish institutions. However, the ability of firms in Tibro to surmount the difficulties shows that this is not impossible. There, inter-company linkages and cooperation, local public agency support, and therefore a capacity for local collective action and the creation of local collective competition goods were able to preserve the structure of the cluster. Though both the sector and the institutional means are different, the approach resembles that of the TV production companies in mobilizing the resources of locality. In that sense, the entrepreneurs of Tibro did not need to take the road that passed through national gatekeepers, because they directly accessed local facilities that were rich in useful potential. IKEA is rather a case of a loose coupling to the Swedish system, using it where it is serving its needs, but internalizing wherever possible, as in the case of financing and vocational training. This demonstrates the specific road of access to resources, bypassing national institutions if necessary, that is available to the big, vertically integrated company.

Finally, this is also the main lesson to be learned from *car manufacture in Zwickau and Győr*. VW and Audi were located in places where public institutions were relatively weak. So the companies were largely able to introduce classical German institutions to the local context where it suited them, but not where it did not, acting in ways that corresponded neither to their 'home-model' nor to local institutions. Like IKEA, this is a strong example of firms as institution makers rather than as institution takers.

These cases also gave us an opportunity to compare a context where West German institutions had in principle been introduced (East Germany) following the collapse of state socialism, and one where they had not (Hungary). Both were regions with a tradition in the relevant sector. Thus, there were dormant capacities that could be revived, allowing the companies not to start from zero. This factor had some relevance: German institutions were more in evidence in Zwickau than in Győr. However, in both cases VW-Audi itself appears as the main institution. Its relations with different tiers of suppliers, and in particular with those that came with it from the west, were the most important forces shaping all issues that we studied. In Zwickau, for example, the dual system of vocational training worked rather well, even without the strong associations normally considered in the west essential to support it, because VW itself was willing to invest in training efforts in order to ensure qualified employees and possibly even to help the region. Similarly, in Hungary Audi favoured a training system that was not very far from the German one, introducing vocational training schools with much the same content as in Germany—but in place of the involvement of social partners was direct control of the training schemes through Audi. Again, VW itself was willing to apply both collective pay agreements and works councils in Zwickau, but it was not concerned that many of its suppliers refused to do so. Audi also encouraged cooperative industrial relations in Győr, but in a rather limited version without strong unions.

Conclusion

For large multinational companies (MNCs)—increasingly dominant in the world economy—that central finding concerning both VW-Audi and IKEA may be the most important one of all: giant, global firms make their own institutions; they are highly effective 'institutional brokers' in Campbell's (2004) sense. This might include regime-shopping to find locations with the most favourable infrastructures, but this familiar idea may assign too passive a role to such firms. They are sufficiently large and transnational to provide the structures that suit their purposes for themselves. While we have here operated largely with a model that sees firms confronting institutional gatekeepers, we have to see them also as having a capacity to *be* gatekeepers, allowing entry to components of national institutions that suit them, barring those that do not, and opening up other routes that bring institutions from far outside any particular country concerned. This is seen most clearly in countries like those of Central and Eastern Europe, where historically rooted national institutions are weak (see, for example, the study of Western European food MNCs in CEE countries by Chobanova 2007). But elements of the same process will be found elsewhere too. This does not mean that these corporations can do what they like wherever they like, as differences between the activities being grouped in Zwickau and those in Győr show. This is where initial regime shopping and locational choice do the preparatory work in selecting a promising location for particular activities. Beyond that point the firms are ready to be institutional entrepreneurs. Further, given the dependence of governments even of countries as economically powerful as Germany or the UK on attracting foreign direct investment, it should not be assumed that they even want to act as gatekeepers defending some past legacy of institutional complementarity—especially given that these legacies are themselves changing quite rapidly at the present time.

The institutional theory of capitalist diversity therefore needs to posit a difference between 'institution-making' and 'institution-taking' firms (for such a dichotomous analysis of the contemporary Germany economy see Höpner 2006). This is not the same as the distinction between firms that respond passively to their institutional environment and those that go in search of institutions to be found elsewhere; as we saw in several of our studies, even relatively small firms can make use of consultants to access information and institutions from outside. These are instances of what we called in Chapter 1, following Lévi-Strauss (1962) or more particularly Campbell (2004), institutional *bricolage*. Large MNCs seem to be able to go one step further than this and design and implement their own supporting institutions. This may mean that, when itemizing cases of varieties of capitalism, we should look, not just at nation states, but at individual large enterprises. Are there Audi-VW, IKEA, IBM, or Nestlé models of capitalism? And what do we know about size thresholds that firms have to pass before they can engage in this largely independent institution-building? These are important questions for future research.

To return finally to the starting point of our work, in Chapter 1 we raised three questions:

1. *Do governance structures of the local economies conform to the national innovation regime of their country, in which they are 'embedded', or do local economies institutionally diverge?* As anticipated, our answer to this has been both enriched and made more complicated by the fact that all four national systems that we have studied here have themselves been in a process of change. Taking that into account, we have found, as summarized above, some cases of conformity to national models, some of deviation from them—though we have also seen that 'deviance' is too strong a word. Very rarely, if at all, did we encounter path-dependent gatekeepers actually preventing institutional innovation where firms and localities had the imagination and resources to generate it—though their existence might have acted as more passive blocks to the search for alternative approaches. On the other hand, there was no simple, one-to-one correspondence between 'successful innovators' and 'unsuccessful conformists': as varieties of capitalism authors have stressed more perhaps

TABLE 8.1. Summary of main findings of the case studies

Cases	Conforming to expected national model	Conforming to alternative models
Furniture	*Germany, Ostwestfalen-Lippe*: but conforms to a changing German model. Virserum?	*Sweden, Tibro*: divergent, even 'defiant' local context (exception A) *Sweden, IKEA*: divergent, even defiant corporate context; creative incoherence; capacity to reach outside national context (exceptions A, B, C)
Motor vehicles	*Germany, Zwickau*: but conforms to a changing German model.	*Hungary, Győr*: capacity of large firm to reach outside a weak national context (exception C).
Biopharmaceuticals	*UK, Cambridge*: but some weaknesses.	*Germany, Munich*: capacity of firms to access non-national resources through market (exception C).
TV programme-making		*Germany, Cologne*: distinctive local context facilitates creative incoherence (exceptions A, B). *UK, Soho* (London): uses distinctive local context to gain creative incoherence in corporate finance, industrial relations, training and inter-firm relations (exceptions 1, 2).

than anything else (Hall and Soskice 2001*a*), different structures suit different economic activities.

Table 8.1 provides a rough summary of these findings, using broad categories of likely non-conforming outcomes anticipated in Chapter 1 (for more detail, see Crouch et al. 2008):

A. Characteristics of local institutions and infrastructure that support forms of economic organization that differ from and may even 'defy' the overall national architecture;
B. Creative incoherences in the difference between national and local, whereby local institutional entrepreneurs are able to produce innovative outcomes, working between the contradictory incentives of national and local institutions;
C. Firms being less bounded by national institutions than theory often assumes.

Our main interest has been concentrated on the expected exceptions, the cases expected to conform to national models being to a large extent a control group. However, there are findings of interest within these control cases. First, in both instances where German firms were expected to do well (furniture and motor vehicles) we had to come to terms with the fact that the German national model itself is not static. Second, being in a liberal market economy has not been enough to guarantee very strong success in British biopharmaceuticals. Third, a remarkable hybrid model has been developing in the British new TV industry, indicating both the relative institutional autonomy of strongly networked local economies, and the weaknesses of a 'liberal' environment for an exceptionally flexible industry.

Among the expected exceptions, we find some examples of all the anticipated sources of variation. Local environments can provide institutional support for sectors that have requirements not normally associated with national models: this is the case of furniture in Tibro and new TV programme-making in both Cologne and London. However, it is only in Tibro that we can really talk of 'defiance' of national institutions. IKEA deviates in all respects. It has a distinctive environment within Sweden, which although locally rooted is really a corporate rather than a geographical environment, and in several respects 'defies' Swedish national institutions. It does this in a way that creates a highly distinctive corporation, and is hence a creative incoherence. And it is a global firm, using characteristics and resources from across the world.

VW-Audi in Hungary provides a further example of how a major corporation can create its own institutions—admittedly here in a country that has not yet acquired a distinctive form of national capitalism. The inability of national institutions to form a 'prison' for firms (assuming that they should want to do so in the first place) is also important in explaining the success of the Munich biopharmaceuticals sector. Here the resources of the locality help firms to network and learn how to access resources elsewhere in Europe and the world that are not provided on the German national scene. Finally, the Cologne new TV industry, like that in London, makes use of dense local networks to produce a creative incoherence.

In our analysis, companies act rationally in response to sector-specific challenges, being partly bound by the existing institutional framework that they encounter, but partly acting to alter it. Two cases can be distinguished. In the first (structurally conservative) case, arrangements of governance in the national innovation and production system prove to be beneficial for the companies and their aim to stand up to international competition. In so far as national institutions help companies to deal with competition on their markets, they will probably try to preserve these arrangements. The key example here is the furniture industry in Ostwestfalen-Lippe and German 'diversified quality production'—albeit in a *nationally* changing form. This is so far in conformity with established wisdom: 'If firms decide to support the regulatory regimes that sustain the comparative institutional advantages of the nation, it is because they also underpin the competitive advantages of the firm' (Streeck and Thelen 2005: 25).

In the second (innovative) case, companies turn away from the national context and develop their own local governance structure. If the national institutional structure is seen as non-adequate or 'non-fitting' to deal with sectorally specific terms of competition, then the internal and external coordination of companies—in reaction to challenges posed by the market—is likely to deviate from the national structure. This is where the potential of local innovation and production systems can be found. The decoupling from the national production system takes place by a differentiation of the local (or corporate) level, which is thereby developing its own governance mode, or by reaching beyond the national context to access resources in the global system, either through individual corporate power (IKEA, Audi-VW) or through local networking (Munich).

2. *Can it be shown that particularities in the governance of local economies contribute to the economic success of these entities?* If departure from national systems were to be found only in failing local economies, the hypothesis of the priority of national systems would be supported rather than refuted. As noted, Table 8.1 enables us to maintain that success can be found in some non-conforming institutional environments. But can we go further and make the stronger claim that conformity with the national system would have led to failure? (It is also possible that, had the local institutional patterns we discovered not existed, other non-conforming institutions would have emerged as functional equivalents; that possibility, impossible to verify, neither supports nor refutes our position, as we are not making any claims concerning the *necessity* of certain institutions.)

Where local actors have clearly striven to construct institutions that departed from national systems, because they found these unhelpful, we probably have enough of a test for our hypothesis. We can make such claims for both the Cologne and London film- and TV-production cases. In both there was evidence of actors making strenuous efforts to establish structures that would avoid certain negative aspects of the national context, particularly in vocational training, where the cases moved in opposite but therefore converging directions. The same applies to Munich biotechnology, where firms took special steps both to find venture capital and to recruit CEOs from outside Germany. The furniture makers in Tibro and, in a more complex way in the IKEA-related firms around Älmhult, also had distinctive structures that 'protected' them from certain aspects of the Swedish national model. Tibro firms used their cooperative networks to give them the collective presence of a large organization, enabling them to access credit and other resources normally available only to large enterprises. Their counterparts in Virserum constituted a very different system of local production and were, for reasons explained in Chapter 4, unable to achieve that level of cooperation and as a result found no way round the problem.

IKEA, though a large firm and therefore partly 'typically Swedish' established unusual corporate governance and made use of the institutional resources of a wide range of other countries. Given that many other large Swedish firms also operate globally, it might be asked if IKEA needed to distance itself so far from its national base. However, most other Swedish MNCs are not family owned. IKEA's strategy of non-conformity stems from an era in which the Swedish national system was even more hostile to family-owned firms than it is today—particularly if of large size. IKEA decided to move its global headquarters and financial base abroad for reasons of taxation and inheritance.[1]

It is even more difficult to judge whether VW-Audi 'needed' its divergence from many aspects of the German model—though, as we have seen, many of those divergences are in line with what is becoming the new, still changing German model anyway. The firm certainly took advantage of the relative weakness of institutional features in Zwickau and, even more, in Győr; but it also retains considerable production in the former Western Germany. VW-Audi certainly gives us an example of the institutional autonomy and creativity of a major MNC. However we cannot claim it in evidence for the stronger version of the claim made in hypothesis 2, which must remain in general unresolved by our research.

3. *Does the divergence of local economies from structural patterns of the national innovation and production system enable us to suggest in which institutional elements local economies may successfully diverge from the national model and in which not?* Table 8.2 sets out the main findings of Chapters 4–7 on this question, again making broad assessments as in Table 8.1. Where the cluster's arrangements seemed broadly in line with the (remember: changing) national models, a tick ($\sqrt{}$); where they clearly deviate, a cross (X) has been entered. Where the situation is ambiguous there is a query (?).

While these can be only rough estimates, there do not seem to be institutions that are more resistant to divergence than others. What does emerge from Table 8.2 is something different and more interesting: as we move from the more 'traditional' sectors to the 'new economy', there is more deviation (or local particularity), irrespective of country. This suggests the reasonable

TABLE 8.2. Patterns of institutional conformity and non-conformity in localized sectors

	Furniture		Car-making		Biotechnology		Film, TV	
	Germany	Sweden[a]	Germany	Hungary	Germany	UK	Germany	UK
Corporate governance	√	√ (T,V) X (I)	Not relevant—branch plants of W. German MNC	X	√	X	√	
Corporate finance	√	√ (T,V) X (I)	Not relevant—branch plants of W. German MNC	X	√	X	X	
Industrial relations	√	√	√ (VW and W. German suppliers) X (local suppliers)	√	X	√	X	X
Vocational training	√	√	√	√	X	√	X	X
R and D	√	√	√	?	√	√	?	?
Inter-firm relations	√	X (T) √ (I,V)	√	?	?	?	X	X

[a] T = Tibro, V = Virserum, I = IKEA.

proposition that the various groupings of institutions that have grown up over time in different places were particularly suited to those industries that had been established earlier in industrial history, and are not necessarily helpful to new industries. That would suggest that these industries will settle more quickly in places where institutions are more able to change—or, to recollect our earlier point, where national institutions do not obstruct firms' access to structures and resources originating elsewhere. Our evidence can throw only incidental light on to this possibility, but it suggests an important new line for future research.

Finally, it is possible to draw some conclusions concerning the relationship between our concept of creative incoherence and that of complementarity. Given our initial definition of the former and economists' definition of the latter, that question is straightforward. Creative incoherence goes against the institutional grain of a system, even transgressing and defying it, not fitting in; complementarity is the consistent mutual accompaniment of two phenomena, such that an increase in the demand for one raises the price of the other. Here the two ideas are opposites: an increase in demand for a deviant institution would reduce the 'price' (or value) of those institutions associated with the dominant system—they are more or less what economists would call substitutes—the opposite of complementary goods in their terms. This relationship is depicted in the straight line in Fig. 8.1: institutional coherence and complementarity rise together. One would therefore expect to find complementarity high when there was a high level of coherence among institutions, that is, in the top right quartile of Fig. 8.1: this is a basic proposition of most institutionalist studies of economies. These studies also suggest

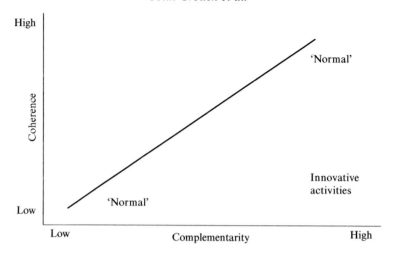

FIGURE 8.1. Relationships between coherence and complementarity in 'normal'
and innovative activities

that, as congruence declines, so does complementarity, leading to lack of fit
and deteriorating performance (e.g. Hall and Gingerich 2004).

However, as argued above, through the findings of our research we have
come to see 'incoherent' institutions as not necessarily confrontational, but
often as part of the internal diversity that rich and lively systems contain within themselves. As such, they may quite usefully 'complement'—in
the everyday and literal meaning of the word—more dominant institutions.
Indeed, we have noted that we should not even assume that the gatekeepers
of national systems strive to keep firms bounded to the range of institutions
to be found within them. They may prefer to leave firms free to find complementarities at the level of a wider European or even global system (e.g. the
ability, within the changed institutions of early twenty-first century Germany,
of Munich biotech firms to access venture capital in London enables financial
markets to complement national German financial arrangements). In these
senses of both terms, creative incoherence here *becomes* a new complementarity. There will of course be many forms of incoherence that are not creative,
but merely things that do not work well; and there will be other forms that
might have been creative had they not been completely rejected by dominant
institutions. These are the historical 'might have beens', alternative futures
that never happened.

Our findings therefore leave plenty of scope for studies of these negative institutional features, both uncreative incoherences and the creative
might have beens. What we have however identified is a potentially opti-
mistic space between these negative alternatives within which Schumpeterian

innovation takes place. It can be defined as that space where incoherence and complementarity cease to be opposites and become identical. As some of our findings suggest, at certain points a low degree of coherence might actually pick up some new possibilities for positive complementarity, indicating the possibility of new formations, which within some new Gestalt might actually come to be seen as new types of coherence. These cases are to be found in the bottom right quartile of Fig. 8.1. There is nothing inevitable about this: the hypothetical graph should best be seen as a scatter plot, with most cases falling along the line, but with the occasional 'rogue' case falling in the bottom right quartile and offering new possibilities. It is here that we should expect to find institutional entrepreneurs active.

Most students of contemporary capitalism consider complementarity between the institutional spheres that make up a national system; once a particular institutional solution for corporate governance is found, for example, it tends to influence the institutional set-up in other spheres (or at least those most adjacent to it) in the manner expected by economic theory: demand for one institution increased demand also for another one that thereby becomes complementary to it. Our present argument suggests that there might be other potential complementarities of this kind which are not normally included in national institutional *ensembles*, but which might well become such if institutional entrepreneurs discover them. In our research we have hints of two possible situations where this might occur: in very new sectors with very new forms of organization (as in the Cologne and London studies); and where Europeanization and globalization radically extend the kinds of institutional combinations that firms can make (as with IKEA, the Munich biopharmaceutical firms, and (to a lesser extent) VW-Audi in Central Europe). Since organizational and technological change as well as increasing globalization are fundamental attributes of the contemporary economy, researchers need to be equipped with methodologies that will enable them to identify phenomena of this kind.

An important aspect of this involves being able to study what we have called here the process of 'institution making' as much as 'institution taking'. This is partly a matter of the mechanisms through which institutional entrepreneurs are able to rely on their broader environment in their efforts to innovate. Our case studies have drawn attention to a number of these. One example, seen particularly in the motor industry study, is the learning that takes place within major international companies who bring 'institution building' expertise into a country. Another is the movement of expertise and skills (in the form of people) across borders. Much of the institutional infrastructure for the Munich biotechnology cluster was built up by Germans with ties to American venture capitalists and pharmaceutical firms who returned from the USA and used their experience to build up new institutions. Another again, which emerges in both the media and furniture cases, is the importance of local collaborative communities and/or networks through which firms learn and act collectively to build up local institutional support infrastructures. Future researchers will discover others.

Note

1. This resulted in an important debate in Sweden over how to prevent large firms like IKEA from voting with their feet, which resulted in changes in the system of regulation regarding corporate finance and governance. Hence, today that degree of non-conformity may seem unnecessary, but it may not have been at the time. In this respect, IKEA is an example of institutional innovation or change in the 'aftermath' of company strategy—how company strategy can affect institutions not only in host countries of MNCs (as in our motor industry cases) but also in their home countries.

REFERENCES

Abelshauser, W. (2000). *Bibliographie zur Wirtschaft Ostwestfalen-Lippes seit 1815*. Essen: Klartext Verlag.

Adelberger, K. E. (1999). 'A Developmental German State? Explaining Growth in German Biotechnology and Venture Capital'. Berkeley Roundtable on the International Economy Working Paper No. 134.

AIM. (2005). *KoordinationsCentrum Ausbildung in Medienberufen*. Download from http://www.aim-mia.de

Alberstat, P. (2004). *The Insider's Guide to Film Finance*. Oxford: Focal Press.

Albert, M. (1991). *Capitalisme contre capitalisme*. Paris: Seuil.

Ålund, S. (1946). *Möbelindustrins uppkomst och första utveckling i Virserum, Tibro och Bodafors*. Stockholm: Möbelvärlden.

Amable, B. (2003). *The Diversity of Modern Capitalism*. Oxford: Oxford University Press.

Amin, A. and Thrift, N. (1993). 'Globalisation, Institutional Thickness and Local Prospects', *Revue d' Economie Régionale et Urbaine*, 3: 405–27.

———— (1995). 'Globalisation, Institutional "Thickness" and the Local Economy', in Healey, P., Cameron, S., Davoudi, S., Graham, S., and Madani-Pour, A. (eds.), *Managing Cities: The New Urban Context*. Chichester: Wiley.

Andor, L. (2000). *Hungary on the Road to the European Union: Transition in Blue*. Westport, Connecticut, and London: Praeger.

Aniello, V. and Le Galès, P. (2001). 'Between Large Firms and Marginal Local Economies: The Making of Systems of Local Governancein France', in Crouch, C. et al. (eds.), q.v., pp. 117–53.

Aoki, M. (1994). 'The Contingent Performance of Teams: An Analysis of Institutional Complenertarity', *International Economic Review*, 35: 657–76.

Arthur, B. (1994). *Increasing Returns and Path Dependence in the Economy*. Michigan: University of Michigan Press.

Artus, I. (2001). *Krise des deutschen Tarifsystems. Die Erosion des Flächentarifvertrags in Ost und West*. Wiesbaden: Westdeutscher Verlag.

Bagnasco, A. (1977). *Tre Italie*. Bologna: Il Mulino.

Bahnmüller, R. (1997). 'Baden-Württemberg: Die duale Berufsausbildung unter Anpassungsdruck', in Regini, M. and Bahnmüller, R. (eds.), *Best Practice oder funktionale Äquivalenz? Die soziale Produktion von Humanressourcen in Baden-Württemberg, Katalonien, Rhône-Alpes und der Lombardei im Vergleich*. Munich and Mering: Rainer Hampp Verlag, pp. 49–104.

Baumann, A. (2002a). 'Informal Labour Market Governance: The Case of the British and German Media Production Industries', *Work, Employment and Society*, 16(1): 27–46.

——(2002b). *Path-Dependency or Convergence? The Emergence of Labour Market Institutions in the Media Production Industries of the UK and Germany*. Ph.D. Thesis, Florence: European University Institute.

Baumann, A. and Voelzkow, H. (2004). 'Recombining Governance Modes: The Media Sector in Cologne', in Crouch, C. et al. (eds.), q.v., pp. 261–82.

Berger, S. and Dore, R. (eds.). (1996). *National Diversity and Global Capitalism*. Ithaca, NY: Cornell University Press.

Berggren, C. and Laestadius, S. (2000). *The Embeddedness of Industrial Clusters: The Strength of the Path in the Nordic Telecom System*. Stockholm: Kungl. Tekniska Högskolan.

Berggren, B., Olofsson, C., and Silver, L. (2000). 'Control Aversion and the Search for External Financing in Swedish SMEs', *Small Business Economics*, 15(3): 233–42.

Bertoldi, M. (2003). 'Varietà e dinamiche del capitalismo', *Stato e Mercato*, 69: 365–83.

Beyer, J. and Höpner, M. (2003). 'The Disintegration of Organized Capitalism: German Corporate Governance in the 1990s', *West European Politics*, Special Issue on *Germany: Beyond the Stable State*, 26(4): 179–98.

Björk, S. (1998). *IKEA: Entreprenören, affärsidén, kulturen*. Stockholm: Svenska förlag.

Bluhm, K. (1999). *Zwischen Markt und Politik. Probleme und Praxis von Unternehmenkooperation in der Transitionsoekonomie*. Opladen: Leske and Budrich.

Blumenreich, U. (2002). *Cluster-Studie Forst and Holz NRW*. Bad Honnef: Hauptverband der deutschen Holz und Kunststoffe verarbeitenden Industrie und verwandter Industriezweige.

BMBF (Bundesministerium für Bildung und Forschung). (2004). *BioRegionen in Deutschland. Starke Impulse für die nationale Technologieentwicklung*. Berlin: Bundesministerium für Bildung und Forschung.

——(2005). *Zur technologischen Leistungsfähigkeit Deutschlands*. Berlin: Bundesministerium für Bildung und Forschung.

Bohman, P. (1997). *Virserums möbelindustri – en 100-årig epok*. Virserum: Virserums Hembygdsförening, Virserums Möbelindustrimuséum.

Bosch, A., Ellgut, P., Schmidt, R., and Trinczek, R. (1999). *Betriebliche Interessenhandeln. Zur politischen Kultur der Austauschbeziehungen zwischen Management und Betriebsrat in der westdeutschen Industrie*. Opladen: Leske and Budrich.

Boyer, R. (1996). 'The Convergence Hypothesis Revisited: Globalization but Still the Century of Nations?', in Berger, S. and Dore, R. (eds.), q.v., pp. 29–59.

——(2004a). 'New Growth Regimes, but Still Institutional Diversity', *Socio-Economic Review*, 2(1): 1–32.

——(2004b). *The Future of Economic Growth: As New Becomes Old*. Cheltenham: Edward Elgar.

Braunerhjelm, P. and Carlsson, B. (1993). 'Entreprenörskap, småföretag och industriell förnyelse 1968–1991', *Ekonomisk Debatt*, 21(4): 56–79.

Brege, S. and Pihlquist, B. (2004). 'Svensk plan möbelindustris beroende av en inhemsk spånskiveindustri samt förutsättingarna för en fortsatt tillväxt', report for Vinnova, 21 March.

——Milewski, J. and Berglund, M. (2001). 'Storskalighet och småföretagande – en studie av strategiska grupper inom svensk möbelindustri', *Vinnova Report VR*, 2001: 41.

Brose, H.-G. and Voelzkow, H. (eds.). (1999). *Institutioneller Kontext wirtschaftlichen Handelns und Globalisierung*. Marburg: Metropolis.

Brussig, M. (2003). 'Institutionen und Organisationen: Bedingungen und Blockaden ihrer Kopplung-Beispiele aus der ostdeutsche Industrie', *Berliner Debatte Initial-Zeitschrift für sozialwissenschaftlichen Diskurs*, 13: 120–43.

Bundesministerium für Wirtschaft und Arbeit. (1998–2004). *Tarifvertragliche Arbeitsbedingungen im Jahr…* Bonn: Bundesministerium für Wirtschaft und Arbeit.

Burroni, L. and Crouch, C. (2008). 'The Territorial Governance of the Shadow Economy', *Environment and Planning C*, 26: 455–70.

Cadbury, A. (1992). *Financial Aspects of Corporate Governance*. London: Gee.

Campbell, J. L. (2004). *Institutional Change and Globalization*. Princeton, NJ: Princeton University Press.

—— Hollingsworth, J. R., and Lindberg, L. N. (eds.). (1991). *Governance of the American Economy*. New York: Cambridge University Press.

Casper, S. (2000). 'Institutional Adaptiveness, Technology Policy, and the Diffusion of New Business Models: The Case of German Biotechnology', *Organization Studies*, 21(5): 887–914.

—— (2002). 'National Institutional Frameworks and High-Technology in Germany: The Case of Biotechnology', in Hollingsworth, J. R., Müller, K., and Hollingsworth, E. (eds.), *Advancing Socio-Economics: An Institutionalist Perspective*. Lanham, MD: Rowman and Littlefield Publishers, pp. 277–305.

—— and Glimstedt, H. (2001). 'Economic Organization, Innovation Systems, and the Internet', *Oxford Review of Economic Policy*, 17(2): 265–81.

—— and Kettler, H. (2001). 'National Institutional Frameworks and the Hybridization of Entrepreneurial Business Models: The German and UK Biotechnology Sectors', *Industry and Innovation*, 8(1): 5–30.

—— Lehrer, M., and Soskice, D. (1999), 'Can High-Technology Industries Prosper in Germany? Institutional Frameworks and the Evolution of the German Software and Biotechnology Industries', *Industry and Innovation*, 6(1): 5–25.

—— Jong, S., and Murray, F. (2004). 'Entrepreneurship and Marketplace Formation in German Biotechnology', paper presented on annual retreat of Society for Comparative Research in San Diego, CA, May 14–15. Available on http://socsci2.ucsd.edu~aronatasscrretreat.

Cheshire, P. and Gornostaeva, G. (2003). 'Media Cluster in London', *Cahiers De L'Iaurif*, 135: 151–9.

Chobanova, Y. (2007). *MNEs in the CEECs: Shaping the Microeconomic Architecture of States in the Context of EU Integration: The Cases of Unilever, Nestlé, and InBev*. Ph.D. Thesis, Florence: European University Institute.

Corbett, J. and Jenkinson, T. (1997). 'How Is Investment Financed? A Study of Germany, Japan, the UK, and the US', *The Manchester School*, 65(1): 69–93.

Crouch, C. (1977). *Class Conflict and the Industrial Relations Crisis*. London: Heinemann.

—— (1993). *Industrial Relations and European State Traditions*. Oxford: Clarendon Press.

—— (2003). 'Institutions Within Which Real Actors Innovate', in Mayntz, R. and Streeck, W. (eds.), *Die Reformbarkeit der Demokratie. Innovationen und Blockaden*. Frankfurt: Campus, pp. 71–98.

Crouch, C. (2004). 'The European Machinery Industry Under Pressure', in Crouch, C. et al. (eds.), q.v., pp. 13–22.

——(2005). *Capitalist Diversity and Change: Recombinant Governance and Institutional Entrepreneurs*. Oxford: Oxford University Press.

Crouch, C. and Farrell, H. (2004). 'Breaking the Path of Institutional Development? Alternatives to the New Determinism', *Rationality and Society*, 16(1): 5–43.

——and Keune, M. (2005). 'Changing Dominant Practice: Making Use of Institutional Diversity in Hungary and the United Kingdom', in Streeck, W. and Thelen, K. (eds.), *Beyond Continuity: Institutional Change in Advanced Political Economies*. Oxford: Oxford University Press, pp. 83–102.

——and Streeck, W. (eds.). (1997). *Political Economy of Modern Capitalism. Mapping Convergence and Diversity*. London: Sage.

——Finegold, D., and Sako, M. (1999). *Are Skills the Answer? The Political Economy of Skills Development in Advanced Societies*. Oxford: Oxford University Press.

——Le Galès, P., Trigilia, C., and Voelzkow, H. (2001). *Local Production Systems in Europe: Rise or Demise?* Oxford: Oxford University Press.

—— —— —— —— (2004). *Changing Governance of Local Economies: Response of European Local Production Systems*. Oxford: Oxford University Press.

——Streeck, W., Boyer, R., Amable, B., Hall, P. A., and Jackson, G. (2005). 'Dialogue on Institutional Complementarity and Political Economy', *Socio-Economic Review*, 3: 359–82.

——Schröder, M., and Voelzkow, H. (2009). 'Regional and Sectoral Varieties of Capitalism', *Economy and Society*, 38(3).

Culpepper, P. D. (2001). 'Employers, Public Policy and Politics of Decentralized Cooperation in Germany and France', in Hall, P. A. and Soskice, D. (eds.), q.v., pp. 275–306.

Czada, R. and Lehmbruch, G. (eds.). (1998). *Transformationspfade in Ostdeutschland*. Frankfurt: Campus.

Davies, P. and Freedland, M. (1993). *Labour Legislation and Public Policy*. Oxford: Oxford University Press.

—— —— (2007). *Towards a Flexible Labour Market*. Oxford: Oxford University Press.

Davis, S. J. and Henrekson, M. (1999). 'Explaining National Differences in the Size and Industry Distribution of Employment', *Small Business Economics*, 12(1): 59–83.

Deeg, R. (2001). *Institutional Change and the Uses and Limits of Path Dependency: The Case of German Finance*. Discussion-Paper, Max-Planck-Institut für Gesellschaftsforschung. Cologne: MPIfG.

——(2005). 'Path Dependency. Institutional Complementarity, and Change in National Business Systems', in Morgan, G., Whitley, R., and Moen E. (eds.), q.v., pp. 21–52.

——and Jackson, G. (2007). 'Towards a More Dynamic Theory of Capitalist Variety', *Socio-Economic Review*, 5(1): 149–79.

Ebbinghaus, B. and Manow, P. (2001). 'Introduction: Studying Varieties of Welfare Capitalism', in Ebbinghaus, B. and Manow, P. (eds.), *Comparing Welfare Capitalism. Social Policy and Political Economy in Europe, Japan and the USA*. London: Routledge, pp. 1–24.

Edgren, G., Faxén, K.-O., and Odhner, C.-E. (1970). *Lönebildning och samhällsekonomi*. Stockholm: Rabén and Sjögren.

Elbing, S. (2006). 'Film- and TV-Production in London: A Coordinated Local Economy in a Liberal Environment?' in Voelzkow, H., Crouch, C., and Leuenberger, T. (eds.), q.v., pp. 253–94.

Elvander, N. (2000). 'Industrial Relations. Internationellt, Svenskt, Allmänt', *Arbetsmarknad och arbetsliv*, 6(3): 139–58.

Ernst and Young. (2003). *Beyond Borders: The Global Biotechnology Report*. London: Author.

Esping-Andersen, G. (1999). *Social Foundations of Postindustrial Economies*. Oxford: Oxford University Press.

European Commission. (2004). *Industrial Relations in Europe 2004*. Brussels: European Commission.

Eurostat. (2001). *Eurostat Jahrbuch 2001: Forschung und Entwicklung*. Luxemburg: European Communities.

Fazekas, K. and Ozsvald, E. (1998). 'Transition and Regional Policy: The Case of Hungary', in Keune, M. (ed.), *Regional Development and Employment Policy: Lessons from Central and Eastern Europe*. Budapest and Geneva: ILO.

Financial Services Authority. (2003). *The Combined Code on Corporate Governance*. London: Financial Services Authority.

Fligstein, N. (2001). *The Architecture of Markets: An Economic Sociology of Twenty-First-Century Capitalist Societies*. Princeton, NJ: Princeton University Press.

Florida, R. (2002). *The Rise of the Creative Class . . . and How It's Transforming Work, Leisure, Community and Everyday Life*. New York, NY: Basic Books.

——(2005a). *Cities and the Creative Class*. London: Routledge.

——(2005b). *The Flight of the Creative Class. The New Global Competition for Talent*. New York: HarperCollins Publishers.

Garud, R. and Karnøe, P. (2001). 'Path Creation as a Process of Mindful Deviation', in Garud, R. and Karnøe, P. (2001) (eds.), *Path Dependence and Creation*. Mahwah, NJ: Erlbaum.

Glassmann, U. (2004). 'Refining National Policy: The Machine Tool Industry in the Local Economy of Stuttgart', in Crouch, C. et al. (eds.), q.v., pp. 46–73.

——(2006). 'Beyond the German Model of Capitalism: Unorthodox Local Business Development in the Cologne Media Industry', in Voelzkow, H., Crouch, C., and Leuenberger, T. (eds.), q.v., pp. 220–52.

Goller, S. (2001). 'Das Herz der Möbelindustrie schlägt in Ostwestfalen-Lippe: Region gilt als "Mekka" der Möbelbranche', *Ostwestfälische Wirtschaft*, 9: 6–8.

Goodin, R. (2003). 'Choose your Capitalism?', *Comparative European Politics*, 1 and 2: 203–14.

Grabher, G. (1996). 'Zur Rolle des historischen Erbes in der Reorganization for Betrieben und Regionen in Brandenburg'. WZB Working Paper No. FS I 96-104. Berlin: WZB.

——(1997). 'Adaptation at the Cost of Adaptability? Restructuring Eastern German Regional Economy', in Grabher, G. and Stark, D. (eds.), q.v., pp. 107–34.

——(2002a). 'Fragile Sector, Robust Practice: Project Ecologies in New Media', *Environment and Planning*, 34: 1911–26.

——(2002b). 'The Project Ecology of Advertising: Tasks, Talents and Teams', *Regional Studies*, 36(3): 245–62.

Grabher, G. and Stark, D. (1997a). 'Organizing Diversity: Evolutionary Theory, Network Analysis and Post-Socialism', in Grabher, G. and Stark, D. (eds.), q.v., pp. 1–32.

———— (eds.). (1997b). *Restructuring Networks in Post-Socialism*. Oxford: Oxford University Press.

Greenhut, M. L. and Norman, G. (eds.). (1995). *The Economics of Location*. Volume I: *Location Theory*. Aldershot: Edward Elgar.

Gummesson, O. (1997). *Därför lyckas Gnosjö. Bygden som har blivit ett begrepp.* Stockholm: Ekerlids Förlag.

Hall, P. and Gingerich, D. (2004). 'Varieties of Capitalism and Institutional Complementarities in the Macroeconomy: An Empirical Analysis', *MPIfG Discussion Paper 04/5*. Cologne: Max Planck Institute for the Study of Societies.

——and Soskice, D. (2001a). 'Introduction', in Hall, P. A. and Soskice, D. (eds.), q.v., pp. 1–68.

————(eds.). (2001b). *Varieties of Capitalism: The Institutional Foundations of Comparative Advantage.* Oxford: Oxford University Press.

Hancké, B., Rhodes, M., and Thatcher, M. (eds.). (2007). *Beyond Varieties of Capitalism: Conflict, Contradictions, and Complementarities in the European Economy.* Oxford: Oxford University Press.

Hassel, A. (1999). 'The Erosion of the German System of Industrial Relations', *British Journal of Industrial Relations*, 37(3): 483–505.

——(2002). 'The Erosion Continues: Reply', *British Journal of Industrial Relations*, 40(2): 309–17.

Havas A. (1997). 'A munkahelyek "áttelepülése" ("szabad áramlása") a jármüiparban'. (Relocation in the car industry). Mimeo. Budapest: Munkaügyi Kutató Intézet.

Henrekson, M. and Jakobsson, U. (2002a). 'Ägarpolitik och ägarstruktur i efterkrigstidens Sverige', in Jonung, L., (ed.), *Vem skall äga Sverige?* Stockholm: Studieförbundet Näringsliv och Samhälle.

———— (2002b). 'The Transformation of Ownership Policy and Structure in Sweden: Convergence Towards the Anglo-Saxon Model?', *New Political Economy*, 8(1): 73–102.

———— (2005). 'The Swedish Model of Corporate Ownership and Control in Transition', in Huizinga, H. and Jonung, L. (eds.), *Who Will Own Europe? The Internationalisation of Asset Ownership in Europe.* Cambridge: Cambridge University Press.

——and Sanandaji, T. (2004). *Ägarbeskattningen och företagandet. Om skatteteorin och den svenska policydiskussionen.* Stockholm: SNS Förlag.

Herrigel, G. (1996). *Industrial Constructions. The Sources of German Industrial Power.* Cambridge: Cambridge University Press.

——and Wittke, V. (2005). 'Varieties of Vertical Disintegration. The Global Trend Towards Heterogeneous Supply Relations and the Reproduction of Difference in US and German Manufacturing', in Morgan, G., Whitley, R., and Moen E. (eds.), q.v., pp. 312–51.

Herrmann, A. (2006). *Alternative Pathways to Competitiveness Within Developed Capitalism: A Comparative Study of the Pharmaceuticals Sector in Germany, Italy, and the UK.* Ph.D. Thesis, Florence: European University Institute.

Högfeldt, P. (2003). 'The Pillars of Corporate Control in Sweden: Dual-Class Shares and Pyramids', unpublished paper, Stockholm School of Economics.

Hollingsworth, J. R. and Boyer, R. (eds.). (1997). *Contemporary Capitalism*. Cambridge: Cambridge University Press.

——Schmitter, P. C., and Streeck, W. (1994). 'Capitalism, Sectors, Institutions and Performance', in Hollingsworth, J. R., Schmitter, P. C., and Streeck, W. (eds.), *Governing Capitalist Economies: Performance and Control of Economic Sectors*. New York, NY: Oxford University Press, pp. 3–16.

——Müller, K., and Hollingsworth, E. (eds.). (2002). *Advancing Socio-Economics: An Institutionalist Perspective*. Lanham, MD: Rowman and Littlefield Publishers, pp. 277–305.

Höpner, M. (2001). *Corporate Governance in Transition: Ten Empirical Findings on Shareholder Value and Industrial Relations in Germany*. Discussion Paper, Max-Planck-Institut für Gesellschaftsforschung. Cologne: MPIfG.

Humphrey, J. and Memedovic, O. (2003). *The Global Automotive Industry Value Chain: What Prospects for Upgrading by Developing Countries*. Vienna: UNIDO.

IKEA. (2004). *IKEA Fakta och Sittror*, www.ikea.se, 1 February.

Jacobi, O., Keller, B., and Müller-Jentsch, W. (1998). 'Germany: Facing New Challenges', in Ferner, A. and Hyman, R. (eds.), *Changing Industrial Relations in Europe*. 2nd Edition. Oxford: Blackwell Publishers, pp. 190–238.

Johansson, A. L. (1989). *Tillväxt och klassamarbete. En studie av den svenska modellens uppkomst*. Stockholm: Tiden.

——and Magnusson, L. (1998). LO – andra halvseklet. Fackföreningsrörelsen och samhället. Stockholm: Atlas.

Jong, S. (2006). 'The Development of Munich and Cambridge Therapeutic Biotech Firms: A Case Study of Institutional Adaptation', in Voelzkow, H., Crouch, C., and Leuenberger, T. (eds.), q.v., pp. 295–315.

——(2007). *The Birth, Dispersion and Adaptation of New Institutions Across Institutional Systems: A Study of the Emergence and Performance of Biotech Firms and Technology Transfer Officers in and Around Publicly Funded Research Centres in Three Regions*. Ph.D. Thesis, Florence: European University Institute.

Kenney, M. (ed.). (2000). *Understanding Silicon Valley: The Anatomy of an Entrepreneurial Region*. Stanford, CA: Stanford University Press.

Kern, H. and Sabel C. (1994). 'Verblaßte Tugenden. Zur Krise des deutschen Produktionsmodells', in Beckenbach, N. and Van Treeck, W. (eds.), *Umbrüche gesellschaftlicher Arbeit*. Göttingen: Schwartz, pp. 605–24.

Keune, M. and Nemes Nagy, J. (eds.). (2001). *Local Development, Institutions and Conflicts in Post-Socialist Hungary*. Budapest: ILO.

——and Tóth, A. (2001). 'Foreign Investment, Institutions and Local Development: Successes and Controversies in Győr', in Keune, M. and Nemes Nagy, J. (eds.), q.v., pp. 94–120.

—— —— (2006). 'From Cathedral in the Desert to Institutional Entrepreneur: The Case of Audi in Győr, Hungary', in Voelzkow, H., Crouch, C., and Leuenberger, T. (eds.), q.v., pp. 184–219.

——(with Kiss, J. and Tóth, A.). (2004). 'Innovation, Actors and Path Dependency: Change and Continuity in Local Development Policy in Two Hungarian Regions', *International Journal for Urban and Regional Research*, 28(3): 586–600.

Kitschelt, H. and Streeck, W. (2004). 'From Stability to Stagnation: Germany at the Beginning of the Twenty-First Century', in Kitschelt, H. and Streeck, W. (eds.), *Germany: Beyond the Stable State*. London: Frank Cass.

——Lange, P., Marks, G., and Stephens, J. (eds.). (1999). *Continuity and Change in Contemporary Capitalism*. Cambridge: Cambridge University Press.

Kjær, P. (1996). *The Constitution of Enterprise: An Institutional History of Inter-Firm Relations in Swedish Furniture Manufacturing*. Stockholm: Stockholm University.

Klikauer, T. (2002). 'Stability in Germany's Industrial Relations: A Critique on Hassel's Erosion Thesis', *British Journal of Industrial Relations*, 40(2): 295–308.

Koch, T. and Thomas, M. (1997). 'The Social and Cultural Embeddedness of Entrepreneurs in Eastern Germany', in Grabher, G. and Stark, D. (eds.), q.v., pp. 242–61.

Krätke, S. (2002). *Medienstadt. Urbane Cluster und globale Zentren der Kulturproduktion*. Opladen: Leske and Budrich.

Kurp, M. (2004). *Filmförderung erreicht Rekordniveau. Etat der Berlinerfilmförderung wurde deutlich aufgestockt*. Download from http://www.medienmaerkte.de

Larsson, L. (1989). *Historien om hur bonden blev möbelsnickare och hur möbelsnickaren i de små röda verkstäderna utvecklades till vår tids moderna industrier*. Tibro: Tibro Förenade Möbelfabriker AB.

——and Malmberg, A. (1997). *Svensk Möbelindustri: kompetens, kontaktnät och konkurrenskraft*, Nutek Rapport R. (ed.), Stockholm: Nutek, p. 54.

Lehmbruch, G. (1994). 'Institutionen, Interessen und sektorale Variationen in der Transformationsdynamik der politischen Ökonomie Ostdeutschlands', *Journal für Sozialforschung*, 1: 21–44.

Lehrer, M. (2000). 'Has Germany Finally Fixed Its High-Tech Problem? The Recent Boom in German Technology-Based Entrepreneurship', *California Management Review*, 42(4): 89–107.

Lévi-Strauss, C. (1962). *La pensée sauvage*. Paris:Agora.

Lewis, E. (2005). *Great IKEA! A Brand for all the People*. London: Cyan Books.

Liebeskind, J., Porter, A., Lumerman, O., Zucker, L., and Brewer, M. (1996). 'Social Networks, Learning, and Flexibility: Sourcing Scientific Knowledge in New Biotechnology Firms', *Organization Science*, 7(4): 428–43.

Lindbeck, A. (1997). 'The Swedish Experiment', *Journal of Economic Literature*, 35(3): 1273–319.

——and Snower, D. J. (1989). *The Insider–Outsider Theory of Employment and Unemployment*. Cambridge, MA: MIT Press.

LO (1951). *Fackföreningsrörelsen och den fulla sysselsättningen*. Stockholm: Organisationskommittén, Landsorganisationen i Sverige.

London–New York Study (2000). Section 2, Chapter 7. *Media in London and New York*, pp. 69–81.

Lundberg, E. (1985). 'The Rise and Fall of the Swedish Model', *Journal of Economic Literature*, 23(1): 1–36.

Lundh, C. (2003). *Spelets regler. Institutioner och lönebildning på den svenska arbetsmarknaden 1850–2000*. Stockholm: SNS Förlag.

Lundvall, B.-A. (eds.). (1992). *National Systems of Innovation: Towards a Theory of Innovation and Interactive Learning*. London: Printers Publishers.

Lütz, S. (2000). *From Managed to Market Capitalism? German Finance in Transition*. MPIfG Discussion Paper No. 00/2. Max-Planck-Institut für Gesellschaftsforschung. Cologne: MPIfG.

——(2003). *Convergence Within National Diversity: A Comparative Perspective on the Regulatory State in Finance*. MPIfG Discussion Paper No. 03/7. Cologne: MPIfG.

Mahoney, J. (2000). 'Path Dependence in Historical Sociology', *Theory and Society*, 29: 507–48.

Manow, P. and Seils, E. (2000). 'Adjusting Badly. The German Welfare State, Structural Change and the Open Economy', in Scharpf, F. W. and Schmidt, V. A. (eds.), *Welfare and Work in the Open Economy. Diverse Responses to Common Challenges*, Volume II. Oxford: Oxford University Press, pp. 264–307.

Markusen, A. (1999). 'Fuzzy Concepts, Scanty Evidence and Policy Distance: The Case for Rigour and Policy Relevance in Critical Regional Studies', *Regional Studies*, 33(9): 869–86.

Marrs, K. and Boes, A. (2002). 'Alles Spaß und Hollywood? Arbeits-und Leistungsbedingungen bei Film und Fernsehen', in Allmendinger, J. and Hinz, T. (eds.), *Organisationssoziologie*. Wiesbaden: VS Verlag.

Mayer, K. U. and Hillmert, S. (2004). 'New Ways of Life or Old Rigidities? Changes in Social Structure and Life Courses and Their Political Impact', in Kitschelt, H. and Streeck, W. (eds.), q.v., pp. 79–100.

Media Guide NRW (2005). Download from http://www.messetreff.commg-nrw 04service01d.htm

Morgan, G., Whitley R., and Moen, E. (eds.). (2005). *Changing Capitalisms? Complementarities, Contradictions and Capability Development in an International Context*. Oxford: Oxford University Press.

Münch, J. (1995). *Vocational Education and Training in the Federal Republic of Germany*. Luxembourg: CEDEFOP.

Nachum, L. and Keeble, D. (2000). *Foreign and Indigenous Firms in the Media Cluster of Central London*, ESRC Centre for Business Research, University of Cambridge, Working Paper No. 154.

Nelson, R. R. (1993). *National Innovation Systems: A Comparative Analysis*. Oxford: Oxford University Press.

——and Winter, S. G. (1982). *An Evolutionary Theory of Economic Change*. Cambridge, MA: Harvard University Press.

North, D. C. (1990). *Institutions, Institutional Change and Economic Performance*. New York, NY: Cambridge University Press.

——(2005). 'Institutions and the Process of Economic Change', *Management International*, 9(13): 1–7.

Parsons, T. (1951). *The Social System*. London: RKP.

Pfeifer, S. (2000). *Branchenreport. Nur nichts anbrennen lassen – Die Küchenmöbelindustrie im Umbruch*. Bochum: ISA-Consult.

——Kremer, U., and Schorn, B. (1997). *Rekon Branchen Report – Die Küchenmöbelindustrie in Ostwestfalen-Lippe*. Bochum: ISA-Consult.

Pierson, P. (2000a). 'The Limits of Design: Explaining Institutional Origins and Change', *Governance*, 13(4): 475–99.

——(2000b). 'Increasing Returns, Path Dependence, and the Study of Politics', *American Political Science Review*, 94(2): 251–67.

Piore, M. J. and Sabel, C. F. (1984). *The Second Industrial Divide: Possibilities and Prosperity*. New York, NY: Basic Books.

Piotti, G. (2002). *Mezzogiorno e Germania Est: politiche, capitale sociale e sviluppo locale negli anni Novanta*. Ph.D. Dissertation. University of Brescia.

Piotti, G. (2005). 'Industria Automobilistica e processi di cooperazione locale: il caso di Zwickau', *Sviluppo Locale*, 25: 31–48.

——(2006). 'Testing the German Model in Eastern Germany: The Case of the Automobile Industry in Zwickau', in Voelzkow, H., Crouch, C., and Leuenberger, T. (eds.), q.v., pp. 162–83.

Porter, M. (1990). *The Competitive Advantage of Nations*. New York: Free Press.

Powell, W. W. (1998). 'Learning from Collaboration: Knowledge and Networks in the Biotechnology and Pharmaceutical Industries', *California Management Review*, 40(3): 228–40.

——Koput, K. W., and Smith-Doerr, L. (1996). 'Interorganizational Collaboration and the Locus of Innovation: Networks of Learning in Biotechnology', *Administrative Science Quarterly*, 41: 116–45.

Pratt, A. (1999). *Technological and Organisational Change in the European Audiovisual Industries: An Exploratory Analysis of the Consequences for Employment*. European Audiovisual Observatory, Council of Europe.

Regini, M. (1997). 'Social Institutions and Production Structure: The Italian Variety of Capitalism in the 1980s', in Crouch, C. and Streeck, W. (eds.) (1997), q.v., pp. 102–16.

——(2003). 'Dal neo-corporativismo alle varietà del capitalismo', *Stato e Mercato*, 69: 388–93.

Reiter, J. (2003). 'Changing the Microfoundations of Corporatism: The Impact of Financial Globalisation on Swedish Corporate Ownership', *New Political Economy*, 8(1): 103–25.

Rhodes, M. and van Apeldoorn, B. (1997). 'The Transformation of West European Capitalism?' Robert Schuman Centre Working Paper. Florence: European University Institute.

Sabel, C. F. and Zeitlin, J. (eds.). (1997). *World of Possibilities: Flexibility and Mass Production in Western Industrialization*. New York, NY: Cambridge University Press.

Salzer, M. (1994). 'Identity Across Boarders: A Study in the "IKEA-world" ', *Linköping Studies in Management and Economics*. Linköping: Linköping University.

Saxenian, A. (1999). *Silicon Valley's New Immigrant Entrepreneurs*. San Francisco, CA: Public Policy Institute of California.

Scharpf, F. (1997). *Games Real Actors Play: Actor-Centered Institutionalism in Policy Research*. Boulder, CO: Westview.

——(2000). *Interaktionsformen. Aktevrzentrierter Institutionalismus in der Politikforschung*. Opladen: Leske und Budrich.

Schmidt, R. (1998). *Mitbestimmung in Ostdeutschland: Expertise für das Projekt 'Mitbestimmung und neue Unternehmenskulturen' der Bertelsmann Stiftung und der Hans-Böckler Stiftung*. Gütersloh: Verlag Bertelsmann Stiftung.

Schmidt, V. (2002). *The Futures of European Capitalism*. Oxford: Oxford University Press.

Schneider, F. (2002). 'The Size and Development of the Shadow Economies and the Shadow Economy Labour Force of 22 Transition and 21 OECD Countries: What Do We Really Know?', paper presented at the Round Table Conference 'On the Informal Economy', Sofia, Bulgaria, 18–20 April. Download from http://www.csd.bgnewsbertschneider-paper.pdf

Schönert, M. (2004). 'Zur Lage der Medienwirtschaft in den deutschen Großstädten 2003', *Monatsbericht des Instituts für Wirtschaftsforschung (BAW)*, Heft 5. Bremen: Institut für Wirtschaftsforschung.

Schroeder, W. (1997). 'Loyalty and Exit – Austritte aus regionalen Arbeitgeberverbänden der Metall-und Elektroindustrie im Vergleich', in Von Alemann, U. and Weßels, B. (eds.), *Verbände in vergleichender Perspektive. Beiträge zu einem vernachlässigten Feld.* Berlin: Edition Sigma, pp. 225–52.

——(2000). *Das deutsche Modell auf dem Prüfstand. Zur Entwicklung der industriellen Beziehungen in Ostdeutschland.* Wiesbaden: Westdeutscher Verlag.

Schumpeter, J. (1993 [1912]). *Theorie der wirtschaftlichen Entwicklung: Eine Untersuchung über Unternehmergewinn, Kapital, Kredit, Zins und Konjunkturzyklus.* 8th Edition. Berlin: Duncker and Humblot.

Scott, J. (1997). *Corporate Business and Capitalist Classes.* Oxford: Oxford University Press.

Silvia, S. (1997). 'German Unification and Emerging Divisions within German Employers' Associations', *Comparative Politics*, 2: 187–208.

Sjöberg, T. (1998). *Ingvar Kamprad och hans IKEA: En svensk saga.* Stockholm: Gedins.

Sjöberg, Ö. and Rafiqui, P. (2006). 'Spatial Differentiation in National Production Systems: The Case of the Furniture Industry in Sweden', in Voelzkow, H., Crouch, C., and Leuenberger, T. (eds.), q.v., pp. 109–61.

Skillset (1994). *Employment Patterns and Training Needs 1993–4. Freelance and Set Crafts Research.* London: Skillset.

——(2002*a*). *Annual Report 2002.* London: Skillset.

——(2002*b*). *Employment Census 2002.* London: Skillset.

Somai, M. (2002). *The Hungarian Automotive Industry.* World Economics Working Papers No. 131. Budapest: Hungarian Academy of Sciences.

Sorge, A. (1988). 'Industrial Relations and Technical Change: The Case for an Extended Perspective', in Hyman, R. and Streeck, W. (eds.), *New Technology and Industrial Relations.* Oxford: Basil Blackwell.

Soskice, D. (1997). 'Technologiepolitik, Innovation und nationale Institutionengefüge in Deutschland', in Naschold, F., Soskice, D., Hancké, B., and Jürgens, U. (eds.), *Ökonomische Leistungsfähigkeit und institutionelle Innovation. Das Produktions- und Politikregime im globalen Wettbewerb.* Berlin: Edition Sigma, pp. 319–48.

—— and Finegold, D. (1988). 'The Failure of British Training: Analysis and Prescription', *Oxford Review of Economic Policy*, 4/3: 21–53.

Stadt Köln (2002). *Medienhandbuch Köln.* 6th Edition. *Die audiovisuellen Medien.* Cologne: Emons Verlag.

——(2004). *Medien-und Kommunikationsstadt Köln. Die Branche im Überblick, Unternehmen, Infrastruktur, Ausbildung, Events.* Leverkusen: Stadt Köln and Industrie-und Handelskammer Köln.

Ståhlberg, H. (1942). 'Några drag ur den sydsvenska möbelindustrins lokalisering', *Sydsvensk Geografisk Årsbok*, 18: 191–205.

Stark, D. and Bruszt, L. (1998). *Postsocialist Pathways: Transforming Politics and Property in East Central Europe.* Cambridge: Cambridge University Press.

Storper, M. (1997). *The Regional World: Territorial Development in a Global Economy.* New York and London: Guilford Press.

Streeck, W. (1991). 'On the Institutional Conditions of Diversified Quality Production', in Matzner, E. and Streeck, W. (eds.), *Beyond Keynesianism. The Socio-Economics of Production and Full Employment.* Aldershot: Edward Elgar, pp. 21–61.

——(1996). 'Lean Production in the German Automobile Industry: A Test Case for Convergence Theory', in Berger, S. and Dore, R. (eds.), q.v., pp. 138–70.

——(1997). 'German Capitalism: Does It Exist? Can It Survive?', in Crouch, C. and Streeck, W. (eds.), q.v., pp. 33–54.

——and Rehder, B. (2003). *Der Flächentarifvertrag: Krise, Stabilität und Wandel,* MPIfG Working Paper Nos. 03 and 06. Cologne: MPIfG.

——and Thelen, K. (eds.). (2005). *Change and Discontinuity in Institutional Analysis: Explorations in the Dynamics of Advanced Political Economies.* Oxford: Oxford University Press.

Sturgeon, T. J. and Lester, R. K. *The New Global Supply-Base: New Challenges for Local Suppliers in East Asia,* paper prepared for the World Bank's Project on East Asia's Economic Future, MIT Special Working Paper, Industrial Performance Centre. Cambridge, MA: MIT.

Swann, G. M. P., Prevezer, M., and Stout, D. (eds.). (1998). *The Dynamics of Industrial Clustering: International Comparisons in Computing and Biotechnology.* Oxford: Oxford University Press.

The Economist. (2005). 'Germany's Surprising Economy. The Reviving Health of a Previously Sick Country', 18 August, p. 9.

Thelen, K. (2000). 'Why German Employers Cannot Bring Themselves to Dismantle the German Model', in Iversen, T., Pontusson, J., and Soskice D. (eds.), *Unions, Employers, and Central Banks.* Cambridge: Cambridge University Press, pp. 138–62.

——(2004). *How Institutions Evolve.* New York, NY: Cambridge University Press.

Töpfer, A. (1998). *Die Restrukturierung des Daimler-Benz Konzerns 1995–1997: Portfoliobereinigung, Prozeßoptimierung, Profitables Wachstum.* Neuwied, Kriftel: Luchterhand.

Torekull, B. (2003). *Historien om IKEA. Ingvar Kamprad Berättar.* Stockholm: Wahström and Widstrand.

Trigilia, C. (2004). 'The Governance of High-Tech Districts', in Crouch, C. et al. (eds.), q.v., pp. 321–30.

UK Film Council. (2003). *Post-Production in the UK: A Study of the Current Nature and Extent of the UK Post-Production Sector.* Available on http://www.ukfilm-council.org.uk

UK Government. (1977). *Progress Report on the Financing of Industry and Trade* (Wilson Report) (Committee to Review the Functioning of Financial Institutions). London: HMSO.

——(1980). *Broadcasting Act 1980.* London: HMSO.

——(1986). *Report of the Committee on the Financing of the BBC.* London: HMSO.

——(1990). *Broadcasting Act 1990.* London: HMSO.

Vitols, S. (1995). *German Banks and the Modernization of Small Firm Sector: Long-Term Finance in Comparative Perspective.* Discussion Paper No. FS I 95-309, Wissenschaftszentrum Berlin für Sozialforschung. Berlin: WZB.

Voelzkow, H. (with Elbing, S. and Schröder, M.). (2007). *Jenseits nationaler Produktionsmodelle? Die Governance regionaler Wirtschaftscluster. Eine international vergleichende Analyse.* Marburg: Metropolis.

——and Schröder, M. (2006). 'Governance of the Furniture Industry in Ostwestfalen-Lippe and Its National Context: A Local Economy Conforming to the "German Model"?', in Voelzkow, H., Crouch, C., and Leuenberger, T. (eds.), q.v., pp. 70–108.

——Crouch, C., and Leuenberger, T. (eds.). (2006). *Local Production Systems in Europe*, unpublished report to Volkswagen Stiftung, Frankfurt am Main: VW Stiftung.

Whitley, R. (1999). *Divergent Capitalisms. The Social Structuring and Change of Business Systems.* Oxford: Oxford University Press.

——(ed.). (1992). *European Business Systems. Firms and Markets in Their National Contexts.* London: Sage.

Wiesenthal, H. (2004). 'German Unification and "Model Germany": An Adventure in Institutional Conservatism', in Kitschelt, H. and Streeck, W. (eds.), q.v., pp. 37–58.

Windolf, P. (2002). *Corporate Networks in Europe and the United States.* Oxford: Oxford University Press.

Winkelmann, O. (2001). *Entwicklungen in der Mitbestimmung: Industrial Relations, Industrial Districts und Netzwerke. Das Beispiel 'Betriebsräte-Netzwerk' im Industrial-District Ostwestfalen-Lippe*, unpublished dissertation, Osnabrück: University of Osnabrück.

Zucker, L. G., Darby, M. R., and Brewer, M. B. (1998). 'Intellectual Human Capital and the Birth of U.S. Biotechnology Enterprises', *American Economic Review*, 88(1): 290–306.

Zysman, J. (1983). *Governments, Markets, and Growth: Financial Systems and the Politics of Industrial Change.* Ithaca, NY: Cornell University Press.

INDEX